Dying Is Not Death

Dying Is Not Death

Lee Hoinacki

Resource _Publications_

An imprint of Wipf and Stock Publishers
199 West 8th Avenue • Eugene OR 97401

ISBN 10: 1-59752-879-X
ISBN 13: 978-1-59752-879-5

Chapters 1 and 7 of the present work appeared in a slightly different version in *Stumbling Toward Justice*, copyright © 1999 by The Pennsylvania State University Press, and reprinted here by permission.

Woodcuts copyright © 2006 by Robert F. McGovern.

Scripture taken from the HOLY BIBLE, NEW INTERNATIONAL VERSION Copyright © 1973, 1978, 1984 by International Bible Society. Used by permission of Zondervan.

Manufactured in the U.S.A.

*In memory of Bernard Hoinacki (1929–1999),
my brother, who taught me that dying
is the way to Life.*

Contents

Introduction

I WROTE THIS book out of a sense of justice, the cardinal virtue understood as St. Thomas Aquinas analyzed it. I owe many debts, among them: to my brother, Bernard, to Ivan Illich, Barbara Duden and German friends, to my parents and other members of my family, to Brother Gerald Morris, C.M., Rose Delaney, and my classmates in the Dominican Order. Therefore I write out of necessity. I cannot not write, I need to express my gratitude.

Therefore I am grateful to the persons in State College, Pennsylvania; Bremen, Germany; Ocotepec, Mexico.

I want to thank the following for critically reading parts of the manuscript: Aaron Falbel, Judith Van Herik, Gene Burkart, Alex Wood, and David Cayley. Their corrections and suggestions greatly helped.

I am especially thankful for the fine woodcuts of the Philadelphia artist, Robert F. McGovern, and for the hospitality of Father John McNamee at St. Malachy's.

The book comprises twelve chapters that look at death today; eleven are stories. The final chapter is a more theoretical examination of a contemporary pathogen, the pursuit of health. The narratives are firsthand or hearsay reports of people dying or preparing for death. Most of these persons were quite close to me.

Many of the stories describe a technological death, and such is interpreted as a perversity one might wish to avoid. Throughout the book my focus on death comes out of the Western tradition of humanism. When appropriate, I present the position of a Christian believer and, specifically, a Catholic.

A perspective on death enables me to make sense of what I see and experience. A reflection on dying may be a kind of key to the craziness of our world.

The writing is influenced by the life and work of Ivan Illich, whom I knew from 1960 until his death in 2002. One chapter, "An Art of Suffering," relates his way of living with pain.

Certain thoughts impelled me throughout the writing of the chapters. For example, the impact of tools on contemporary life. Tools, in progressive thrusts, came from dim lost origins, went through millennial developments and, as technology, recently burst into hegemonic control. Perhaps they're not neutral, perhaps it's time to become apprehensive.

Is there no escape from tools? Am I doomed to a Promethean fate, bound to a rock, a vulture feasting on my guts each day? Is modernity really a nightmare that imprisons me?

Perhaps in Greece a seer succumbed to a false dream: Mind work is more noble than body work. The West embraced this vision and Christianity sacralized it—my hands cannot be calloused.

Further, I am faced with questions about gene technology. Do transgenic manipulations directly deny the inviolability of nature? Do the questions relate to death, to *my* death?

Health often appears inscrutable. But the truth of the human condition remains the same: I suffer pain; I am afflicted with impairments; I will certainly die. Some undergo greater pain, others more debilitating disorders, but all face death. Many, mesmerized by the glitter of high-tech "solutions," pathetically believe in fix-it drugs, mistakenly think all pain an evil to be suppressed, and seek to postpone death at almost any cost.

A dramatic testimony to the reality of power is found in a 1970 work of Luis Buñuel, *The Milky Way*. The movie is idiosyncratically based on a pilgrimage to Santiago de Compostela. In the late Middle Ages the route to Compostela was called the Milky Way because that galaxy appeared to show one where to walk.

In one of the many surrealist scenes, Buñuel portrays the Marquis de Sade sexually violating and torturing a young girl. The viewer sees only the child's bare foot and ankle, secured by a leg chain, and hears her repeated cry, "Je crois . . . je crois . . . " In the face of de Sade's calculated cruelty, she continues to express her belief in God.

One cannot help but see the truth of this exercise of power in her tenacious firmness. All the pain, degradation, and shame inflicted by de Sade could not shake her faith. Buñuel, a great director in film history, depicted an unforgettable image. Through it I am irresistibly moved by the young believer's stubborn affirmation of reality.

Does emphasis on medicalization and legalization give even greater legitimacy to the replacement of sin by therapy and rules, contribute to making a therapeutic society even more hegemonic?

I see a world awash in fantasy, confused illusions that modern Western medicine has made us more healthy. Such beliefs reflect reality only in a sense defined by the system itself. The medical system thrives through the hubris of professional aggrandizement and the public's learned greed for consumption. People largely lost in a rootless and fractured world devoid of true culture are despairingly fear-ridden.

To the extent I participate in conventional patterns of consumption, I directly destroy the only livable niche we know. I write my ineradicable epitaph: "Necrophilia was his ruling passion."

Lee Hoinacki
Philadelphia
October 2006

1

To Die My Own Death

FIRST I saw his hands, gripping the bars tightly. Old hands, hands scared and marked by nearly fourscore years of labor. The fingers were not delicate, the nails not pampered. A remark of my mother's, remembered from a distant childhood, came to me. "Clean your nails," she gently reminded him, as we got ready to go to church on Sunday mornings. And then he did something that shook my youthful and overly-tender sensibilities, he cleaned and pared his nails with his sharp pocket knife!

My eyes returned to the silent figure confined behind the bars of a hospital bed, hooked up to various machines—*I* felt sick. What have they done to someone who has lived honorably among us? What is this treatment called care? Does it invite or demand a complaint, a cry? Has what began as a humanistic impulse gone awry? Is it time for well-meaning concern to be challenged by a prophetic voice screaming out to the world: This is not just! This man is owed the dignity his life and work merit! Who is guilty of imposing this shameful end on a praiseworthy citizen? Overwrought, I was unable to look calmly at my father in this strange new place. I never before felt so strongly my affection for him.

He opened his eyes, saw me, and closed them again. I was unable to speak. Did he recognize me? Why didn't *he* speak? What was he thinking? A kind of terror slowly enveloped me. But I was too confused to do anything except stand there in dumb silence. What could I do anyway? I needed time . . . no, I needed knowledge . . . perhaps understanding . . . or wisdom . . . ultimately, inspiration, grace.

Later—was it minutes? Hours?—the room darkened. The hospital noises, the racket of efficient technology, became somewhat muted. I sat numbly and stared without any focus, my mind a jumble. When I first arrived at the hospital, after traveling several hundred miles from my farm, the physician gave me a report. I immediately recognized much:

a series of categories strung together in the desiccated non-language of a textbook, what passes today in some circles as value-free objective knowledge. There are seemingly serious claims that such a laundry list reveals reality. But I asked myself: What had that description to do with what I saw before me? Unless . . . Was this *not* my father, then? Has my father been transformed into some other creature, one that fits the needs of modern medicine? Has he already gone? But without dying? Creeping terror again.

I stayed on through the hours of the night, searching for light in the darkness. I hoped to run into him there, among the shades . . . I waited . . . I was quiet . . . then, slowly, images floated up before me, some vivid, sharp; some still opaque, playing with me. I have been in hospitals before, many times. I thought I was over familiar with these places, skeptical of their promises, hardened against their illusions, confused by their personnel . . . so often I found decent people working in an indecent setting. Now I felt something new. I appeared to be lost in a labyrinth; the shadows advanced and receded. Then a startling scene, with its story, came into clear focus.

I had been here in my hometown some weeks earlier with my son, Ben—a regular trip to see Grandpa and the family. One day we went together to visit an old aunt in the nursing home. She had no children, her husband was dead, but family members regularly dropped in to see her. Entering the main door, we discovered that it was lunch time. So we headed for the dining room where we knew we would find Aunt Frances with the other ambulatory people. There they were, all seated at their assigned places, four to a table, looking down into their laps, waiting quietly for their meal. I had noticed, during previous visits, that the same old people faced one another at the tables three times a day, until death, but seemed never to carry on a conversation, and often never spoke a word to one another. As Ben and I came into the room, a slow-motion electric shock hit almost everyone. Like Pavlov's dog, each hoary head slowly raised up and bleary eyes sought us. The pathetic plea was familiar to me; it was repeated every time I visited the institution. As I walked past the glassed-in TV lounge on my way to Aunt Frances's room, the eyes of each person, expectant, tried to focus in and hold my eyes. Their lips moved, seemed to mumble. Were they questioning me? Are you my husband? My son? Have you finally come? Are you coming to see me? Confusedly, painfully, perhaps guiltily, I turned and forced myself to look straight ahead, down the corridor, until I reached Aunt Frances's room.

That day, making my way through the tables, I seemed to be walking away from rather than toward our aunt. The room moved out, the pitiable creatures rose up to become vague figures in a distant panorama, like faded and unrecognizable clones of Munch's painting, "The Scream." I felt troubled, anxious. But I knew from previous visits that the dining room population represented the most "presentable" patients. If one were to peer into the rooms of the bedridden on the second floor, a much more shameful sight awaited. There, one really doubted: Is this doubled up body a person? Is that still someone's mother?

Once, another aunt was on this second floor, and my sister and I came at lunch time to help her eat (my sister and brother took turns doing this every day). Some of the old folks could be put in wheel chairs and brought to a common room for their meals. While my sister helped our aunt eat, I noticed another old woman being fed by one of the aides. The aide filled a large plastic syringe with what appeared to be mashed up baby food. She then forced open the old woman's mouth, stuck the syringe in, and pressed the mouth full with the pap. After the woman swallowed, the procedure was repeated—until she was sufficiently stuffed. I had to work at controlling myself so as not to retch. It seemed obvious to me that the creature sitting there had long ago understood, somewhere in her soul, that her time had come. Instead of a vain struggle against the timely opportunity to embrace death, she stopped eating; she did what her nature and person required. Perhaps she was unable to explain this prudent action in words, but she knew what to do, she understood the laws of the universe, she was ready to obey them. But a recent service invention, the caring system, intervened, transforming her from an obedient child of God into an object for the consumption of services; her body was still of some use to the economy; it helped support a huge new growth industry, nursing homes. These enable "do-good" people to participate in an artificial extension of consumption. Ivan Illich wrote:

> Socially approved death happens when man has become useless
> not only as a producer but also as a consumer. It is the point at
> which a consumer, trained at great expense, must finally be writ-

ten off as a total loss. Dying has become the ultimate form of consumer resistance.[1]

Seeing that woman in the nursing home, and knowing other persons who have tried to die by not eating and drinking, I understood the necessity that society invent a Doctor Kevorkian, inevitable that people find a way to have doctors kill them. Techno-medicine has created a race of freakish prodigies far beyond the imaginings of science fiction and Hollywood, for these creatures were truly human at one time. Some people, finally, begin to revolt, begin to demand death in place of suffering monsterhood. But many have been technologized, to some extent made into technological artifacts. In everyone the pattern of technological death is deeply engrained. People have had their knowledge of how to die obliterated through a lifetime of treatments by professionals. Now comes the final request, a kind of solution: "Through your propaganda and interventions, reaching back to before I was born, you have made me what I am . . . I am your invention, your product. Now, I've had enough; it's time to die. Kill me. That's your obligation, since you have created me . . . Into your hands I commend my spirit . . ."

But modern life is not wholly determined by techno-science; insurance companies demand a part of the action; bureaucratic procedures are still required; other experts must be consulted; rationales must be devised; the appropriate poison or instrument must be selected; papers must be filled out; all the requisite signatures must be obtained. Only then can the killing take place.

It is fitting, I suppose, that death in a technological society occur in this way. After all, one of the principal effects of modern science is to make each person more and more helpless, to increasingly remove any vestige of autonomy. Death should fit this pattern, should be totally under the control of caring professionals and conscientious bureaucrats. Compassionate doctors cannot renege on their responsibility at the last moment. No one should be permitted, simply, to stop eating and drinking.

I was gazing upon the final scene in modern institutional care—the inevitable result of Western scientific progress, the success of accepted medical intervention, indeed, the picture of what is today called a right! If only the ideologues and technological fanatics could stand here and *see*. They think of time as an irreversible line, at times interrupted, at

[1] Illich, *Medical Nemesis*, 206–7.

times continuous. The line proceeds through discoveries and inventions. So, in time, because of progress, we are always at the summit, always on the cutting edge, always enjoying state-of-the-art performances. And, of course, we are never wrong for the naïve, banal reason that we are living in the present moment. Therefore, we are *permanently* not only right, but righter than was ever before possible. How neat! How logical!

But I have a feeling that something terribly miscarried. This scene was never imagined. No one had thought it necessary to meditate on Dante's Inferno before going off to medical school, before inventing yet another wonder drug to prolong life. As I looked at the figures in the nursing home, I saw a new race of technological zombies, pitiful Frankenstein freaks in wheelchairs and beds, each one artificially kept alive to a great old age through a lifetime of medical treatments, beginning before birth and generally intensifying as the patient becomes ready to die. Someone's father, or grandmother, an individual with a name, now lived on as an abstract example of longevity. So this is what the statistics tables refer to! Apparently, however, no one can see these cruel crimes; people are blinded partly because they are participants. Most share in the guilt because they live off the industry—believing in its science, buying and ingesting its products, getting rich off its profits. Almost everyone is complicit. No one is free to step aside, to stand outside the illusions of modern medicine, to find an independent place from which to see what is there. Each has become a prisoner.

I stop myself. Perhaps the shock of seeing my father in a hospital bed had unhinged me. These thoughts might be only the bizarre associations of a promiscuous imagination inflamed by an emotionally-heightened night. Perhaps I just need some sleep. St. Clara Manor, where our aunt now lived, is in many respects an exemplary setting. A new building, designed for this purpose, filled with light, color and efficient arrangements for the latest technological treatments. Various activity programs were offered each day. Volunteers came to entertain, clergy to minister. Since this was a small town, many of the employees knew the patients and their families. Every time I went to see different relatives over the years since the institution was founded, I ran into others also visiting elderly members of their families. Many of the younger generation, like my brother and sister, remained in the town of their birth and were able to maintain close contact with their old. Perhaps I just do not understand how care functions today.

5

But why do I feel so badly if my father is receiving the best that an enlightened profession can offer him? Why does the well-run nursing home upset me? Why does this hospital make me sick? Is there some insight here beyond the realization that those I love are getting close to death? Am I on the edge of some perception that I must desperately attempt to comprehend? . . . out of love for those near me. I cannot believe this is a good way to die. Death should not take such grotesque forms. Is there some relationship: the more control the more horror? Or, is technological death only the modern version of what all humans have had to face? Death, in any form, is always cruel, or senseless, or unjust, or painful, or lonely, or terrifying; perhaps I don't understand anything about the Christian prayer for a good death. It is claimed that with modern medicine one lives longer. Yes, something continues. But what is this creature that hangs on? Anyway, length of life has nothing to do with a good death; of that I am certain. Further, I strongly suspect that a so-called longer life is used (unconsciously, I hope) by the medical profession to extract yet more money, more power, from the public; old peoples' bodies are used to promote the project. As the insurance companies became more dominant over the treatment of patients at the end of the twentieth century, the profit aspect became more prominent. The desires of Midas are still strong, greed continues to be alluring, often compelling; the ancient capital sin allows one to overcome any revulsion about benefiting from human misery. But I must concentrate on what is taking place in front of me. The truth of my life at this moment will be found there.

What I see, in and around my father, is the noisy drama of a technological death. But isn't that a matter of more or less, just like life in today's world? No one is completely free from the possible distortions and perversions of technological intrusions. How judge? I've heard that the Amish use a rule of thumb: How will the adoption and use of this technology affect our local community? But almost no one among the rest of us belongs to such a community. We must seek another criterion. That can be found, I came to think—even today—in the notion of a self. How will the technology affect the self, my self?

The self exists to the extent that the subject is autonomous, not heteronomous, in sensing, perceiving, imagining, thinking, knowing, speaking and acting. The critical task, vis-à-vis technology, is to determine whether, how, and how much technological devices are corrosive of selfhood. In this sense, I can hold that the self is precious. The self is also given a measure of time on earth, independently of my thoughts or desires. Years of medications and therapies, however, sometimes frantically intensified at the end, can alter my time. Is this a particularly serious technological seizure or theft of my self? Is this one of the great institutional evils of our time?

The hours pass; I watch my sleeping father. I immediately left my work and came when my sister called me. She lives with him, caring for him in the family home. Although he became less and less active in the last few years, he required almost no attention. He was accustomed to look after himself, especially after the death of our mother some years ago. The morning after my arrival, I again met with the physician, a new man in town, but my sister liked him. Our old family doctor, with his fingers yellowed from chain smoking, was long dead. The young man spoke to me; he gave me a conscientious report. But it was the speech of an ex-medical student, mouthing the logic of his textbooks, skirting infantile fantasies of omniscience. Then, with obvious feeling and concern, he ended, "Unfortunately, we cannot predict the exact outcome."

"Thank God!" I countered—impulsively, passionately, almost shouting. "Thank God the world and its creatures are such that you cannot predict what will happen!" Startled, his eyes revealed a mixture of fright and puzzlement. Who was this wild man irreverently confronting him? Where was the respect and deference to which he had already become accustomed? But then the entire expression on his face changed— he was intelligent enough to understand the meaning and implications of my outburst. He looked down at the floor, turned, and slowly walked away in silence. He gave the impression of being an honest man.

I walked the few blocks from the hospital to my father's house; the town was a comfortable size. When I grew up there, I seemed to know a lot of the people. But now so much had changed; now so many were strangers to me. I recalled a recent visit. Dad asked me to take him around to pay his bills. Never in his life did he have a checking account. He believed credit cards to be some kind of financial deception, designed to trick you into buying and to keep you in debt. He seemed not to believe in consumption. Each month he personally visited the various offices to pay his bills with cash: telephone, electricity, gas, water and sewage. Monthly, he had only utility charges, annually, only a tax bill. He did not believe in debt and, through self-denial, thrift, and hard work was able to pay cash for everything he bought. He believed if he didn't have the money, he shouldn't buy it. Formerly, he rode his old bicycle in this monthly ritual—it would have been a waste to start up the car for such errands. But now he was too feeble to ride his bike—he had already sold the car a couple of years earlier—so I drove him around town that day in my sister's car, substituting for her.

I arrived at his house. It was surrounded by large trees, all planted by him years ago, now covering the yard with shade. How many trees he has planted for the neighbors and different members of the family! He found almost all of them in the few wooded areas still left around the town. He believed he should look there first, and only pay for nursery stock if the kind of tree he needed could not be found. He knew all the local species of trees, knew how to dig up one in "the wild," and how to transplant it successfully. How attractive the property looked! But as I approached the house I saw that the shrubbery needed trimming; this kind of chore he could no longer do. Neglecting such work, though, was not the significant fact. Rather, in the last years, he had lost interest—in almost everything. I realized this was a fundamental change in the way he had always lived. I had no recollection of ever seeing him idle, doing nothing. Nor did he ever go to a movie, or any other amusement event, and never to a restaurant. Apparently, he felt no need to be entertained or to eat out. During his vacation, he worked on our or some family member's house—there was always some carpentry, painting or electrical work, landscaping or gardening to be done.

During the past few years, he spoke progressively less each time I visited him. Nevertheless I went to see him regularly. I liked to visit his home; it reflected a life I came more and more to respect and admire. I also wanted to hear what he had to say. I believed he had a certain repertoire of stories, memories from his life, which he would tell me. But he was not the kind of person who, on any certain day, would sit down with you and relate one or more of his stories, if you bluntly asked him. Like other people I know who have good stories to tell, he seemed to follow some secret, idiosyncratic inner rhythm; one could not command or force such a memory. I had to be prepared to wait, to practice a great patience. Genuine stories are not commodities one can pick up in a supermarket. He told them, one at a time, when he was moved. I could only come, sit, and relax. When he was completely silent, I would know that it was the end; he had finished the last story . . . it was time to die.

Later, I returned to the hospital to keep vigil and found him awake. Seeing me, he asked whether I got the corn grinder; then he seemed to sleep again. He had a grinder he used to crush corn to feed the birds in winter. He gleaned the corn in a farmer friend's field each fall. He wanted me to take the grinder to prepare corn and grain for the baby chicks on my farm. It would be difficult for him to imagine buying ready-prepared chick feed which, I guess, is the custom today. Strange, that he should think of that; it was weeks since he had asked me to take the grinder. How could he come out of the medication, the drugged sleep, find himself in a truly strange place, he who had known only his own bed almost all the nights of his long life, and speak nothing but words of concern about literally helpless creatures, day-old chicks without a mother hen? I had expected to hear some complaint, or the pitiful meanderings of a disoriented old man. I sat down, and emptied my imagination and mind. Perhaps he had yet another story to tell me. As the noise of the hall traffic, the machines, the loudspeakers, died down, a kind of silence settled on the small hospital. In this quiet darkness, I saw something about the truth of his life . . . and his death. There was a final story! When the physician arrived on his morning rounds, I told him what I had heard and seen:

He is obviously more in our hands than his own, I maintained. For him, this is a violent change from the way he has lived; this places a direct responsibility, first of all, on me and the rest of the family, but also on you. You have the opportunity to actually do something for him, for this man. That means to be a physician here you must ignore many of your simplistic textbook concepts and formulas; you must try to look at the man before you. He is not a patient, that is, not a generalized, categorical abstraction. Let me give you one small example to illustrate what I'm talking about. This is something altogether typical of his life; I've just spent all night reflecting on it.

Many years ago he bought and single-handedly tore down a large, old, two-storied frame house. He did this in his spare time after finishing work at the post office each day. Then he tried to salvage all the materials; if possible, nothing would be wasted. He intended to use everything he could in the construction of a new house.

The old one had plastered walls, with old-fashioned laths underneath. He carefully cracked all the plaster, removed the rough-sawn laths without breaking or splitting them, and took out all the nails. He tied the laths in bundles and stored them—I don't remember where; it was a large house, there were many bundles.

Over the years, with a hand plane, he turned those thousands of laths into smooth, finished strips of thin lumber. Out of these he made lattice fences for our yard, and for the yards of relatives and friends. It is almost inconceivable that one man could stand over his workbench the countless hours, slowly doing all this hand labor, all those years. But he could do it because that was the shape he gave to his life, that was the kind of active life he chose to lead. He understood the quiet satisfaction and joy of making something. He practiced a craft. Many years ago, Marx tried to describe what happens to a man when he can no longer be a craftsman. Dad was also carrying out an imaginative recycling years before the concept was invented. His kind of recycling meant that he himself, through a highly labor-intensive action, found a way to turn waste into a useful and attractive artifact for many others. With his finely cared-for hand tools, he stood at that solid homemade workbench during many hours of his lifetime, turning out everything from bird houses to doll houses for family and friends.

Several years ago, you people said he had a cancerous bladder and it should be removed; you took it out. Then, about a year ago, some specialist claimed he needed a pacemaker; you installed it. I suppose you would claim that modern medicine extended his life. Well, it did *something* to him. In this time since you people have interfered in his life, he has drastically altered the way he lives. At eighty-eight, he gets up each morning at six o'clock and cooks some oatmeal for breakfast, the practice of a lifetime. But then immediately returns to bed! This he has never done before. In these years you have given him, he arises at midday and in the evening to eat what my sister prepares. The rest of the time, he sleeps or lies in bed—all day, all night, with one exception. He gets up to go to church on Sundays. He has stopped his lifetime habit of reading in the evening; he no longer watches television. He has become a different kind of being; he is not the same man he was; I cannot recognize him. We—you people, my brother, sister, myself—have made him into what we see lying there in that room. Who or what is that?

He has never been articulate in a conventional sense. But he has always spoken, in his own time, in his own way, and he speaks now, clearly, unequivocally. He's trying to tell us that it's time to die. He's been telling us that for the last several years. What could have been more obvious, more indisputable? Yet I was too blinded to see . . . too much wrapped up in myself, I suppose. We have artificially, probably sinfully, lengthened his life. Doing this, we assaulted him; we violated him. We've turned him into a creature fit only for suffering and the consumption of medical treatments. Now you people would like to try something else! To intensify and prolong the infliction of pain!

Well, he's had enough. There will be no exploratory surgery or any further invasion of his body. When he says he is in pain, give him an anodyne—immediately. No waiting. Is that clear?

He has lived in pain for years. One had only to see the grimace on his face when he got up out of a chair—always silently, never complaining. Sometimes, when I saw this, I would ask him, "Does that hurt you? Are you in pain?" he always answered, "No." If he says he is in pain now, then simply accept his word. You have no way of imagining his agony. But from the way he has consistently lived, if he now speaks of pain, then he is indeed *in extremis,* and it is our duty to help him. Once, when visiting him at his home, I went to the medicine cabinet looking for an aspirin. There weren't any; none in the house; no medicine of any kind! He was then over eighty.

We must face an ominous and terrifying thought: What he suffers now may be the unmistakable result of repeated medical interventions, these modern wonders of up-to-date care. Such misery is utterly unnatural, horrifyingly perverse, way beyond what is man's lot to suffer in this life. In this man we can see the pain inflicted on many under the modern rubric of care; we can look into the face of evil.

But seeing is highly problematic for everyone in today's society. I can't expect you to see the truth of this man. It would be necessary to have lived with him, observed him over many years, to see him. To see another is a wondrous thing, a grace, something quite outside the realm of the professional gaze. So you'll have to look at him through my eyes. Then you'll see him, insofar as it is given to you, and you will no longer be dealing with a patient, but be looking at someone's father. Your responsibility is clear, unambiguous: Your job is to help him die, that is, to leave him alone.

I did not speak calmly, and I probably made harsher remarks about institutional medicine than I remember, but at the end of my tirade I offered something of an apology. I told him I was speaking principally and directly about the world from which he came, the world of so-called care systems that endlessly multiply monsters, not about him personally. By this time, I imagine, he was quite bewildered by the polemic.

The darkness and silence of my nocturnal watches turned out to be radiantly eloquent. My father made himself known to me, and revealed something about the world in which I live. I now saw more clearly, because he led me into the experience of it, that the high-tech medical industry, in its beliefs and ambitions, practices and myths, incarnates what I have traditionally understood as hellish, fiendish. My father had become one of the countless victims of the madness that is modern medicine; he was imprisoned in a demonic torture chamber. With an anguished, sick feeling, I realized he had indeed become a patient. Now anything was permitted.

It is generally believed that the actions of the Nazis were evil. For example, I have heard of the extermination camps, and I visited one, Auschwitz. After slowly walking through the gate, under the words in iron letters: *Arbeit macht frei* (work makes you free), across the yard, into the buildings, I sat there, alone in the late afternoon of a somber, overcast winter day, in silence, and wondered . . . Hitler's program of hatred and horror selected only certain well-defined individuals; one could see a frightful rationale in it; it was not mindless mass murder. The Nazis never made a mistake in the persons selected for the camps. In one of the display cases at Auschwitz there was an opened log book: each person's name, sex, and *Beruf* ("profession") was accurately written. But a technological death makes no such fine distinctions. Everyone might just as well be a despised Gypsy, a hated Jew, an intransigent Jehovah's Witness, or a homosexual; it wouldn't make any difference. Everyone in the affluent sectors of our world, even before birth, is a potential guinea pig for genetic screening and other medical intrusions; after birth, for drugs, organ transplants and an ever-lengthening list of scientific manipulations and experimentations. Everyone, unless the money runs out, is coerced or pushed, throughout life, to become a technological construct, a suitable subject for a scientific death.

The rational Nazi order helps greatly to understand what all people have most in common today: a greater or lesser encirclement of their ways of perceiving, feeling, thinking and acting by ever more ingeniously complex and unintelligible technologically generated instruments and organizations, monitors and agents. What I saw in the nursing home, what I saw in the hospital, is of another order, significantly distinct from that of the Nazis. In a sense, there can be no comparison because the differences are too great. Today, the torture is inflicted for the other's good, and with almost everyone's approval. The action is honored by the society, the technologically-supported institutions praised and celebrated by nearly all reasonable people. Few, however, note the extent to which all are increasingly rendered helpless by the technological project.

Independently of the persons affected, the interventions are now necessary, integral parts of the megamachine, of the system. Further, one's final days come out of the very organization of society, this is the way the society functions. Death comes, not by turning on the gas, but by turning off the apparatus—ultimately, according to the indications of the machines and only secondarily from the judgment of the technicians, never from the dying person or the family.

In my experience of the last few years, I had learned something about how the industrial mode of production is applied to farming and learning. In a painfully personal encounter, I now learned something about technological medicine. All actions related to these notions come out of an institution. Are these institutions, then, some kind of lie? All of them equally? Are they an unnatural project? Is this one of the principal sources of evil today? Is this where I should look to see a contemporary form of the devil's schemes St. Paul warned us about?

> For our struggle is not against flesh and blood, but against the rulers, against the authorities, against the powers of this dark world . . . (Eph 6:12)

All modern institutions owe their existence and growth partly to the idea of rights. Any declaration of rights, universal or specific, is highly suspect. As Simone Weil pointed out:

> The notion of obligations comes before that of rights, which is subordinate and relative to the former. A right is not effectual by itself, but only in relation to the obligation to which it corresponds, the effective exercise of a right springing not from the individual who possesses it, but from other men who consider themselves as being under a certain obligation towards him. Recognition of an obligation makes it effectual. An obligation which goes unrecognized by anybody loses none of the full force of its existence. A right which goes unrecognized by anybody is not worth very much.[2]

Her insight into the slogans proposed by French intellectuals in 1789 undercuts today's arguments in defense of rights. Discussions about the denial of rights, claiming that people have a right to education, to an efficient food system, to health care, to employment and so on, in addition to their dubious character with respect to the concept

---

[2] Weil, *The Need for Roots*, 3.

itself of right, may be a deadly distraction. There may be much more pressing social imperatives: for example, to submit to critical examination these institutional forms, together with the so-called need for such all-encompassing intrusions in peoples' lives.

At the hospital, I quickly learned that constant and alert observation was necessary to protect my father from normal care procedures. For example, a young woman came in the room to take a blood sample, a routine practice, often repeated, I'm told. My father winced and groaned as she sought yet again to find and puncture an old vein. When I saw what she was doing, I jumped up and demanded, "Why are you doing that?" "We need blood samples for the lab tests"—what could be more obvious? "No, you don't," I shouted angrily. "You'll never take another blood sample from him."

I strode to the nursing station, peremptorily gave them the order, and asked to see the physician when he appeared. Later, confronted with the stupidity and cruelty of the procedure, he admitted that it was unnecessary. And so it stopped. By staying at the hospital as much as possible, and questioning everything they wanted to do to him, I was able to prevent further useless torture. Finally, he was left in peace—to die.

Many patients do not feel competent or courageous enough to question and challenge medical personnel. Further, weakened by illness and/or age, they are unable to confront the physician. Others, regardless of the number and frequency of family visitors, have no one to examine the sense of *every* procedure and pill, no one to defend them. But what must be the cruel loneliness of those isolated patients who have no loved one to sit with them day and night? For long hours they are alone with the rhythmic regularity of the beeps and blinks, the maddening absurdity of a machine's cold company. Perhaps those who die alone in their apartment or home, unattended by any professional, are more blessed.

While waiting for my father's death, the physician and I had several good, "clearing the air" conversations. Speaking together shortly after our early meetings, he presented me with two questions which, he pointed out, are quite different before and after the procedures involved are begun. "Do you want us to feed him if he stops eating and drinking? And, do you want us to use resuscitation measures?" As the eldest, I discussed the matter with my brother and sister and, getting their agreement, I told him, "No resuscitation measures of any kind, and no intravenous feeding or hydration." Since we were not always there twenty-four hours a day, it was necessary to be quite explicit before the occasion arose.

Once, he expressed his fear, implying that we might sue him because he had neglected to carry out some possible test or procedure. He was confused by having to deal with a family that wanted no unnecessary medical treatment which, in this case, meant no further "curative" measures at all. He had difficulty believing he was dealing with a family that regarded such suits as morally wrong; therefore, out of the question. At another time he worriedly explained how government and insurance company bureaucrats review physicians' records, and he might be penalized by them for failing to utilize available means to treat this patient. It seemed to me this was *his* problem, not ours.

Toward the end of our vigil, the physician confessed that if it had been his father, he would have acted in the same way. As I suspected, he wanted to be a good man; in his work he still retained some shreds of decency, in spite of the training, in spite of the nefarious business that employed him. Perhaps in an attenuated way, he was similar to Oskar Schindler. Schindler, a very *worldly* man, at great personal risk, saved several thousand Jews from the gas chambers.[3]

In the hospital I regularly noticed bits and pieces of cheer or kindness in the actions of employees. Can one speak of some kind of balance? Do these remains, these vestiges, of a gentler way of living, where one person touches another, takes time for another, attempts to see another, prevent the malignant forces of modern institutions from plunging the world into an organized hell? Interestingly, and perhaps importantly, in my experience of hospitals, universities and other such places, it is generally the employees at the bottom who most often act in ways that acknowledge the client or citizen as a singular person, someone with a name, a face, a history different from that of everyone else, someone to whom one can be kind.

At Penn State University Ivan Illich lectured to college students on the character of modern institutions. Touched by Illich's words, a young woman afterwards raised her hand and asked a question: "What do you suggest we do?" Illich saw something in her eyes, in her person, and immediately answered, "You have a summer vacation. Get a job in a public hospital at the bottom of the employee hierarchy, for example, emptying bed pans, and try to see, make the attempt *to see*, the people you serve, the personnel, the way the institution works." He passed on to the next student's question.

---

[3] Keneally, *Schindler's List.*

The central issue coming out of this experience then appeared before me: How do I protect those I love from the demonic in its specifically modern forms? The answer lies, I believe, in the practice of loving familiarity. This requires time and patience; one must learn to see, to listen. One needs to acquire the habit of being aware of the other, sensitive to the other's nuances. In my case, after a lifetime of casual indifference, I was somehow moved during his last years to be more attentive to my father, repeatedly visiting him, waiting for him to speak, listening to him, attempting to learn the shape of his life. When I knew this, when I knew *him*, I would know how to help him die. I would also find the courage to confront the professionals. So much depends on the intensity and accuracy of this very particular, personal knowledge. One has to know the other intimately. For example, while sitting there beside him, letting the images and events come up out of my memory, hour after hour, I saw something I had forgotten, and I saw it in a completely new light.

My father was born in a rural area of Poland, but his parents emigrated to America when he was two years old, and he grew up in Lincoln, Illinois, a small town where he remained all his life. The pull toward the soil, toward working in the soil, was strong in his peasant blood; his ancestors' experience of living on the land in the old country had been there for many generations. All the time he was married, a time when he carefully saved sufficient income, he wanted to buy a small farm.

His first job, which he began after finishing grammar school, was in a local greenhouse, working with plants. Near his home he maintained a large garden that took up two city lots. After his marriage, both he and our mother worked in the plots. I remember, as a child, complaining about having to help him in that garden. I see now that he and my mother tried to be self-sufficient in providing food for the family. They had the help of others, too. My maternal grandmother still lived in the country and had chickens. Fried chicken was a frequent Sunday dinner. When hogs were butchered, farmers on my father's rural mail route gave him gifts of fresh sausage.

All of us in the family were fortunate. Although we grew up in the Great Depression, Dad had a permanent job in the post office. It did not pay much in those years, but was quite sufficient for a thrifty family. In addition to his salary, he also provided meat for the table in winter. Out of old, discarded lumber, he made a large number of box traps to catch rabbits. After getting permission from the respective farmer, he would place the trap in a hidden place, but where he could see it from the road. As he drove his mail route, he could also run his traps. If he found a tripped trap with a rabbit, he put it in a burlap bag. But he had to be extremely careful when checking the traps. Once, a trap contained a skunk. When he arrived home, he took out the catch of the day, skillfully cut the animal's throat, affixed the back legs to two nails, then skinned and gutted the carcass. During the Depression we always had wild rabbit several times a week in cold weather. Dad was afraid of catching rabbits in warm weather because of the danger of disease. Extra animals, cleaned and ready for cooking, were given to family and friends.

But living in a farm town and working a large garden was not enough to satisfy his longing for the land. He located a small farm not far from Lincoln that was for sale, and wanted to buy it. He would keep his job, but we would move there to live, and he could become a part-time farmer. He carefully explained his plan; the seriousness of his desire was evident to all of us. But our mother said no; and she was adamant. She grew up on a farm, the eldest of four daughters. No sons who lived were born to my grandparents. So the girls had to work hard that the family might pay off the farm mortgage. Now Mom had married a man in town who already owned a house there—he had first built a house, then looked for a wife. She was happy with town living and never wanted to return to the country, except to visit. So, Dad denied what was probably the most powerful longing of his life out of love for his wife. After once bringing up the idea of moving to the country and seeing it shot down, he never mentioned it again. Nor did he ever manifest any resentment. On the contrary, insofar as I could remember, he threw himself single-mindedly and conscientiously into giving his wife, all of us, the best kind of home possible.

With three children, the house he had brought to the marriage proved to be too small. So they bought an old two-story house because of its good location on a corner, intending to tear it down in a few years. Together, they then designed, and hired a contractor to build, a new house on that property, utilizing much of the material from the old place.

As the children were leaving home, Mom talked about yet another house, a kind of "dream house" with everything conveniently on one floor, on the other side of the tracks, a better part of town. She was unreservedly and patently untroubled about her vocation. Before marriage, she had worked as a bookkeeper in an office. But from the day of her wedding, she devoted herself enthusiastically and joyfully to the job of homemaker and housewife. Although as a young woman she knew how to drive a Model T Ford, she never once drove the newer models that came out after she took up housekeeping. Although I don't know the kind of excitement Dad felt for the new house—I was away in the Marines and then in college—from the results I could see that he thoroughly enjoyed making the new home one of the most attractive properties in the neighborhood.

I also remembered other such actions—the ways in which he repeatedly and consistently reached out to his children, relatives, friends, and neighbors, in light of the respective ties that bound him to each of them. I had no memory of him acting in terms of self; he seemed to have nothing of a modern self about him. But I also remembered many small ways in which he asserted his independence. For example, his first automobile, purchased before his marriage, was a black Model T Ford, the only color available. He stayed with black Fords all his life, in spite of our arguments in favor of some other make or color each time he bought a new car.

In so many ways, he appeared to reject the modern world, the world which, finally, turned against him and attempted to rob him of his death. Reflecting on the actions of his life, I searched for their pattern, their meaning. Then the concept came to me from out of the Middle Ages. For a thousand years, philosophers and theologians had tried to talk about the Trinity. One of the ideas that some of them came up with was that of a *relatio subsistens*, a subsistent relationship. According to the tradition in which they worked, the two words were contrary to one another, the expression was illogical, nonsensical. A relation only exists between two things, it has no existence of itself. And *subsistens* means totally independent existence, neither needing nor admitting anything else. These men used the notion of a *relatio subsistens*, then, to talk about the Persons of the Trinity—each existed only as a relation to the other two. No one could exist for itself.[4]

Since my father was a man of deep faith—which I noticed, for example, from the way he prayed—I would expect him to express his faith directly in the way he lived; and he did. His life made the ancient concepts sensible—accessible to my sense experience—as the ideas in turn marvelously illumined his life. His final gift to me, then, was this:

[4] See Aquinas, *Summa theologiae*, I, q. 29, art. 4, corp.

To some small degree I was enabled to act as he had acted, to focus my attention on someone else, not on myself . . . I helped him die his own death.

2

An Afternoon's Gift

THE GREYHOUND bus arrives at my final destination; I get off, re-
trieve a bag from under the bus, and stretch. Now that I'm over
seventy, I sometimes feel the ride more achingly than in former years.
But this was not an arduous trip; I only traveled from State College
to Bloomington, Eastern Pennsylvania to Central Illinois. One night
on the bus is no strain at all, although perhaps I don't sleep well. Two
nights, however, are a kind of limit; after all those hours in a bus seat, I
begin to feel a continual desire for a bed . . . which means I'm also per-
sistently distracted from the book I'm reading.

I have to be careful not to fall into a certain complacency, which inevitably veers off into a kind of self-righteousness. True, it's better to take
a bus rather than a plane . . . if I'm interested in the effects on my soul
and, secondarily, on the condition of the earth . . . but walking is better yet, as I learned in Spain, when I covered a greater distance on foot
than just now by bus. To get to my destination, Compostela, I needed
thirty-two days, whereas the present journey took less than two days.
Then, I was midway to seventy; now I'm nearly midway to eighty . . .
differences.[1]

Walking alone across Spain, cleaning my mind through reading
nothing during that month, emptying my imagination of its usual images, I was able to reflect on various dimensions of moving through space
and time. I came to believe that *any* travel needed to be questioned.
A primary concern for one who wanted to believe and participate in
the Incarnation, for example, was to find and insert self in my proper
place, my fitting home, the spot where I belonged, and remain there.
My identification with the Incarnation is in proportion to the depth of
my living in Creation. That, in turn, is dependent on familiarity with

---

[1] Hoinacki, *El Camino. Walking to Santiago de Compostela.*

my surroundings, and commitment to a specific place. I can't achieve all that traveling hither and yon.

I felt I had to walk to Compostela because some internal voice called me to that place, called me to make a journey already blessed by the feet of probably more than a million pilgrims, walking from all over Europe in the last thousand years. Yesterday, I got on a bus and made a trip to visit my family. This seemed an appropriate reason to leave my temporary home, my place in Pennsylvania.

Over the years, I have found that bus travel in America is significantly different from air travel. Bus passengers are from a lower economic level; in America, except for the Pacific Northwest, most of my fellow passengers are black; almost all the people I've met on a bus are there either to visit family or to find a job. Vacationers do not usually take a bus unless it is specially chartered. Criss-crossing most sections of America over several years, I have only one complaint: the quality and price of food. This has doubly pained me: To see people who display no signs of affluence putting their money into vending machines or handing it to a clerk at the cash register of a McDonald's. I'm moved to reflect on how simple it is to carry an empty water bottle and decent food bought *before* I get on the bus. It's easy to acquire nutritious and cheap provisions for the time I'll be on the bus, and in most places it's possible to refill a water bottle free and as often as I want; I don't have to buy junk food.

The bus no longer stops in the small town, Lincoln, where my family lives, so I will get off in a neighboring city about thirty miles away. My sister will pick me up, but she has a baby-sitting job and can't make the trip until about five hours after the arrival of the bus. When I spoke to her on the phone, I didn't tell her how long I would have to wait, only that I would arrive in Bloomington before she could meet me, that I had a book, and that there is a McDonald's nearby. I asked her to look for me there.

The bus station is a tiny building that seems to be open only for the sale of tickets just before bus departures; there is no space inside to sit. However, there are some small trees close by, surrounded by concrete benches and tables. One need not stand in the sun on a hot day. For five hours, though, I decide to be more comfortable; from past experience, I know that the concrete benches get harder with time. I pick up my luggage and walk about seventy-five yards to the McDonald's. Inside, I buy a small soft cone, sit at a table in a quiet corner, and open my book, Simone Weil's *Waiting for God*.[2]

After about an hour a young woman comes to my table and asks if I am waiting for my order. Absently and quickly glancing up, I say, "No, thanks, I'm just waiting." I don't actually look at her, but a vague thought flits through my mind: She must be an employee checking on customer needs. Then, while continuing to read, a puzzling idea interrupts me: Customers get their orders at the counter after paying . . . How could I be waiting for an order? But I don't pursue the question.

An hour or two later, a young woman—perhaps the same one— approaches and asks if she can get me anything. "No, thank you," I answer, "I'm waiting for my sister who will meet me here." This time I look up at her, and catch myself continuing to stare after she smiles, turns and walks away. Now I'm intrigued. Something tells me she's the same person who came earlier. Why does a McDonald's employee come to my table twice? and, Why that same person?

I noticed that her face is not quite "right," it's slightly awry or irregular. Further, her body appeared somewhat misproportioned, rather lumpy, almost misshapen. She walked away with an awkward swaying motion, maybe revealing a little limp. She definitely does not come anywhere close to matching fashion model norms for body shape and facial features. I slowly reach the conclusion that she is what people call handicapped. I'm pretty certain she would not do well on a conventional intelligence test. But something very unusual, quite striking, shines out from her person: she's attractive, and obviously quite open and friendly.

After leaving McDonald's with my sister, I continued to think about the worker. Certain facts were simple and clear. She was the only employee who came up to me in those five hours and she was the only one handicapped. Trying to remember the other workers, I think she was the only employee so endowed. It seems highly probably that the other young workers noticed I was there. Carefully considering my two short contacts with her, I decide she was not sent out to check on me, nor was she moved by curiosity.

For a few moments, my attention was completely fixed on her. All the nuances of her manner indicated that she acted out of a single motive, a pure heart: She wanted to reach out to me, to help me. Although

---

[2] Weil, *Waiting for God*.

I was a total stranger, my welfare appeared to be uppermost in her sensibility; she was solely interested in *me*.

The certainty of this conclusion was confirmed by the book I was reading at the time. Simone Weil places great importance on attention:

> If there is a real desire, if the thing desired is really light, the desire for light produces it. There is a real desire when there is an effort of attention. It is really light that is desired if all other incentives are absent.

I was attentive to the young woman because I desired a light, the light of understanding who she was in that situation. The certainty of my perception is also confirmed by Simone Weil's observation in the same book:

> Certainties of this kind are experimental. But if we do not believe in them before experiencing them, if at least we do not behave as though we believed in them, we shall never have the experience that leads to such certainties. There is a kind of contradiction here.[3]

There was some spark, some light, in the young woman's face and eyes, her very actions, her person. She did something beautiful, but what kind of beauty was this? How make sense of it? Seeing me, a solitary stranger, she reached out. I can only conclude that her action was one of truth and goodness, the very truth and goodness I find in the Gospel. But I keep coming back to the light in her eyes, which appeared to project a certain ineffable beauty.

Two mutually reinforcing actions came out of me: I perceived some spark that indicated a trace of some further reality, perhaps what an Aristotelian would call a form, a modification of her person that made her a certain special kind of person; further, I was held there, I couldn't just drop her. According to Hans Urs von Balthasar, I was enraptured. "If all beauty is objectively located at the intersection of two moments which Thomas [Aquinas] calls *species* and *lumen* ("form" and "splendor"), then the encounter of these is characterized by the two moments of beholding and of being enraptured."[4] A form, what Medievalists called a *species* (a "likeness"), through my seeing, revealed a comeliness, a *species* transformed into *speciosa* (what is beautiful), because of a certain splen-

---

[3] Weil, *Waiting for God*, 107, for both quotes.
[4] Balthasar, *Seeing the Form*, 11.

dor shining out from her. I feel I must return to Greek thought and the Middle Ages for the concepts to describe our meeting.

The young woman's beauty opened my seeing to a series of analogies: Her disorder—stumbling a bit, handicapped—was like the disorder of nature, or the disorder of the Bible, both hiding a higher order, a truer beauty. If I were to hear the *Divina Commedia* read aloud, I would get only gibberish—its meaning would be hidden from me because I do not know Italian. I would be deaf to its poetic beauty. This is similar to the "ignorance" of Socrates seeking his *daimon*; perhaps like St. John of the Cross, plunging into the dark night of the senses and then of the soul, seeking the Spirit. The Anthroposophists hold to a truth: They see the soul/spirit/beauty hidden in the handicapped person whom they welcome into their Camp Hill communities. The lack of *self* consciousness of the young woman, her conventional foolishness in approaching me, a stranger, can be understood in the foolishness of Dostoievsky's *Idiot*, indeed, in the Russian tradition of the Holy Fool.

I experienced a vision of beauty in that McDonald's. I was also granted an infinitely more inclusive seeing: What I saw was a *way* to faith, to faith in the eternal reality of beauty, together with truth and goodness, as transcendentals and, further, as an entry to faith in God. Everything in the world that is fine and beautiful is an epiphany, a radiance and splendor breaking out from a veiled or hidden depth of being. Ultimately, for the believer, the epiphany is a revelation of God in the lovely (*speciosa*) forms found in the world.

The young woman revealed reality to me: God is to the soul what the soul/mind is to the senses; through her, therefore, I saw a relationship between me and God. My belief in the Incarnation further shows what happened to me that afternoon in McDonald's: God is to the Word what I am to words. As in the story of Adam I, too, possess a capacity for naming. I enjoy this ability through grace, namely, through my belief in the Lord. I have acquired a participatory power.

The *esse*, the existence itself of all these analogies is based on my faith, and that means a kind of obedience to God, to the Spirit running through the Hebrew Scriptures and discernible elsewhere, too, for example, in Socrates and the neo-Platonists. Once the Incarnation occurred, once Christ became man, all nature and history became filled with redemptive images—for the person graced with faith.

As I mentioned, the young woman came up to me while I was reading Simone Weil's *Waiting for God*. She writes about beauty: "Beauty is the only finality here below." Later, she explains that this is true,

> Because beauty has no end in view . . . here below there are no ends. All the things we take for ends are means. That is an obvious truth. Money is the means of buying, power is the means of commanding. It is more or less the same for all the things that we call good.
>
> Only beauty is not the means to anything else. It alone is good in itself, but without our finding any particular good or advantage in it. It seems itself to be a promise and not a good. But it only gives itself; it never gives anything else.[5]

That is what I experienced in that elfin, misshapen child, that young, unusual worker. She had nothing to give me except her beauty.

Reflecting on that afternoon, I was confused by its extreme ambiguities. When I look around, I see that our ways of living are making the earth an uglier place, whether I consider the rising proportion of involuntarily destitute people in the world or the destruction of Creation. Sitting in McDonald's, and in the midst of depressing thoughts, a dazzling comeliness broke through. Sorrowfully, however, I cannot but agree with Simone Weil in what I read while waiting there.

> Today one might think that the white races had almost lost all feeling for the beauty of the world, and that they had taken it upon them the task of making it disappear from all the continents where they have penetrated with their armies, their trade and their religion.

McDonald's certainly stands for Americans' drive to establish their markets everywhere while the ideology of a so-called free market reigns powerfully. As the principal arms merchant on the globe, America penetrates deeply into most other countries. The American Way of Life establishes its hegemony, either in "happy" realization or frustrated desire over all who see the television and cinema screens throughout the world. And yet . . .

> And yet at the present time, in the countries of the white races, the beauty of the world is the only way by which we can allow God to penetrate us . . .

[5] Weil, *Waiting for God*, 165–7, for both quotes.

She later adds that

> ... a sense of beauty, although mutilated, distorted, and soiled, remains rooted in the heart of man as a powerful incentive. It is present in all the preoccupations of secular life. If it were made true and pure, it would sweep all secular life in a body to the feet of God, it would make the total incarnation of the faith possible.[6]

As I become more conscious of myself as a modern person, I am also more aware of myself as an instrumentalized person. Perhaps someone once picked up a stone and threw it at an animal, in self-defense or out of hunger. Perhaps Prometheus stole fire from the gods and provided humans with this wondrous instrument. Perhaps Ellul's notion of *la technique* is the instrumental means dominating and controlling the lives of all today, as his argument leads me to conclude.[7] Whatever be the patent or qualified truth of these statements, I feel that the contemporary world is so arranged that almost everything is instrumental, with the result that, ultimately, each of us is in danger of becoming completely and irrevocably instrumentalized—all my actions, thoughts, desires, dreams, "ends." Nevertheless, the dismal reality of a plastic world was blown apart for one instant that afternoon: A young woman, whose name I do not know, whom I'll probably never see again, graced me with her beauty and thereby freed me for a fleeting moment from an instrumentalized life, thereby pointing the way to a richer reality.

A further aspect of the ambiguity of my experience is a large question: Why? Why was this young woman afflicted with her debilities? Why are there such apparent imperfections in the world? Failures of nature, perhaps? But, paradoxically, the very blemish that caught my attention was simultaneously an entry into the recognition of beauty.

I was driven to ask a question that has troubled many throughout history: Ultimately, why does evil exist in the world? With St. Augustine, I can think about evil as the lack of a due good; it has a strictly privative character; something that should be present is missing. Simone Weil is explicit and consistent in her remarks on this question. For example, in the book I was reading she writes,

---

[6] Weil, *Waiting for God*, 162–3, for the three quotes.
[7] Ellul, *The Technological Bluff*.

If we examine human society and souls closely and with real attention, we see that wherever the virtue of supernatural light is absent, everything is obedient to mechanical laws as blind and as exact as the laws of gravitation. . . .

The mechanism of necessity . . . from our present standpoint, and in human perspective, it is quite blind. If, however, we transport our hearts beyond ourselves, beyond the universe, beyond space and time to where our father dwells, and if from there we behold this mechanism, it appears quite different. What seemed to be necessity becomes obedience. . . . In the beauty of the world brute necessity becomes an object of love.[8]

If I follow her thinking, I recognize that the young woman's condition derives from certain causes, which are termed causes of nature. Simone Weil never wavers in her opinion that " . . . nature is at the mercy of the blind play of mechanical necessities."[9] Ambiguity becomes mystery if I try to enter the terrain where necessity becomes an object of love. Since I am much less gifted than Simone Weil, I find myself drifting toward the medieval expression, "credo quia absurdum est," I believe because it is absurd. She simply states where perception of the absurd takes one:

Impossibility—that is, radical impossibility clearly perceived, absurdity—is the gate leading to the supernatural. All we can do is knock on it. It is another who opens.[10]

Thinking about the impact of the young woman on me, I later picked up the Gospel of St. Matthew and read the Beatitudes again. She seemed to fit them, for example, "Blessed are the pure in heart, for they will see God" (Matt 5:3–10). But it was also necessary to reread Matthew's comments on the Final Judgment (Matt 25:31–46); she appeared to fit there, too, for example, "I was a stranger and you took me in."

I had the sensation of seeing these familiar words for the first time; further, they metamorphosed into a pressing actuality, a jolting truth. I discovered something further: My "seeing" was a very different kind of seeing; I've never understood words the way I understood these; I've never *seen* in such a manner before. Abruptly, I knew that the Beatitudes, in the particularity of my situation, don't point to someone "out there,"

[8] Weil, *Waiting for God*, 129.
[9] Ibid., 119.
[10] Weil, *The Notebooks*, vol. II, 412–13.

in the sense of referring to, describing, naming, or stopping at some other. Rather, someone out there brings the words to me, down to me, inserting them deep in my self, in my being. She looked at me; I was the stranger she took in; she saw me purely, that is, she saw God. If that happened, and I am convinced it did, then she gave me an inestimable gift, that I might become her!

I'm uncertain about how creation is the occasion of grace. Therefore, I don't know how to say the young woman *blessed* me, that she in some sense gave me a special grace, the grace that opened these scriptural passages to me. But I know that, because of her, I have seen truths hitherto hidden from me, and my seeing was an experience that filled all of me. She revealed me to myself, told me who I was or, rather, who I can be. With this knowing, I also felt a strong desire: that the truth of the revelation *be* me; I wanted to become the truth of the words.

As never before in my life, the scriptural passages came alive for me through the young woman's gift. I then understood why it was necessary for me to sit in that McDonald's on that day for so many hours. I came into immediate contact with the finally unfathomable mystery of necessity, the necessity that Simone Weil asserts is the rule of the universe. Given—in a limited sense, knowable—certain physical causes, it was necessary that the young woman be born misshapen. But in a way I cannot understand, the physical necessity is consonant with a higher eternal law, the governance contained in God's Providence.

Today, however, an intense international competition whose winner will walk away with unprecedented fame and wealth threatens to rule the life sciences. Fantasist scientists and publicists who dream of the benefits of eugenics want to ensure that no person be born "abnormal." Eugenics, as both theory and practice, seeks to eliminate handicapped persons from the world; the necessity I saw, the necessity that occasioned my vision of beauty, would no longer exist.

I am a citizen of the country that pioneered eugenic sterilization, a country where the first law authorizing such practices was passed in 1907. The Supreme Court upheld this statute in 1927. It is said that the eugenic sterilization law of California influenced the Nazi policy of 1933 and the following years. The revelations and revulsions that came out of Europe after the defeat of the Nazis did not adversely affect government-authorized sterilization in the American South. After a Congressional inquiry, such a policy was stopped only in 1973.[11]

These programs had a double purpose: to get rid of undesirable people and to improve the "race." That has meant to eliminate those whom the science-based experts designated as degenerate, and to promote the propagation of allegedly superior people. Some would claim that the Nazis gave eugenics a bad name. That, I suspect, is behind the spurious distinction some try to make between eugenics and genetic counseling. Those in favor of such counseling go to extreme lengths to distance themselves from the Nazis. It's true; they are not Nazis. What they propose is infinitely worse. Under the cover of a series of contemporary fallacies, for example, a skewed understanding of reproductive "rights," choice, freedom, and individual liberty, the scientific, governmental and media promoters advocate the use of sophisticated technological interventions and esoteric statistical formulae to convince a miseducated, confused and fashion-driven public that the future of *their* child's physical and mental character should be in *their* hands. That means, in the hands of ambitious and aggressive techno-scientific expert practitioners.[12] It's difficult to hear the small still voice questioning: What about Creation? What is its origin? What is its end? What is *the* good?

Genetic manipulation, including genetic engineering and counseling, are designed that the young woman I met in McDonald's may never come to exist on this earth. These modern sciences are organized to circumvent this kind of necessity in nature, to create a new kind of "human," based on *statistical* necessity. All such efforts are directed to one end or outcome: to deny the beauty I experienced. If that were to happen no one will ever see what I saw. I ask myself: Is the ultimate purpose of public health policy in many so-called advanced nations to remove beauty from the world? For I believe it to be true that the world needs *this* beauty, the beauty of the young McDonald's worker, that beauty exist at all.

If those who place career first succeed in eliminating the beauty of the handicapped, an infinitesimal but essential part of an infinite whole

[11] Kevles, "Grounds for Breeding," 3–4.

[12] See Pfaff, "Eugenics, Anyone?" 23–4. Pfaff discusses "the consequences of professedly value-free science," claiming that "the horror becomes greater: those allowed to be born are decided on the basis of sex, medically-defined 'defects,' or any trivial excuse. And there are no principles or limits, no way to get limits to be acknowledged."

will have been destroyed; a necessary component of a higher, admittedly mysterious good, will be missing. In medieval philosophy truth, goodness and beauty, as transcendentals, are one, ontologically. In Creation, they constitute a fragile whole that anyone of us can violate. Our raison d'être is not to chip away at them, but to desire and seek them. I fear the beauty I saw that afternoon in McDonald's will disappear from a world governed by *la technique*. In seeing the beauty of the young woman, I was given an insight into the beauty of the universe, the beauty of the cosmos. Further, I *saw* the unity of truth and goodness and beauty in their transcendental character . . . they exist in Being, the reality believers name God.

3

Dying Is Not Death

Belief and Sophistication

IF I want to believe in the Gospel, desire to act in a way so that, if the Incarnation had not occurred, my life would make no sense whatever, what do I do about the influence and impact of technology on me and the world? How do I answer the disturbing questions I sense prowling around in the ever-changing shadows? As a sat in my room in Bremen, Germany, reading and reflecting, I received a letter from my brother about two weeks before Christmas, 1998.

This was most unusual, for I could not remember having received a letter from Bernard before, although I had left out hometown over fifty years earlier, and lived in various countries in Latin America and Europe. In our family, letter-writing was always a gender-specific activity. First my mother, then my sister, wrote all the letters. My father and brother read my regularly sent letters, but never answered them. Because of my difficulties with technological instruments in general, and especially with those mediating between me and someone about whom I cared, I never used the phone, except in extreme emergencies.

On that December day, Bernard did not depend on Elizabeth, our sister, to write me his news (our parents were dead by this date). Looking back, I see that *he* took the initiative, as he would continue to do for the rest of his life. His letter was dated December 16, 1998. What to make of the fact? On December 16, 1999, he died.

Beginning in secondary school, I have been writing; in the last dozen or so years, every day. Many times, as teacher or friend, I have helped others write what they wanted to say. I suppose it's accurate to note that I read many books, probably too many. Bernard, I suspected, almost never wrote, and probably read few books. Because of this and, more importantly, because of the content itself, I found the way he expressed himself in the letter most unusual; I had never come across anything like the "style" of his writing. Style, of course, is not the proper word. Perhaps his manner of writing was analogous to what I once noticed in the public talks given by a friend, an Irishman: He was not looking over his own shoulder when he spoke; he manifested a radical unself-consciousness.

It's my strong belief that most people are like myself: We are almost always looking over our own shoulder. "How'm I doing?" I constantly ask myself. How do I look? What impression will I make? The list noting the various aspects and degrees of self-awareness can be extended quite far. Such an attitude was totally absent from the letter; he simply achieved a directness I never thought possible. Although I had never read such a text, I somehow recognized what I was mulling over: a transparent revelation of a self unaware of what it was not disclosing. I was surprisedly exposed to what I would have maintained to be a near impossibility . . . but it happened! Among the sparse sentences I read:

> This note is to let you know about my medical condition. I am having difficulty in swallowing solid food. I went to the doctor for an examination . . . he told me I had a tumor in my esophagus. It is also cancer.

His local small town doctor in Lincoln arranged for him to see a specialist in a nearby large city, Springfield. After all the X-rays, Bernard wrote, the doctor said " . . . he can see no more cancer in my body [that is, except for the one tumor]." The physician proposed to cut out the tumor, "lift up my stomach and reattach it to the esophagus. The doctor said this is a common practice performed each day . . ." in that city. (Bernard never submitted to the surgery.)

From Bernard's report on the words and actions of the doctors, I recognized a sharp division between his and their position. The separation, insofar as I could tell, held true throughout the year, while each party became more and more extreme in its stand. Each side progressed in its own direction: Bernard advanced, going deeper and deeper into reality; the doctors, too, advanced, proceeding deeper and deeper into unreality, into a fantasy world, the world in large part created by modern technology.

I have witnessed doctors wandering around, seemingly busy, seemingly knowing what they are doing, but in reality, lost, truly out of touch with the person before them, out of touch with what is happening to that person, out of touch with where that person is going. Many doctors have been turned into a new kind of zombie, perhaps related to the nerds attached and addicted to their screens. But, as I realized more fully in the course of that year, Bernard was the first person I had met who cut through all the hype, all the false promises, all the occult incantations of medical experts, all the superstitions of the medical system.

He ended his "letter": "I hope you have a good Xmas."

Two more letter/reports arrived before the end of the year. The division I saw in the first letter held its course: Bernard facing what lay in front of him, the doctors shifting about in never-never land. One doctor spoke a version of truth: "He said I had 3 options—radiation—surgery—chemotherapy—or all three." From what I have heard, this is a contemporary ploy of some physicians: Let the patient decide! This means, apparently, that the patient is in charge; it's his initiative that ultimately counts.

As I immediately saw, the doctor gave an incomplete list of options, thereby attempting to falsify Bernard's world. Starting with the most radical option—to walk out of the office, rejecting altogether the Weltanschauung of allopathic medicine—to a number of alternative routes one can choose, Bernard actually faced a large array of options. Later, I searched for an answer to the question that hung over all these absurdities throughout the year: How did Bernard see through the deceptions? He was just an ordinary person—or so I imagined. He enjoyed watching TV, was a Chicago Bears fan, and regularly played penny ante poker with his friends. He and his wife liked to shop and eat out occasionally.

Reflecting on myself, it seemed I lived in an unreal world, the world of books. I believed one needed to read a lot of sophisticated critiques of the technological project to know what was going on. Further, one needed to know something about the Greeks' teaching on hubris to view with proper skepticism the fantastic claims of the medical system, to be able to strike through the vanities and exaggerations. For those who accept the Scriptures, immersion in the wisdom of Ecclesiastes provides a penetrating light.

Later, the more sophisticated tests (for example, an MRI) show " . . . a small amount of cancer in a bone in my left leg. He [the doctor] said it was insignificant." More deception . . . deliberate lies? Bernard laconically notes, "It [the cancer] may be spreading in my body."

In a letter written shortly after the first of the New Year (1999), he mentions undergoing chemotherapy, adding, "I feel fine with no pain," but he gives no details about the chemotherapy treatments, except for their number and duration. He writes that his doctor took more X-rays and, "He said the tumor has not enlarged. It has stopped growing." I interpret this to mean that the doctor is fostering another illusion: The treatment is effective, Bernard is getting better, perhaps he will be cured . . . whatever that might mean. The division remains in force.

The Transcendent

Then I received a letter, written on February 1, 1999, which completely changed my views: of my brother, of my studies, of the opinions of technological critics, of the world, of the universe, of the Beyond. Ever since I received that letter I have felt it is not for me alone, but also for my friends, for fellow Catholics, for those confused by the chaos of our age, and for all persons who ask questions. Since the day I read the letter, I've thought about it; I've tried to understand what I should do with it. That comes down to mean, essentially, how to share it, how to share this inestimable gift.

In just under two months from the original news, the diagnosis of a cancerous tumor in his esophagus, he wrote me a different kind of letter, one like none I've ever seen or heard about in my life. From what he wrote, I see he is no longer in the doctors' offices, no longer in the medical system, indeed, no longer in the world of sense and everyday experience. He has grasped a truth which, perhaps, few ever suspect before their death. He has understood and felt something the greatest thinkers known in history have struggled to know, perhaps even to experience. All this from a man who lived in the one house he and our father, with the help of his future wife, built. A modest house in a subdivision of other modest houses. A journalist, glancing at the neighborhood, would immediately categorize it: yes, of course, lower middle class.

The letter begins: "This is a letter of love. Love of my God, you, Liz, Jeff, Ethan, Kallie, and Marilyn, my wife." In addition to his wife, he has named the living blood relatives of his immediate family.

He's uncertain . . . either the malady or the medication has occasioned a change in his thinking. But he has no doubts about the source of this thinking.

I tell Marilyn that God puts these thoughts in my mind. I do not go out and pick them and put them there. When I dream I do not go out and pick the dream I wish for. God puts the dream in my head. I believe that God has given me a gift, to see Him better, understand your work better. See Elizabeth and the rest of the family in a more loving way.

Sometimes I think God said, "Come follow me; I want you in heaven with me today." And I said, "Good Father, I have been waiting a lifetime to see you. To get away from all this sin on earth and be happy in heaven where there is no sin and everything is good."

I hope to see my Mom and Dad again. Marilyn and I are closer to each other now than all the 37 yrs. of our marriage. I do not think that Marilyn or I could love another person more than we love each other now. God has brought us stronger together with his and our love.

People who knew our father rather well were accustomed to remark that he was almost totally inarticulate. He did not have much to say, and never, to my knowledge, ever spoke of his intimate thoughts, wishes, and dreams. I always believed that Bernard inherited this characteristic, and that I, who endlessly speak and write about what is in my mind, was a maverick in our family, in a family otherwise universally chary of revealing emotion or internal thought. At the end of the document, he wrote again of the love of his wife for him. Among the expressions at the end of the letter, he concluded:

What more love does a man need to have? . . . God bless you all for loving me [he again explicitly names God, our mother and father, and the living members of his immediate blood relatives].

For just over half a year after the initial diagnosis, Bernard wrote other letters, too. They were reports in which he simply listed visits to doctors, tests taken, results, doctors' interpretations of these findings, and therapies administered. All the letters included the phrase, "I feel good," or, "I feel o.k." Occasionally, his comments caused me to stop and reflect. I again asked myself, "Where is he getting these insights? What is the source of his courage to accept them?" For example, in a letter written in March, he said:

With my illness I feel I know you better, also my family, God, our Church, my marriage, all life and death better. I think God has given me a gift with my sickness. I know now that my life and marriage is better than it has ever been. I think of you, my Dad and Mom each day.

As Bernard appears to penetrate reality more deeply, so the doctors escape farther into their chimerical world. After 288 hours of chemotherapy, interrupted now and then by various tests, such as X-rays, his principal doctor, after examining him again, said, " . . . everything looked O.K."

At this time, Bernard wrote:

If I only get two months or two years [more], I have accepted it. I know my body will not live forever . . . I feel good about my sickness and I am not depressed. I do not believe my life is in the hands of my doctors but God's. God gave me my life and he will take it when the time comes. That will be a great and happy day for me to see God.

His doctor, who had said that "everything looked O.K.," suggested he see the radiologist! . . . to start radiation treatments! From further tests, they told him they found cancer in his blood, in his left and right leg and, "I may have other cancer in my body." But the doctor had said, " . . . everything looked O.K."

In July, he got new X-rays, and five doctors examined them. The chief radiologist commented, "everything looks good." He added that Bernard "should not need any more treatments." Bernard mentions that the weather is hot but, "Since I had chemotherapy, the heat does not bother me."

Celebrating Lent

In 1999, the beginning of Lent, Ash Wednesday, occurred on February 17th. Shortly before that day, I had decided that each day during Lent I would think about the letter he wrote me on February 1st, and attempt to understand what he so generously shared with me. After a morning prayer and reflection, I would write him. I continued this daily practice throughout Lent, writing the last letter of the series on Easter Sunday, April 4th.

Catholics have traditionally imposed on themselves some form of penance, a mortification, a "dying to self," during the forty days of Lent, as a small act of preparation for the great feast of Easter. For example, those in religious orders might cut out all meat during the holy season. In the past few years, perhaps succumbing to self-indulgence, I have tended to adopt rather comfortable exercises. Since I am usually writing something or other every day, it was no real sacrifice to direct a daily letter to Bernard.

Shortly after the first of the year, I was again thinking about doxology, the praise of God. In Catholic tradition, raising one's voice, mind, and heart is especially emphasized in the liturgy, the formal public worship of God. The most elaborate and solemn expression of the liturgy occurs annually in Holy Week, from Palm Sunday to the end of Lent, Easter. I decided I would attempt to participate in the Holy Week liturgy in the best possible manner I could imagine.

Living in Germany, I did some searching, and approached people who knew the various places in Europe where the liturgy was carried out with great perfection and solemnity. I had decided to end Lent in a way that seemed most fitting and profitable: to witness the ceremonies of Holy Week in a monastery. What is the best monastery to experience the beauty of the liturgy? Knowledgeable people mentioned the Benedictine monastery at Einsiedeln, a short distance from Zürich, Switzerland, as one of the outstanding monastic sites for the quality of their chant. I wrote the guestmaster, asking him to reserve a place in the monastery for Holy Week.

Rereading copies of Bernard's letters, I was reminded of the impact the letter of February 1st had on me. After reading that letter, I could not accept the guestmaster's friendly and affirmative answer to my request. The monks at Einsiedeln would raise their voices, rhythmically bow, stand, and sit in the exercise of a magnificent week-long doxology with or without me. Since the monastery is famous throughout Europe, and liturgy-loving persons flock to such places for Holy Week, by not going I was probably ceding my room to a more faithful participant. My brother, without the advantages and discipline of a focused monastic tradition and life, has given me a dramatic example of someone striking through the various distractions and illusions peculiar to our times to reach a transcendental truth of our faith in the face of death. Pampering my own so-called religious sensibilities by traveling a great distance to a famous monastery appeared manifestly embarrassing, maybe even shameful. I immediately went to the local travel agent and asked her to get me the cheapest possible flight to the U.S. a couple of weeks later.

Bernard showed me what I thought I knew from the study of medieval philosophy, but had never really understood: *agere sequitur esse* (action follows being). I had tended to believe that I first had to articulate or spell out a truth before I could act or, strictly, *be*; it turned out that I really believed that *esse sequitur agree* (being follows action). Yes, Bernard acted, but he acted out of who he was, what he had become, what the Medievals called his *quidditas* ("whatness"). This was the source of his action and words.

Sitting at my desk, I had come to think that a cancer diagnosis was a good thing. With it, I would definitely know that I was going to die, perhaps sooner rather than later. But my actual experience of knowing others with a diagnosis was troubling. I had friends who, in the face of such a diagnosis, continued to create the fiction that they only suffered from some passing illness which would, indeed, pass. I had seen them maintain such an attitude right up into death! Other friends placed all their hopes in doctors and the medical establishment. They seemed to firmly believe they could fight and conquer cancer! They accompanied their doctors into a progressively darkening fanciful realm.

As I wrote Bernard, he reminded me of an old story reputed to be from Italy or Sicily. The story may be a piece of popular folk wisdom to illustrate a universal truth particularized by the contours of a certain people. There was a dangerously bitter feud between two families, perhaps what is called a blood feud. Some grave offence had been committed by a young man in one of the families. Brothers in the injured family worked out a plan to get revenge . . . to violate the young offender in the worst way they could imagine, to hurt him as seriously as you can harm anyone in this world.

They got their sister to seduce the young man. When the seduction actually occurred and the couple were in the height of their pleasure, the brothers killed the young man, believing that if he died at that moment, he would die in a state of mortal sin (committing the act of fornication). Not having the time or being able to repent his sin, he would be damned to hell for all eternity.

Whether the story is literally true is not the issue; it expresses a truth, a truth about the unknown, the afterlife . . . if one believes in the Gospel. From Bernard's letter, I saw that he had embraced the truth of his death out of a genuine belief in the words of Christ. He understood what it is to prepare for a good death.

The options presented to Bernard by his doctor do express a truth, if they are well understood. Mainstream medicine, faced with cancer, offers only three possibilities: a doctor can try to cut it out (surgery), burn it out (radiation), or poison it (chemotherapy). One can accept these measures as a true response to a human malady as long as one is under no illusion that they constitute a "final" cure; there is no *final* cure—for either living or dying; there is no cookbook recipe. In terms of joyful living, even when one is immersed in desolation or misery, the theological virtues remain: faith, hope, and love, and certain acquired moral virtues, as required from moment to moment, such as courage or humility. One in truly dire straits is confronted with the necessity of seeking outside, that is, transcendental, intervention.

I saw from Bernard's letter that both he and Marilyn understood this. They fully knew there is something more basic than the chemicals and the burning, namely, their fundamental attitude, stance, faith, in front of the whole situation. Both of them *knew* where they stood, they were on solid ground: They needed to bridge the "distance" between time and eternity.

As Bernard admitted in the letters, the treatments had great power—to harm, to kill; otherwise, they would not be effective against cancerous cells. I wondered about his doctors. Never before in history have doctors possessed such power. In proportion to their thoughtfulness and conscientiousness, they must stand in awe, or aghast, at such dangerous interventions. I could understand better their approach: giving Bernard the three available options, and letting *him* decide which one he wished to pursue. Such an approach made it easier for them to live with themselves . . . no matter what doctors do, all their patients die.

Often, however, patients' discomfort or extreme pain is unnecessarily prolonged by the treatment; they live beyond their time. Such could be good if the person has worked out a personal art of suffering, and chooses to undergo the pain and anguish. The historical record is replete with believers who have accepted, even welcomed, physical and mental affliction, with hearts fixed on their Lord, the abandoned Jesus. The idea and practice of an art of suffering are historically recoverable. But, as with all arts, one needs to accept the desirability of this art, to know the "rules," and acquire the skill to apply them. Because of a nefarious psychologization in the air today, an art of suffering appears perverse to many. If one or a few were to seek to practice such an art, the truth remains: it is the most difficult of all the arts known to the various cultures.

From Bernard's ingenuous reports of the doctors' comments, I saw that these men evidenced no awareness of the hard reality of an art of suffering. Rather, they appeared firmly ensconced in a fabulous world. Perhaps they had reached a state of self-delusion, a state that formerly assigned people to bedlam. I again asked myself: Where is Bernard getting the light and strength to recognize the deceptions and stand up to the system?

In the seventeenth century, a great and complex controversy raged among Catholics in France, and the opposing positions can still be discerned today in the moral reasoning of thinking persons. Grossly, one can speak of rigor versus laxity. Historically, the rigorists have inclined toward a community (or church) of the perfect. The other side has tended to hold that one must be more lenient, one has to take people where they are; one cannot make impossible demands; often, one must go along with what is less than ideal.[1]

What I found, through knowing him, and this knowledge was wonderfully confirmed by the letters, was that Bernard showed me how both extremes are true, and come together. He lived an ordinary life, he enjoyed the small pleasures of middle-class affluence, he maneuvered his way through a very imperfect world. Suddenly, he was faced with the extraordinary, he came face to face with the most terrifying difficulty each of us must confront: how to die well. At this moment, tolerance or accommodation is of no help; one needs a surplus of severity, perhaps heroism, considering the delusions and false assurances of the medical system. Bernard proved himself capable of facing this trial.

A Pilgrim Destiny

Toward the end of Lent, I was back in the U.S., at State College, Pennsylvania. On my walk to the university office each morning, I directly faced the rising sun. Seeing the sun shining through the still leafless tree branches, and enjoying the gratuitous pleasure of this natural beauty each morning, I marveled at the loveliness. I recalled other sunrises. For example, once I awoke and basked in the scene, looking out the window of a Greyhound bus as the night slowly retreated and the

---

[1] Among the many books on the subject, one can begin with Kolakowski, *God Owes Us Nothing*.

changing sky in a treeless Texas plain colored and brightened . . . so much beauty in the world . . .

Each morning I also thought of Simone Weil's opinion about the necessity of such phenomena, the *necessity* of the world. She held that everything which happens in the world does so by an absolutely strict necessity.[2] So, in a physical sense, the sight of the sun rising each morning is to look at a quite ordinary phenomenon. How many people do I know who, lost in wonder, watch the sun rise each morning?

I saw, from Bernard's letters, that he regarded the existence and growth of the tumor as necessary, as necessary as I considered the sunrise. One might argue that the two necessities are highly dissimilar; one lovely and pleasant, the other, frightening and painful. But one must accept each necessity; they are both natural. Ultimately, it makes no more sense to rebel against one any more than against the other. One could, however, harbor feelings of anger or resentment about the tumor. But all such emotional releases were absent from Bernard's letters. He progressed from information to knowledge to peace to wisdom . . . to gratitude.

To recognize his situation truly Bernard looked *beyond* tumors and sunrises, beyond the world itself; he knew *where* to look to find understanding. He thereby gave me an example of *how* to act when one faces an extremely terrifying personal crisis.

Shortly after Easter, I was in Illinois to see Bernard and the rest of the family. I returned again at the end of the summer, and was able to help the family celebrate Bernard's seventieth birthday on September 2, 1999. Two months later, I was back in Germany. I had bought a round-trip ticket, calculating a return date in December, thinking that Bernard would not live beyond that month.

Meanwhile, Bernard had stopped going to the hospital, had stopped seeing doctors altogether, and was enrolled in a hospice program. On the first visit of the hospice nurse, Bernard told him there was no need to stop by the house, since he (Bernard) felt reasonably well, though weakened. As it turned out, Bernard did not see a doctor in the last two months of his life, a fact I considered a definite blessing. He had followed the conventional course of cancer treatment with a growing and maturing awareness that such procedures are severely limited in effectiveness and scope. While still able to enjoy the pleasures of being with

---

[2] Weil, *Gravity and Grace*, 90–98. See also *The Notebooks*, vol. 2, 403.

his family and making modest outings with his wife, he accomplished the final radical and definitive act every seriously ill person must complete: to turn one's living completely around, to abandon efforts at cure and long only for palliative care.

At one moment, a cousin of ours who lives in a Chicago suburb called and told Bernard she could get him an appointment with one of the best-known oncologists in Chicago, a man so busy that you needed special influence to see him. Bernard said, "No, thanks. The only thing he can do is tell me I'm dying; I already know that."

Several days before I was scheduled to catch my return flight to the States, Elizabeth called to tell me the hospice nurse thought Bernard was rapidly going down. I immediately took the streetcar to the airline counter at the airport and asked to change my ticket. The young woman worked hard to find a loophole, since I had a cheap ticket that could not be changed.

On a Sunday, December 12, 1999, after an overnight bus ride from Pennsylvania, I arrive at Bernard and Marilyn's home . . . briefly greet family gathered there . . . go into the bedroom and find Bernard in the bed he and Marilyn had shared for the thirty-eight years of their marriage . . . I'm uncertain what or who I see on the bed . . . two bumps holding up the sheet catch my eye . . . later, I notice they are his hip bones . . . his arms and legs like shrunken and wrinkled reeds . . . where other men have a stomach or belly, he has a deep hollow . . . he has not eaten in days . . . now and then he takes a few small ice chips . . . usually, his eyes are closed, covered with a damp wash cloth . . . he opens his eyes . . . a very slight flicker or perhaps almost a gleam that I almost miss . . . he recognizes me . . . I sit down . . . and wait . . . straining to absorb his presence . . . focusing my attention on him . . . on my seventy-year-old brother . . . is this the person who shocked me with that letter? . . . will I finally come to know him?

After some hours, I arise and walk into the kitchen. Marilyn and Jeff, their son, hand me a one-page photocopy, asking that I read it. Going through the words, I notice they are watching me closely. Why?

It's a recent article from a professional geriatric journal. The principal point: dehydration can be medically beneficial for a dying person; the hospice nurse gave them the article.[3]

---

[3] Taylor, "Benefits of Dehydration in Terminally Ill Patients," 271–72. See also Ganzini, "Nurses' Experience with Hospice Patients Who Refuse Food and Fluids to Hasten Death," 359–65; and a commentary: Jacobs, "Death by Voluntary Dehydration—What

Later I hear that their closest friends, a husband and wife, acting out of an assumption found in the minds of all medicalized mentalities today—that means, almost everyone—voiced a strong criticism: Marilyn should take Bernard to the hospital where he would be given a proper IV, medication, professional care, and so on, all under the supervision of *doctors!*

Such well-intentioned critics . . . Do they ever consider that the actions they advocate might prolong one's time on earth a few minutes, hours, days, and transform a human death into a medical statistic? Such voices, especially those coming from friends, can deeply and insidiously inflict guilt.

I speak to Marilyn and Jeff . . . "Simply look . . . see what signs he gives; people in his place generally know what is best, they *know* whether they should eat or drink, whether they 'need' any liquids. He doesn't have to make a speech or explain . . . he is telling us exactly what to do."

During that first night in their home, about 4 a.m. Monday morning, Marilyn awakens me—she is sleeping in one adjacent bedroom, I in the other—Bernard wants to cross the hall to the bathroom!

Later, Marilyn tells me he had refused to put a portable commode next to his bed and they had both rejected the offer of a bed whose ends can be lowered and raised. They did not want to turn their home into a hospital!

I suggest that Marilyn order a hand urinal, and urge her to return to bed, then take up a turn to watch at his bedside. I'm still feeling the effects of jet lag . . . my time entering their time.

Marilyn's boss gave her an indefinite leave of absence from her job at the County Clerk's office. It's a small town, people know one another, it's possible to interpret rules generously.

We're near the end of Advent. The Church invites us to meditate on time, an endless subject for reflection. Bernard seems to be moving in a different time, not a clock time; perhaps I can enter his time, perhaps I can enter the time of Advent; his time appears to be coinciding with the time of Advent. A few days ago, he told Marilyn he had completed saying all his prayers, he was now ready to die. This must be to live in the time of Advent . . . to live in the time of the Lord's coming.

the Caregivers Say," 325–26.

Contemplating his face, especially the eyes, I think I see the *facies hippocratica* (Hippocratic face).[4] How clear it is! How plain to see! There is no doubt, his face and eyes are eloquent, expressing a terrible "I don't know" . . . "I'm confused" . . . "I'm fearful" . . . "What is happening?"

He questions, but does not expect an answer. Further, the questions are *not* rhetorical queries; they are real, and insistent. At the same time, beyond all asking for answers; he knows there is no answer, no explanation . . . only the frightening wonder of this strange between-worlds time where he now moves and lives.

He's able to urinate in the hand urinal; no catheter! He's hooked up to only one tube, for a breath of oxygen.

No reproductions on the walls of the bedroom, nothing expect for a conventional "sick call" crucifix over the bed, what one often sees in the homes of older Catholics.[5] I had always wondered about a crucifix in the bedroom . . . Here it seems appropriate, a proper image.

Marilyn says he was waiting for me to arrive . . . perhaps the ice chips served this end, too.

As one approaches death, there is nothing one can take along. So, Bernard's body is perfectly prepared: No need for a stomach . . . he's effectively ready to die. The large hollow between his hip bones, a living trope, the ruling metaphor of his dying, the fitting symbol . . . divesting himself of everything, including the bulk of his body, in preparation for the final journey.

He depends on Marilyn and Jeff, but his needs are slight, almost non-existent. He gives new meaning to Thoreau's ideal about reducing one's needs to the minimal.[6]

Now and then he opens his eyes and looks, perhaps to see who is here, but says nothing . . . only the silent look.

One night, he removes the oxygen tube. Is this to tell us something? That he no longer needs oxygen? How careful we must be . . . not to violate his person by knowing "better" because of our superior strength.

---

[4] Hippocrates, *The Theory and Practice of Medicine*, 42–5. See also: Levine, *Hippocrates*, 23–9.

[5] Such a crucifix opens and, inside, one finds two candles and cotton (for absorbing the blessed oil on the priest's fingers). When people died at home, Catholics kept a sick call set for the time when a priest came to anoint the dying person.

[6] Thoreau, *Walden and Other Writings*.

I sit, saying the Rosary. It seems best to say only the words of the prayers, over and over, to make no effort at meditating on the mysteries. The occasion/time calls for action, saying the words, not for quiet, not for orderly meditation.[7]

Marilyn and I take turns during the night . . . sitting, watching, at his bedside. I notice she is there more than half the time. I'm able to be there, but think it better to defer . . . for thirty-eight years of fidelity and love, she takes precedence. If I strive for equality of time, I will no doubt be unable to enter the time of Bernard, the time of Advent.

The longer I keep vigil at his bedside, the more I become convinced that one grammatical form is a kind of key to enter the reality Bernard lives. So much needs to be seen, understood, as a verb, *not* as a noun . . . Bernard is dying, that is, he is living. I am sitting, seeing, speaking the words of the Our Father, the Hail Mary, the Glory Be.

Friends and relatives are bringing or sending cooked dishes for us to eat; they are given the opportunity to draw near, perhaps to enter, the Advent time of Bernard. He gives them this gift . . . infinitely more than their action of preparation and delivery of food.

Sitting there, I feel overcome by a strong wish, a pressing desire, a firm hope: That my kids, Ben and Beth, be given the privilege, the gift, to see my dying as I now see Bernard's dying . . . they would then complete the generational cycle that began with their conception and birth, a cycle usually broken by the medical system, a cycle one needs to complete to live a human life, a full life. At this moment in the cycle, Bernard is teaching me so much. I feel that, in some way, his experience enters my body, mind, heart, soul . . . What better inheritance to give my children than the experience of my dying!?!

Here, so many are active; in a hospital, only the professionals actively participate in dying. The patient, relatives, friends dumbly lie or sit. Again, I am reminded of the wisdom of Bernard and Marilyn. Only at home, and only keeping the routines of their home, can they, the family, friends, actively take part in his dying.

Marilyn says he is becoming weaker . . . he is moving toward death!

Bernard is just *there*, being himself, but he also exists in each person's ability to see, in their eyes, in their looking . . . he exists as we see him, for he does not look at himself. I suspect, further, that he does not

[7] The usual method of saying the Rosary is to meditate on the mysteries of Christ and Mary's lives while reciting the Our Father, Hail Mary, and Glory Be.

reflect on himself, he is far beyond such exercises, he is just there, to be seen by us. The question, then, for each of us: Do I truly see him as he is?

If a person has been influenced by photos—I tend to say, infected by photos—that person may not be able to see Bernard now. In outward appearance, he presents himself very differently from the "normal," the photographed Bernard. Later, at the funeral home, the director asks Marilyn, for a color photograph of Bernard. The people doing the embalming need to know how he looked! How curious, how strange.

It seems, then, that funeral directors prepare or create false images out of cadavers, following the picture presented by a photo. So, embalmers become skilled in the creation of visual conceits. At the wake, no one will ever see Bernard, the Bernard I see, hour after hour, the Bernard with so much to offer those who can see, the Bernard ready to share an infinite treasure. Perhaps those of us given the opportunity to see him now, to see him in his passage from life to death, will forget what we saw. If so, we will have lost the truth of Bernard, for the way he lives now is the way he *is*.

What bizarre result of the chemicals and devices, the fantasies and perversions of our age: to be hidden from everyone after your death! Is this some frightening violation of the memory of a person known and loved by us, inflicted on him when he's dead, defenseless? Is this a sin against which I should rail? Is this a truth, too, which Bernard is teaching me? He, silent . . . I, silent . . . but much moved by thoughts.

I know that here, in the small town where Bernard is well-known, many will come to the wake, more than come to the house now, more than will come to the funeral Mass, more than will go to the cemetery. But only a few of us are privileged to get a glimpse of Bernard's *facies hippocratica*. At this moment, Bernard is instructing us through his silent face: in what we should *do*, in what we should *be*. The means of his actions: a fearful and questioning face, a shrunken and distorted body. Many will look at him after the cosmetic work of the embalmers, but he will be *absolutely* silent, they will see nothing except the waxen lies of the cosmetician's art. Is this yet another example of the deceptions in our "culture"?

His friends, distant relatives, and acquaintances of the town, who will only see what remains of Bernard at the wake, will remain stuck in their nouns, in their fancies, will not experience an eventful shock that might move them to live in the verb where Bernard now moves. The truly important hermeneutical task of interpreting his face, the stick arms and legs, the deep hollow of his "belly," will never occur for so many deprived persons. How many they must be! In all the cities and towns of America, in all the sectors of the world affected by the modern way of death, people suffer a new poverty.

In the history of all peoples, death changes over time. In Europe, for example, one can identify the periods of the *ars moriendi* (the art of dying), the Dance Macabre or Dance of Death, a "Natural" Death, a Clinical Death, an Intensive Care Death, a Nursing Home Death, a Doctor-Assisted Suicide/Death.[8] Thinking about this small part of the historical record, and sitting with Bernard, I feel that, age after age, greater and greater cruelties have been progressively inflicted on the dying person and all who have any contact with him.

As I watch Bernard, I see a wasting, a wasting away of someone I barely knew. His appearance in these days may be *the* image of the grotesque today. Elizabeth told me that some friends, quite close to Bernard and Marilyn, have not come to see him, protesting that they cannot "take" seeing a sick person. I wonder . . . I suspect that what lurks in their heart is the idea of disgust, upsetting them beyond what they imagine they can stomach. They fear being reminded of their own mortality, they flee from any dramatic confrontation that possesses the power to present them with the possibility of their own death. For such people, the grotesque could be a vision of the true.

So many send their relatives off to the sterile and impersonal high-tech world of the medical system. There, hospital employees are extremely careful to prepare the patient before visiting hours; the visitors must never view anything "disgusting." True, such procedures are most effective in the more expensive institutions. I have witnessed the very opposite, more the reality of human diminishment, in the wards and hospitals where welfare patients are confined. In the more costly facilities, all possibility for being disgusted has been wiped out, sanitized.

All the actions of Bernard at this time appear necessary . . . that he get out of time, that he enter Advent time. My specific behavior, too, is necessary. For example, one needs to avoid sitting stupidly in a hospital waiting room. In Bernard's situation, action is the only way for me to enter the realm of the good, the realm where Bernard now dwells.

---

[8] Illich, *Medical Nemesis,* 179–208.

Again, the Rosary seems the perfect prayer for this place . . . time . . . activity. I need the *feel* of the beads, an action more elementary or basic than reading words in a book. Speaking the words, moving along the beads, my action grounds me, roots me where I should be rooted.

I find myself repeating the Our Father over and over. I don't follow the order of ordinary Rosary recitation. Slowly, I go deeper into each word, the phrases of the prayer penetrate my soul more thoroughly, the sentiment and meaning of the prayer become richer, more certain. It's as if I come to the prayer for the first time . . . a revelatory time—perhaps the time given me by Bernard.

I experience a wonderful spontaneity, freedom. It's a feeling other than what I have known. Paradoxically, I never tire of repeating the Our Father. At the same time, I feel I can continue to go farther and farther into the prayer; going so far, I may get into the time of Advent. Through Bernard's presence and, I assume, his action, I come to know prayer as never before in my life.

I feel I'm now living out the truth of what I learned from our dad. I am becoming who I am, ontologically . . . indeed, transcendentally . . . I slowly become what I saw in our father, a living *relatio subsistens* (a subsistent relation).

In the Middle Ages, thinkers dared to write about the principal and most unfathomable truth of their and, I hope, my faith: the reality of the Trinity, basing themselves on Aristotelian notions of substance (from the verb, *subsistere*, that which stands under; that which exists of itself; for example, this chair) and relation (*relatio*, that which only exists *between* two substances; it has no real existence; it's an *ens rationis*, a reality of the mind, not an *ens reale*, a real entity; for example, I am Bernard's brother). From this idea, they formed the concept of a *relatio subsistens*, a subsistent relationship which, in strict logic, in the logic to which they adhered, is a contradiction in terms. The Father exists *only* in the relationship to the Son and Holy Spirit; the Son exists *only* in the relationship to the Father and the Holy Spirit; the Holy Spirit exists *only* in the relationship to the Father and the Son.[9]

In God's Providence, each of us is invited to become a *relatio subsistens*, to lose our "I" or ego, to become only what I am in relation to those from whom I come, who come from me, who share the same origin, or who are joined in friendship. I am *only* the son of my father

---

[9] See Aquinas, *Summa theologiae*, I, qq. 27-31.

and mother, the father of my two children, the brother of my brother and sister, the husband of my wife, the friend of my friends. My reality, my truth, is found *only* in these relationships, not in the modern notion of a self. This older kind of self is the authentic self I am free to create. Further, the ultimate reality of my self is only realized in my relationship to the infinite, to God. This relationship legitimates, in an ontological sense, all the other relationships, as I see from the letter, a truth Bernard powerfully perceived.

My perfection, my very being, exists *only* in the realization of my relations, not in a self interested in self-potential. My happiness exists in the exercise of actions like the one that occupies me now, accompanying my brother on his final journey.

From seeing the face of Bernard, I realize that the *facies hippocratica* is not, contrary to the way it has often been interpreted by non-believing Greeks and other physicians, a "face of death." True, Bernard's eyes, when he opens them, seem to express fear or terror, but I don't know what lies behind his eyes. I *feel* a great comfort in seeing them; I know his face stands between two worlds, between two times. For me, the face is necessary as an introduction to the reality of the other world, the world of Advent. His *facies* is the face of the promise of life, the Life offered by the Christ. This appears clear from his face's changing character, its transitional nature. I seem to intuit that toward which it points.

Again, Bernard instructs me: I learn what is and what is not loss, what is and what is not gain.

Marilyn says that the visiting hospice nurse suspects that Bernard is going through a period of depression, another modern buzz word, a recently discovered—or invented—phenomenon. In the past weeks, Bernard was not interested in TV, or local news of the town. I wonder . . . What could be more sensible? Did he not report, "I've said my prayers . . . I'm ready . . . "? What a silly idea . . . depression!

At 4 a.m., on Thursday, December 16th, one year exactly from the date of his first letter to me, his hands and feet twitch or move a bit; otherwise, he appears lifeless. I wonder . . . is there a time when he moves from acting to just being? Corresponding to this movement, we would need to learn from him . . . to learn from our experience of him . . . to learn that we, too, should go from acting to being, simply, "to be there," to live in someone's presence . . . we in his presence . . . he in our presence.

After a full breakfast of bacon and eggs, prepared for Jeff and me by Marilyn, I return to Bernard's room. Sitting next to the bed, Rosary in hand, I continue repeating the prayers, over and over. After a time, I get up and lean over him . . . I can detect no signs of his living . . . there is no motion at all . . . only a quiet stillness. I call Marilyn. She, also, can discern no indication that he lives.

I notice the ends of his thin fingers . . . they have turned gray . . . one arm lies on the bed, the palm turned up . . . I raise the hand . . . and drop it . . . it falls like an empty and lifeless glove. The grayness then seems to advance to cover all the skin of his emaciated body.

I get my Breviary, and recite the *Proficiscere*, the prayer for the dying, written in the ancient Latin that goes back to St. Jerome, one of the most beautiful prayers of the Church. "Go forth, Christian soul, from this world: In the name of God the omnipotent father who created you; in the name of Jesus Christ, son of the living God, who suffered for you; in the name of the Holy Spirit who was poured into you . . . "[10] How grateful I am that I have the Latin text with me, that I can comfortably read it, that it catches me up in its magnificence.

Puzzlement

Having come back to America after living pretty much as a recluse in Germany and Mexico for about ten years, I was confused. What were the cues? The meaningful signs? How orient myself? How get my feet on solid ground? What society was this? I had difficulty recognizing the world around me.

Living outside the country, generally staying in my room, surrounded by books, I had gradually formed a set of ideas and insights, propositions and judgments which, I believed, made sense of the world and my place in it. The society, as I conceptualized it, is dominated by its tools; technological devices, often viewed as magical wonders, reign

---

[10] The rest of the prayer: In the name of the glorious and holy virgin Mother of God, Mary. In the name of blessed Joseph, the distinguished spouse of the same virgin. In the name of the Angels and Archangels. In the name of the Thrones and Dominations. In the name of the Principalities and Powers. In the name of the Potencies, the Cherubim, and Seraphim. In the name of the Patriarchs and Prophets. In the name of the holy Apostles and Evangelists. In the name of the holy Martyrs and Confessors. In the name of the holy Monks and Hermits. In the name of the holy Virgins and of all the Saints of God. May you be in peace today, and dwell in holy Zion. Through the same Christ Our Lord. Amen.

supreme. There are no limits to what one can imagine; perhaps there are no limits to what one can carry out.

Some commentators suggested that the notion of a market, a *free*, unrestrained market, is the engine driving technological development, the making of ever new products.[11] In addition, the forces of the market determine the character and extent of institutionalized social services. In both areas, most people have become consumers, consumers of ready-made packages.

But the word, market, is little more than a pop label, apparently useful for some as an ideological whip-term. Innocent of much contact or interaction with the realities of economics, I nevertheless came to believe that I needed a more analytic term, a concept that would tear open the real world for me. I began to arrive at such a concept through the notion of "disembedded"; a modern society is a disembedded society.[12] Specialization and apparent autonomy divide up and isolate activities that, in a more embedded society, are intertwined; there is more meaning in such a society for people and their actions are lived as an interconnected whole. In modern societies, economic transactions are more and more independent from, for example, cultural and religious norms. With the almost universal use of money, people playing the market can dedicate themselves to dealing in the abstraction, currency value. Those with the resources and skills can become day traders, although such actions may have an adverse effect on the viability of a company and hence on the jobs of many employees. As in this instance, independence is highly restrictive and often more apparent than real; independence serves some more than others.

Suddenly I understood, but mostly through hearsay, not through direct experience, that avarice comes to dominate, not only a few very affluent modern traders, but many who have nothing to lose except for a few dollars' savings, or who can risk nothing more than their current salary.

A curious paradox is at work. In those societies that were more embedded, where money as such had less importance, curbs on the development of avarice were stronger.[13] In our societies, on the other hand, such curbs are almost non-existent. For example, how often does

---

[11] Judt, 3; Fukuyama, *The End of History and the Last Man.*

[12] Polanyi, *The Great Transformation.*

[13] Foster, "Peasant Society and the Image of the Limited Good," 295–315; Mauss, *The Gift: Forms and Functions of Exchange in Archaic Societies.*

a Catholic congregation hear a homily on usury as a sin? And yet, according to the Church's teaching, the character of present-day interest was at one time considered the serious sin of usury. In the tradition of Catholic moral theology, still current, at least in the books, avarice is one of the capital sins, namely, one of the most serious offenses against God, a sinful disposition resulting in immoral actions from which yet other sins are generated.

My studies showed me a world tyrannized by technology, one where people are deprived of their natural inclination to learn, to create, to look to the past, to walk softly on the earth. For example, schools are designed to deliver uniform learning packages, electronic gadgets restrict the user to the manipulation of programmed options, history is presented as a kind of nostalgic diorama that is made to amuse, resource gluttons such as SUV's are aggressively promoted as tickets to freedom and excitement. Paradoxically, the extremely dispossessed retain the ability and liberty to stand on their own two feet and achieve by acting; the affluent can buy packages. In the essentials of living, the higher you are on the money scale, the more you are passive. In terms of a more traditional, that is, active life, many in this "upper" realm are, effectively, dead.

From my books I "saw" that the fit is demonic: the capital sins—pride, envy, avarice, anger, sloth, gluttony, and lust—have become institutionalized. People apparently glory in the fact that sin has become respectable. For example, old-fashioned patriotism, what the Medievalists emphasized as a virtue deriving from justice, and named piety (*pietas*), has often been deformed into nationalistic chauvinism and, as such, honored by some.

Largely restricted to my books and articles, I saw no hope; the world appeared doomed. My few contacts with up-to-date practices and institutions only confirmed my view: the production of goods seemed aimed principally at the despoliation of the earth; the production of services at the despoliation of the earth's people. Further, a reality like global warming ominously indicated the symbiotic relationship between so-called goods and ever more encompassing services. Destruction seemed to be built-in.

My puzzlement increased when I got up from my desk and ventured out to meet new acquaintances who somehow still survived in this modernized inferno: I met persons who were decent! How could such be? Everything I read pointed to diminishment, to the ruin of the earth and the strangulation of its people.

Information

Never before in history has so much information been available to such a large proportion of the population. For example, there seems to be no limit in the production of print media. If one is competent to do searches on the Web, the amount of information to be accessed in cyberspace appears to make possible one of the heretofore unrealizable dreams of hubristic fantasizers: an actual infinity exists!

Given the fact that many people's imagination and thinking have become largely mathematized, they lose sight of the crucial distinction between information and knowledge. Information is never equivalent to knowledge; more information is not necessarily better. Beyond knowledge, there is a further and more important reality, wisdom. Understood as a gift, it was acknowledged and respected by thinkers in ancient Greece and the Middle Ages. Numbers, however impressive, can never give one wisdom. I fear that the perspective and reality of wisdom enters the awareness of fewer and fewer people today.

Numbers, in so many varied contexts, rule. What is a country's GDP? How many pounds do you weigh, and how does this compare with your height? How many volumes does the library hold? How many murders were committed in the city last year? But I, too, am infected; I am tempted to see how far I can extend the list! Such a mindset is the mathematization of mentalities. One of the effects is the decreasing ability to think, that is, to seek knowledge, knowledge being a contextual and multi-dimensional probing into the reality of what appears to be a fact. For example, what can I know about the New York stock exchange? The context and dimensions I select will depend on where I am standing, where I have come from, the character of my preparation for the question, my interests, and these directly touch and derive from Aristotle's final cause, the ultimate goal, the transcendental raison d'être of my life. Such finality also gives shape and meaning to my specific question. But all that is to look at only one side of the task. For knowledge, I still need to conceptualize and investigate what are termed the objective facts, for example, the effects of the stock exchange on citizens' sensibilities and the operation of free food kitchens.

To perceive well what is in front of me, what is "out there," is much more than a perennial issue. All those called philosophers have faced and attempted to address the matter. Each person, perhaps more problematically today than ever before in history, must supercede seemingly insurmountable obstacles . . . simply to see.

Francis Bacon was a major thinker who, after the Middle Ages, attempted to make a list of distorting factors, what he called, Idols, a hindrance to the acquisition of knowledge. He died in 1626, and some think of him as marking the origin of modernity. One might say that he is the first modern. He was certainly one of the first Europeans to accept and popularize the notion of progress. He devoted his considerable talents to the promotion of science, understood as an inductive technique to gain control over nature. As such, he is still alive and vital among us.

For me, however, his supreme importance for our time lies in a unique and novel idea and its realization: instrumentalization. The actions he advocated, from scientific experiments through the manipulation of other men's passions to the very utilization—at times, shamelessly—of himself, were designed with some further end in view. Bacon vociferously repudiated the Aristotelian and medieval idea of "leisure as the basis of culture," to paraphrase the title of Josef Pieper's book.[14]

Ironically, one of Bacon's principal ideas is particularly pertinent to what I write: the Idols. For Bacon, Idol is a figurative term for difficulties or fallacies that prevent or distort one's perception of reality. Although he discusses the Idols in different works, and varies in his description of them, writers of monographs today tend to place them under four headings: the Idols of the Tribe; the Idols of the Cave; the Idols of the Marketplace; and, the Idols of the Theater.[15] Although there are few points of agreement between Francis Bacon's thought and mine, his *intent* in listing and describing idols is as important for me today as for him in Elizabethan times. Today, the idols are more numerous and more powerful; Bacon's exposition appears naïve in the light of contemporary distortions, falsities, blindnesses, and superstitions.

Today's idols are different, but certain constants remain, for example, the seven capital sins; they are alive and well. I also maintain that an inclination existing in every person, sometimes called "original sin," is real, although the strength and configuration of its presence or urging

[14] Pieper, *Leisure the Basis of Culture.*
[15] Patrick, *Francis Bacon,* 7, 20–1, 28–31.

differ from person to person. For my purpose I believe it is sufficient to point out the importance of the mathematization of mentalities which, to a greater or lesser extent, affects most people in all highly differentiated societies.

Except for some at the very bottom of the socio-economic pyramid, and a very few in isolated and marginalized religious and academic enclaves, wisdom is absent from our world. Wisdom means a view of reality from the Other Side, from the Beyond, from what "lies" outside metaphysics or ontology. The position of thinkers in the Middle Ages was that wisdom means seeing as God sees. That demands, therefore, that such a sense or view of reality come as a gift from the Beyond, from God. Strictly speaking, namely, accurately speaking, wisdom does not result from study or orderly meditative practices; it's a gratuitous gift. But one can prepare oneself: The most proper disposition for its reception is probably humility, a virtue unknown to Aristotle.[16]

Technologization

Those who attempt to understand an age or epoch sometimes speak of a dominant metaphor. What literary trope or image is widely important? What figure deeply affects the people of this time and place? For example, one can see from the magazine pictures cut out and pasted on the wall of her cubicle that, for Anne Frank, Hollywood stars were an important image, maybe even a dominant metaphor, for her fantasy life.[17] Many people in the U.S. accept the notion of celebrity as a dominant metaphor. Because certain persons, often through the concerted efforts of publicity agents and the collaboration of the media, fit my idea of a celebrity, I will look at the image—since I don't know the person intimately—with respect, maybe with adulation. I may also be moved to alter my appearance and/or behavior.

A dominant metaphor, if it be such, always has some effect on the people exposed to it. They might even become like camp followers or groupies. Although the degree and character of the effect are empirical facts, it is difficult to verify such facts. They are subjectively spe-

---

[16] Aquinas, *Summa theologiae*. II II, q. 161, aa. 1–6. St Thomas explains why Aristotle does not list humility among the virtues in art. 1, ad 5. The relevant place in Aristotle, *The Nichomachean Ethics*, Book 2, vii.

[17] I saw the pictures, cut out of newspapers and magazines, pasted on the wall next to where her bed was located. The wall is preserved in the Anne Frank House in Amsterdam, which can be visited.

cific to each person, different for each person; further, they wax and wane. Perhaps the best way to determine a dominant metaphor's effect is through a disciplined introspection; that may also be the only certain way.

Observation and reflection lead me to conclude that there are various dominant metaphors in American society, some more important than others. Further, they never affect all sectors of the population equally. Every person is affected by a complex of images and, in any individual, the conformation of images will change, in composition and intensity, over time. Those persons who practice a rigorous examination of self can become adept at discovering such metaphors and, according to their partially inherent, partially developed strength of character, can largely determine or even eliminate the images' influence. Proceeding in this direction, one fulfills a necessary but not sufficient requisite for realizing human freedom.

If such be the truth of freedom, I feel myself in danger of being overcome by sadness, of tending toward despair. Reflection on this possibility, however, leads me to take great comfort in a truth found in my tradition: mercy. Mercy is the greatest virtue, inclining the merciful to remove or wipe out every defect of the miserable. St. Thomas Aquinas teaches that mercy is proper to God, above all manifesting his omnipotence.[18] My belief, therefore, is the foundation for a rational judgment on the reality or existence of my freedom.

The metaphor germane to my argument is technology. It becomes a dominant metaphor through the technologization of the self. Persons having any contact with the principal and most attractive tools of our age, technological devices, are tempted to imagine themselves as realizations of technology.[19] For example, I can think of myself as an immune system; a woman, after submitting to the procedure to obtain a sonogram, can imagine herself a receptacle for the digital print-out; I can see myself as a camcorder; I can believe myself to be a processor of information, and so on. A list of examples would extend toward infinity.

The phenomena associated with or attributed to dominant metaphors are not new, historically. Ancient Greeks and Romans, for example, formed anthropomorphic images of their gods and took these as prime exemplars, that is, as what a human being should look like.

[18] Aquinas, *Summa theologiae*, II II, q. 30, a. 4, corp.

[19] Ivan Illich often spoke of this possibility. The most extended argument for the position can be found in Duden, *Disembodying Women*.

Over the centuries, Christians have elaborated various images of Jesus Christ, and acted to conform themselves to these imaginings. One of the important conceptions at the beginning of the modern era was a new mechanical metaphor based on the theories of Descartes, who died in the middle of the seventeenth century. Man as machine, as a dominant metaphor affecting peoples' notion of themselves, still pervades much of contemporary consciousness.

Powerful refinements of this generalized image are at once singular and multiple. Everyone in a highly differentiated society is constantly surrounded with various technological artifacts. Through one's use of, insertion into, being embraced by, such devices, one's imagination and rational abstract thought are affected, perhaps quite strongly.

Partly because of similarity of purpose—they are always proposed as means—all artifacts participate in a clear commonality. But the ends will be multiple, some more immediate, some more remote. Because of a difference in immediate ends, technological artifacts are diverse. If the more remote end is principally economic, to make more money, very different artifacts will share this commonality. For example, a fork, a computer, and a car are all means to some end. I can use both the computer and the car to make money. For those troubled with commodity fetishism, both the computer and the car can become ends. Some theorists of technology, such as Jacques Ellul, maintain that technology, as *la technique*, has become *the* end in our societies.[20]

Proof for the existence and power of technological artifacts as dominant metaphors influencing or even determining one's image of self can be easily obtained through introspection and observing the behavior of people around me. For example, I can do physical exercises needing nothing more than a couple of square yards of floor space and a bit of time, or I can believe that I need to be attached to a machine; I can become an adjunct of that machine, effectively regarding myself as a part of it, I can become a cyborg. Such seeing can become all-embracing. A complex of technology "out there" becomes internalized through self-imposed images. It may be more meaningful to speak about a technological system in this sense, rather than as a set of objective structures. On both sides there can be breakdowns or gaps. Through the technologization of self, however, I run the risk of losing my very humanity. Logic is helpful here: A cyborg is not a human.

---

[20] Ellul's argument is found in a number of his books, for example: Ellul, *The Technological Bluff*.

Believers

The Christian believes that Jesus Christ is one person in two natures, human and divine. Jesus walked the earth; he is the visible way to the unseen, unknown and, most rightly speaking, unknowable God. These truths are clearly revealed in the Greek Scriptures, the New Testament. Through the Incarnation, the Second Person of the Most Holy Trinity, assuming human flesh, thereby sanctified all human flesh, every human being. Therefore, a believer unconditionally respects every other, each other person.

The texts of the New Testament, which the believer accepts as a revelation of truth about the Beyond, about the unknowable notion, God, are clear and consistent on the nature of the human person. Among these texts, the letters written by St. Paul are a principal source for truths about the sanctity of the person—in a very particular way of imagining this sanctity. The relevant passages of St. Paul explicitly use the concept, body, that is, a human body, the body assumed by Jesus Christ. This body is identified with *my* body and, in a powerful metaphor, that is, a metaphor at once a trope and literal truth, St. Paul writes of body, referring to the Church, the community of believers.

Many of the most transparent texts of St. Paul are found in his first letter to the Corinthians. For example, he reminds the believers in Corinth: "Do you not know that your bodies are members of Christ himself?" (1 Cor 6:15) Then, in one of the most powerful teachings in the New Testament on this matter, he asks:

> Do you not know that your body is a temple of the Holy Spirit, who is in you, whom you have received from God? You are not your own; you were bought at a price. Therefore honor God with your body (1 Cor 6:19–20).

St. Paul also points out how the believer's body is infinitely, transcendentally, different from the non-believer's body. That is, my faith utterly transforms my body:

> Now I rejoice in what was suffered for you, and I fill up in my flesh what is still lacking in regard to Christ's afflictions, for the sake of his body, which is the church (Col 1:24).

The difference is established *only* through my generous acceptance of suffering; the acceptance becomes possible only through the infusion of God's love in my heart.

Acceptance means I have made a choice. As a person of faith, I know I must somehow assent to the Lord, which means, to participate in his sufferings. That means my action is *for* certain others, members of the body of Christ who stand in need of my pain. This is an integral part of my vocation, my calling. Those for whom I suffer cannot live the only life that matters, life in the Lord, without my participation in the divine plan. My life is described by St. Paul in yet another text:

> We always carry around in our body the death of Jesus, so that
> the life of Jesus may also be revealed in our body (2 Cor 4:10).

Finally, St. Paul also sees the body in its ultimate place in the Christian's belief. In his first letter to the Corinthians, we find "his most eloquent exposition of the life of a true believer . . . a Himalayan peak of world literature."[21] Among the ringing phrases of this wondrous paean, St. Paul reveals the position of one's body/person in the divine dispensation: "If I give all I possess to the poor and surrender my body to the flames, but have not love, I gain nothing" (1 Cor 13:3).

The fact that St. Paul perceives the person in terms of the body is doubly significant. First, his usage highlights the reality of the Incarnation: God did take on human flesh, he assumed or took up a human body. Secondly, emphasis on the body directly confronts and rejects a historical temptation, at least as old as recoverable records. The temptation: to make a dichotomous distinction between matter and spirit, assigning matter to the realm of evil, spirit to the realm of good. After reading St. Paul, no believer can accept a heretical tendency still very much present in Christianity today, perhaps more powerfully, certainly more subtly, than ever before.

The contemporary world, through technologization, has progressed far beyond the world of Zoroastrianism, founded in the sixth century, B.C., by the prophet, Zoroaster, and widespread in the early years of the Church when it was known as Mithraism. In Zoroastrianism, a cosmic struggle takes place between the god of light, Ahura Mazda, and the god of darkness, Ahriman; each human participates in this conflict.[22]

Witnesses to Christ's reality, from the time of St. Paul until today, consistently teach and practice a belief altogether other than the conflict of Zoroaster. The ways in which this belief is realized and expressed are

---

[21] Cahill, *Desire of the Everlasting Hills,* 136.

[22] See, for example, Runciman, *The Medieval Manichee,* 3–25, 171–180.

as various as the believers themselves. For example, a recently deceased Orthodox nun, Mother Maria Skobtsova said, "each person is the very icon of God incarnate in the world."[23]

For a believer, any technologization of the person, or of one's body, immediately raises a disturbing question: Is some kind of sacrilege being committed here? The word is derived from *sacrilegus*—one who steals sacred things. Its dictionary meaning: "a technical . . . violation . . . of what is sacred because consecrated to God" (*Webster's Ninth*). According to the New Testament, every person and, more specifically, every person's body is consecrated to God. The question then becomes: Does technologization violate the person or the person's body?

Many things affect my person and my body. It is precisely the task of my reasoning power to find the distinction between what is harmful and what salutary, what helps me reach my goal and what not, what leads me toward the imitation of Christ and what takes me away from him. In my tradition, this reasoning power and the practices to act on it are worked out, refined, and perfected through asceticism, the disciplining of my senses, interior and exterior, of my reasoning, and of my willing, wishing or desiring.

Reflecting on the lives of good people I have known, I see that, at their death, they had become *virtuous* persons, their asceticism had enabled them to reach a certain wholeness; they died a beautiful death. What I have experienced is confirmed by what I have read: Good hearsay knowledge is in conformity with good experiential knowledge. It's of some importance to acquire both kinds of knowledge. That is one certain way of going beyond information and reaching into true knowledge, especially if I go from direct experience to indirect hearsay and discover that they agree.

One Believer

Apparently through being with my brother I was given a bit of true knowledge. After his body was taken away, I sat and reflected . . . and again asked myself: How did he do it? How did he come to see so clearly? How did he come to act so courageously? Why was his dying so utterly different from others I have witnessed, others who were conventionally learned people, others who expressed a sophisticated critique of moder-

[23] The quote is found in Ellsberg, *All Saints,* 145. A more complete story of Mother Maria Skobtsova is found in Smith, *The Rebel Nun.*

nity but who, I had to conclude, did not know how to die well. How to "explain" what appeared to be humanly impossible?

In the months following Bernard's death I returned to the teacher I most respect, St. Thomas Aquinas. In his greatest work, the *Summa theologiae*, I think I found a response to my questions. There, St. Thomas writes about grace: what it is, why it is necessary, what it effects.

No one has ever seen grace and, strictly speaking, you cannot feel its presence. Ultimately, its reality rests on my belief. But I've seen its effects, recently in the drama of Bernard's dying. Grace is a brightness of the soul (a *nitor animae*), a gratuitous gift given by God, a participation in the divine goodness. None of these terms, beginning with the notion, God, is comprehensible. They are all inferred from the effects of grace, effects that are abundantly manifest—if one has the eyes to see. St. Thomas also says that grace is a certain special light of the soul that raises one above the condition of one's nature to a participation in the divine good.

In this section of his work, St. Thomas assumes that human nature has been corrupted by the sin of our first parents (the complex matter is fully treated in another part of his book). Therefore, we find ourselves with a double need: that our nature be healed, and that we be able to go beyond our natural powers to reach a supernatural or divine good.[24]

Knowing something of Bernard's life, and the circumstances surrounding him in that mid-western town, I can find no rational reason or argument to account for his insights and actions. But from the profound fidelities of his life, the exemplary lives of other witnesses to grace during the past two thousand years, and the teaching of churchmen like St. Thomas, I can reach a certain conclusion: I cannot but posit the reality of grace in Bernard's living and in his dying. Because of a truth finally inscrutable, I know that Bernard was especially favored, that is, loved, by God. This is one of the many truths before which I can only stand dumbly, bow my head, and wonder.

Afterthoughts

An often cited opinion of Aristotle: All people naturally seek happiness.[25] However, there may be insuperable difficulties in determining the exact

---

[24] On the sin of our first parents: Aquinas, *Summa theologiae,* I II, qq. 82, 85; on grace: Ibid., qq. 109-113.

[25] Aristotle, *Nichomachean Ethics*, Book 1, iv.

meaning of happiness. "Naturally" presents similar obstacles, but I may be able to overcome them. Naturally means what comes with the way I'm made, with, simply, the way I am. I take it as highly probable that everyone else also seeks to avoid misery, pain, unhappiness.

In the America I know, I notice that nearly all people place a great emphasis, and many actually shape their behavior, in terms of their health. What is the basis for this concern?

One position holds that Aristotle's dictum was most perfectly elaborated in a tradition beginning with Greek thinkers and continuing, often fitfully, until today, with the question: What is the good life? The question generally assumes a corollary: How live the good life?

Reading the Hippocratic Oath and the body of writings associated with the name of Hippocrates, I found that health appeared to be an essential component of the good life in the ancient world, necessary for any general notion of happiness.[26] But, while sitting next to my brother's bed, being present to his dying, I've come to question the conventional interpretation of the Greeks' question and answer.

Since the pre-Socratics, many have studied the question: What is the good life? If I am confronted with the issue today, I can immediately reach for the most direct and powerful means possible: I can look to my own experience. If I am unable to reach my experience, or have none, I can turn to another. This tactic is usually called education, and it's claimed I can thus learn something. The one from whom I learn knows from personal experience, or from someone else's experience. It does not require much reflection, or a complicated thought experiment to conclude that most of what I have learned is not based on my own experience, nor on the experience of another, but on a confusing line of "authorities" reaching back into infinity—at least, for the old questions.[27]

Is experience so very important? Before accompanying Bernard's movement toward death, I would not have known what to say. Now I do. I think it accurate to say that the experience of coming closer and closer to Bernard in his dying was the most important one in my life, for I felt, in the farthest recesses of my being, what it means to live.

The most certain answer to so many Americans' concern, the response most likely to approach the truth, is not based on philosophical writings, not to be found in either learned or popular books, not to be

---

[26] Hippocrates, *The Theory and Practice of Medicine*, v–viii, and the Oath of Hippocrates, 4.

[27] Marquard, *In Defense of the Accidental*, 71–89.

heard in the opinion of another, but in the experience of "seeing," of seeing someone progress toward death. The necessary and sufficient conditions for this seeing reveal its character and importance. The only ones I know, however, are the ones I experienced; I can describe them.

Being with Bernard opened up a new elaboration of the idea of a Christian vocation. The word means, a calling (*vocare*, to call) and, some years ago was usually confined to a call to the priesthood or the religious life. Then various persons in the Church attempted to expand its meaning to include many other callings to which God might invite one, for example, to marriage, to be a farmer, and so on. I believe it is now necessary to recognize that every believing Catholic has a vocation, a calling, to accompany the dying of another, a relative or friend. The other *needs* that individual presence of the body, the Church of Christ. I need to be there if I am to love, if I am to learn how to answer the ancient questions: What is the good life? and, How do I live it? But the truth of what I learned should not be confined to believing Catholics. All who ask questions about happiness and the good life can profit from Bernard's action in dying.

I accompanied Bernard in the last days of his journey. From what happened to me, I know that it was essential that I be there out of affection and obligation, that this strong bond bind us together. I could not not be there; I had no choice. If I had dropped in just to visit him, to look in on him, to observe him, he would not have been able to give me anything, whereas he left me an inestimable gift.

Further, he needed to be in a "free" space. I had not come to see a death but to participate in a dying, and for that *he* needed space, the space which, I strongly suspect, is not available in conventional institutional settings, as I pointed out above.

Then, I needed time, lots of ordinary time, to adjust my eyes, to be able to see Bernard. Some speak of the necessity of a life-long *askesis* (asceticism) to purify the eyes that one be able to see today. I feel this is true. The attractive and ugly, enticing and repulsive images that pierce so many eyes, simply make seeing difficult or impossible.

What I saw lying on the bed during those hours had little relationship to photos of Bernard. Indeed, I might have objected, cried out, "No, no, that's not him! He never looked like that!" What I saw when he opened his eyes and stared about wildly bore no resemblance whatever to any eyes I had ever seen, was utterly unlike any image of a man's eyes: *But I needed to see them* . . . otherwise, I would never have seen the movement, the movement toward a different time, to a time beyond the time we ordinarily experience. Something cleared my eyes sufficiently so that I just barely saw him, only faintly grasped his action, but deeply sensed his going.

I feel I know what Aristotle reached for, what the philosophers have studied and written about, what many Americans devote so much time and money seeking. "Happiness" is too fleeting and shallow; "the good life" too abstract and cold; "health" too illusory and false. I recognize now that, during his last days especially, Bernard was perfectly in consonance with himself and his place, with the movement in which he went forward to his death.[28]

Throughout the writings of Simone Weil the term, proportion, occurs over and over.[29] What I saw in Bernard must be what proportion means at this time; he lived in perfect proportion; there was a lovely fittingness, a gracefulness expressed in his actions and being. I suspect, then, that the notion of proportion must hold true throughout one's life. There's a proportion to being born, to growing up, to living, and so on, until one reaches the proportion of dying. As I saw with Bernard, the proportion of dying can shine forth with a particular beauty.

I also came to recognize that, ultimately, truth lies in the time beyond time, and from that "place" someone bound to me can reveal fragments of that truth through his experience. This bit of truth is a wordless gift from that bonded other, given to me through my quiet but timely and alert presence.

---

[28] Some writers have been able to express an approximation of what I witnessed. One of the best is Unamuno, *The Agony of Christianity*, especially 5–6, 16, 79–80.

[29] See, for example: Weil, *The Notebooks*, vol. 1, 49; vol. 2, 508.

4

Jerry in the Evening

GETTING ON a bus in State College, Pennsylvania in the late 1990s, I set out to visit a friend, Brother Gerald Morris, S.M., a resident at an old folk's home outside Dayton, Ohio. I took a night bus to arrive early the next morning, leaving all day Saturday to find my way out to the St. Leonard Center. Two decisions of the journey were influenced by Jerry's remarks and example: take a bus, and travel at night. Jerry often traveled by bus; that was the means people at the bottom of the socio-economic pyramid used. In the 1960s, when Jerry and I worked in Cuernavaca, Mexico, I once heard him say, "If I can, I always take a night bus. I can thus sleep on the bus, saving the expense of a hotel room." He acted accordingly. Forty years later, I still remember what he said. Several times I have been able to follow his example, even to traveling between Pennsylvania and Mexico, and crossing the United States from coast to coast. These were good times; I read books, met and talked with a great variety of people, and formed many impressions of the two countries' landscapes from the windows of a bus.

Arriving in Dayton quite early, I had plenty of time to wash and shave. Bus station rest rooms always have a sink and sometimes have hot water! I need carry only a small bar of soap and several paper towels. While rinsing my face, I noticed a dapper but rather poorly dressed man enter. We exchanged greetings, and then he mumbled something about the awful behavior of kids today. There had been a story in the papers about some young boy who murdered his grandparents. After mentioning this news, my companion started to wash his face. Then, interrupting himself, he exclaimed: "What these kids today need is what I had—a school where the good nuns are not afraid to use the stick. There's too much permissiveness, not enough strictness. Nobody makes these kids shape up." Out of the corner of my eye, I noticed that he carefully blackened his substantial moustache, remarking to me that this was necessary

" . . . to make me look younger." He also mentioned that he lived as a street person.

From the driver of a city bus stopped near the Greyhound station, I learned how to get to the suburb where the St. Leonard Center was located. Buses did not run very often on Saturdays, several transfers were necessary, and it was a long way to the old folks' home; it took almost three hours to arrive at the neighborhood. Looking around for the Center, I came upon an open real estate office. Kindly people inside directed me to my destination, a few blocks away.

Walking through acres of grass lawn, I approached the large complex of buildings, then found the central office. A man there gave me the name of Brother Gerald's building. After I entered, attendants pointed out the location of his room. I knocked and walked in. Jerry was shaving with an electric razor. I greeted him warmly, and stepped up to give him a solid *abrazo* (hug). As I advanced, I caught a flicker of confusion in his eyes—"Who is this?" But in a moment he recognized me, and his face broadened into the smile I had known for so many years; he was genuinely delighted to welcome me. I had not written I was coming, for I thought it more in Jerry's spirit of adventure to surprise him.

He continued working the razor around his face, explaining that now and then "they" told him to shave. He feared that if he didn't do it, a worker would shave him with a straight razor and take advantage of the opportunity to slit his throat from ear to ear. I instantly saw that Jerry had not lost his unique sense of humor. In the years since I last saw him in Mexico, he had definitely aged and appeared rather decrepit, but the spirit I knew still burst out.

With an artificial hip that had worn out, Jerry could take a few steps, using his wheelchair for a walker. To go farther, he sat in the chair and moved it forward by "walking" his feet along the floor; his legs, from the knees down, were still usable. He took me on a tour of his floor of the building, obviously proud of it. I had been extremely apprehensive about how he would feel in such a place, confined to the routines of institutional living. During the years we were together in Mexico, Jerry enjoyed a great deal of autonomy in the way he structured his time and living quarters. It was always an adventure to ride with him in his old Volkswagen bus. Inside and out, it boasted of some homemade Rube Goldberg-like accessories. The emptiness of his room indicated that Jerry had changed from the man I had known for so many years.

First, he led me to the chapel, which is actually a good-sized church with stained glass windows reaching high into the sky. He obviously wanted to begin my visit in the chapel. I had the strong impression that he expected me to devote a few moments to prayer. Then he enthusiastically showed me the nearby snack bar, offering me coffee and cookies or donuts. He opened the door of a refrigerator to display all the cold and frozen treats available at any hour of the day. Jerry eagerly demonstrated that all one's spiritual and physical inclinations were bountifully supplied. I was surprised. The Jerry I knew was quick to pick out any fault or lack in his surroundings. But here he appeared genuinely pleased with everything. He gave no evidence whatsoever of the complaints one sometimes hears from old people.

At the hour for lunch, he led me to a large dining room, well-lighted naturally by windows that filled one wall. Most tables had places for four persons, some round ones seated six, and all had a clean white cloth and a small bouquet of flowers. Single men and women, retired priests, religious such as Jerry, and couples who were completing many years of married fidelity gathered in what appeared to be an attractive institution. Everyone was dressed for lunch; I guessed that much of the morning was given to getting ready to appear in the dining room. The women were carefully coiffed and, when they were younger, would have worn gloves for tea in the afternoon and for the theater in the evening.

I remember only one person who caught and held my attention: an ancient, thin, fragile-looking priest, who sat perfectly upright and displayed delicate table etiquette. Jerry told me that those living out their time here included people of all faiths, or none, although St. Leonard's was owned and operated by the Roman Catholic Marianist Community. I was hungry and ate a substantial lunch, but Jerry took only soup and a dish of Jell-O. Encouraged to eat more by the kindly attendants, he refused, saying, "I'm getting too fat . . . I can't get my pants buttoned shut."

When I asked him about his false teeth, he answered that he was uncertain where they were, perhaps in some drawer. From what I could determine, he seemed never to put them in, oblivious to his appearance. I wondered which was more comical, the vanity of the street person's moustache or Jerry's unconcern with sunken cheeks and mouth.

Gesturing toward the windows of the room, he excitedly praised the view. I looked and looked, but failed to see anything to arouse my interest or admiration. Outside I saw a small flat prairie field with a few scattered trees and houses in the distance, a *most* ordinary scene. What did he see in this drab mid-western landscape? Further, I knew that his eyes were seriously failing; could he see out the windows at all? Or had he reached a kind of seeing that was beyond my power to perceive or imagine? He was a man, I recalled, who had lived and traveled among the more spectacular scenery of Latin America, who had been through Europe, who, I knew, was capable of recognizing and appreciating the beauty of nature. He would not have been fooled by what lay outside the window. I concluded that he intimated another kind of looking.

I asked him about his medication. He was uncertain, casual, off-handed. Yes, there were pills of some sort and perhaps he took them every day. He appeared uninterested. He just swallowed whatever they gave him. I was talking to a very old person unconcerned about his medical treatment. My wonder grew: What kind of man had my old friend, Jerry, become?

I asked if there were anything I could do for him. "No." Or, if I could send him anything. "No." He had everything he could possibly desire. As far as he could determine, he neither needed nor wanted anything. He offered me some winter clothing; it was impossible for him to wear all the stuff in his closet. "You take it!"

I remembered that we had often gone out in Cuernavaca, for example, driving downtown in my small Volkswagen, to get a dish of ice cream or a beer in the evening. I asked if he would like to go out for a cup of coffee . . . or a drink; I could call a cab. I had heard that people confined to institutions like this one welcomed the opportunity to get out. But no, he was quite content to remain here, on this floor of his building where everything he could wish for was found. What had happened to the small breaks in institutional routines we had so much enjoyed together? Jerry was not exactly the person I remembered.

He had a small room and bath; his meals were served in the dining room at the same hour every day; he always sat in exactly the same place, opposite the same people. He was in an institution; all was governed by a gentle but strict routine. Everything was done for him . . . but he was old, with a worn-out hip. He must have been in pain, at least sometimes. Others I have known with this condition suffer great pain. When I asked him about it, he at first acted as if he didn't understand the question. Finally he answered that he felt fine. Could I take his response literally? Again, I asked myself: Who was this man?

He remarked several times how pleasant everything was in the Center, how kind and thoughtful were the attendants who worked there. As we passed other residents in the hall, he greeted each with an old-fashioned jocular remark. Sometimes he introduced me. Later he briefed me on who they were. He knew everyone and had a kind and appropriate word for each.

I asked if he watched TV. "No." That, too, did not seem to interest him. Nor did he desire to read newspapers or magazines, but perhaps he did read. I noticed a book I had written, *El Camino: Walking to Santiago de Compostela*, on top of several others in his room. He said his favorite activity was to station the wheelchair at the crossroad in the hallways and just watch the people go by. This appeared to be one of his principal daily practices. I saw that he also enjoyed joking with the personnel and flirting with all the women caretakers.

He pointed to a wall at the end of the corridor, asking me if I could see what was there. It was an undistinguished image of the Blessed Virgin and her Son, Jesus. Jerry said that, seeing the figures, he was reminded of their lives. Thinking about them, he prayed every day that he might do God's will, as *they* had done. I could not but be struck by the timbre of his voice, by the firmness and ingenuousness of the statement. He spoke with a clear straightforwardness, without self-consciousness. I involuntarily caught my breath, realizing that this was what people mean by artlessness, simplicity. Some would call it purity of intention. From all I saw that day, I recognized that he hid behind no vagueness. "The will of God" was not a cover to aggrandize self.

Others might speak of sincerity and authenticity. But I remembered something I had read somewhere, a devastating criticism of the very idea of authenticity and sincerity. As I recalled, the argument was arrayed against a subjectivity that can hide a refusal to look at and accept the notion of truth "out there," which can disguise a manner of acting that seeks nothing so much as self. Ever since reflecting on that criticism I have been wary when some author mentions "authenticity." If someone claims that a person I know is authentic, I am on my guard. The term is better left to advertising copy.

From Jerry's behavior, I saw there are two sides to the matter and that both must be taken into account: One must look at the objective truth *and* consider the heart of the actor. In the person before me, there was a clear correspondence between the truth of doing God's will and Jerry's direct approach to this truth in specific, concrete choices.

On the bus to Dayton to visit Jerry, I began reading a book that had been on my wish list for a long time, Saul Bellow's *Mr. Sammler's Planet*. Seeing Jerry again, I recognized that a passage in the book appropriately fitted his situation. I had read just the "right" book during my journey. Mr. Sammler

> . . . was in the Forty-second Street Library reading, as always, Meister Eckhart.
>
> "Blessed are the poor in spirit. Poor is he who has nothing, He who is poor in spirit is receptive to all spirit. Now God is the Spirit of spirits. The fruit of the spirit is love, joy, and peace. See to it that you are stripped of all creatures, of all consolations from creatures. For certainly as long as creatures comfort and are able to comfort you, you will never find true comfort. But if nothing can comfort you save God, truly God will console you."

Bellow goes on to write, "Mr. Sammler could not say that he literally believed what he was reading. He could, however, say that he cared to read nothing but this."[1]

Since Jerry was a good friend, old, confined to a wheelchair, unable to leave the building alone, I repeatedly asked him, in different ways, if I could do anything for him, get him something, send him what he lacked. He always answered, "No." He needed nothing, wanted nothing. I saw he was detached from all the final little "necessities" that tie one down, that stick one firmly to the world, that imprison one in oneself. I recognized that because he lived in a state of abandonment, he was at peace, he was joyful. I was amused to see that one of his old practices remained: Outside his room he had put up a large hand-lettered message, "Smile . . . and give your face a rest."

A friend with whom we worked in Mexico, Ivan Illich, wrote in the 1980s on the modern notion of needs. He believed the idea of socioeconomic needs came out of post-World War II theories and their application in what was called Third World development. Concomitantly, the purveyors of both goods and services designed and offered their products in ever more expensive packages. For example, one can see the differences by opening the hoods of pickups, looking inside doctors' offices, or examining school staff plans in 1960 and 2004.

---

[1] Bellow, *Mr. Sammler's Planet,* 230–31.

Certain social concepts come to the fore at different times, empha-sizing various aspects of change. Historically, prominence has moved from reform to evolution to progress to development to growth to sus-tainability. Many authors have documented the undesirable effects of these changes, for example, global warming, genetic depletion, various kinds of pollution, the breakdown of immunities, and the millions of new DPs (displaced persons, a term from World War II), more properly named homeless fugitives.[2]

Writing in the 1970s and 1980s, Illich pointed out that although people would find it difficult to survive environmental changes, the more serious issue was the horror of living with the habits of needing that the idea and practice of development or progress or growth had established in one's notion of self and society. From one perspective it was possible to say a transformation had occurred, people had moved from being *homo economicus* to *homo miserabilis*; they changed from economist beings to miserable beings, that is, to creatures utterly depen-dent on the delivery of institutional goods and services. Illich wrote of people, principally in the industrialized world, experiencing a change in their human nature. For many, Aristotle's concept of a rational animal no longer applied. Rationality, for the Greeks and later thinkers, meant that one was free to examine and choose between possible alternatives. Under a regime of scarcity, driven by the desire for so-called basic needs, one is no longer free and rational. In Illich's opinion, many have become needy addicts.[3]

After World War II, many social scientists and politicians, Non Governmental Organizations (NGOs) and individuals, devoted them-selves to socio-economic development. Eventually, all aspects of de-velopment or change were reduced to one: the magic bullet, growth. Superstition reigns in the corridors of intellectual and political power. Through an historic refusal to accept necessity, many became enamored with, or enslaved to, the idea of needs. They believed and felt in their deepest being that they had basic needs. It was the strongly held opinion of Illich that perhaps the most pernicious legacy of post-World War II socio-economic thinking and practice was the idea of needs. The true believers still exist; they are legion.

---

[2] See the work of Lester Brown, for example: Brown, *The Earth Policy Reader*.

[3] One of the most succinct expressions of Illich's argument is found in his essay, "Needs," in Sachs, *The Development Dictionary*, 88–101.

No industrial nation proposes a policy of zero economic growth. Further, I am aware of no serious and sustained questioning of the notion of growth; no postmodern obfuscation challenges this new status quo. Growth also makes all people touched by it needy. But Jerry, an old man in his wheelchair, contradicted the modern consensus. He did not believe he had rights or entitlements. He had rejected what everyone takes for granted, what forms the foundation of many peoples' sense of themselves. As I reflected on Jerry and his surroundings, it appeared obvious that, of all the people I know, Jerry was the least needy. He had gracefully thrown off modernity's shackles, he had gloriously escaped affluence's traps, he was free beyond what I thought possible.

So I learned something about the writings of Illich that I had not seen before. What he is saying, in his articles and books, can be best understood somewhat as one "sees" the parables of the Gospel, that is, there is a point, and you either get it or you don't. But "to get" the point Illich is making, one must move into two dimensions, that of knowing and that of living. To read Illich seriously, to understand what he has written, one must both capture the meaning, and then *do* something. In this sense, Jerry was a true student of Illich, he had fully understood the point of Illich's writing on needs, he had seen and then acted. I saw that Jerry lived with impressive integrity. He might not have been able to articulate this as I have done, but I understood that his intelligence may have reached more deeply than that of recognized scholars with whom I've discussed Illich's work. Jerry revealed a kind of knowing that is particularly apt, that fits the substance and mode of Illich's writing: Jerry's knowing was solidly grounded, carnal, fleshly.

I learned something further from Jerry. There is a sense, I now believe, in which Illich's insight into the character of needs today is one of the most important points in his writing. I have long believed that many persons' freedom is often superficial or even non-existent. Those who apparently have the means to be most free may be the ones most lacking in freedom. The issue is directly related to the modern belief in and addiction to needs. Not getting Illich's point about needs, not living in detachment, that is, free of needs, is to erect and maintain an insuperable barrier to personal freedom. Here, perhaps, one can simply speak of "either-or." I am needy . . . or free.

There are many people I know, people who profess to respect Illich's thought, to be influenced by him, even to be his faithful students. But I must conclude that Jerry was one of the most impressive readers of Ivan

Illich I've ever met. Jerry surprised me; he taught me something about learning. When he and I worked together in Cuernavaca, many persons regarded him as something of a clown, definitely a likeable person, but not terribly bright. No one expected him to make any contribution to the various philosophical or social or historical questions being discussed and written at CIDOC. My friendship was based on respect for his person; I, too, never thought of him as endowing the world of thought. But there, in the old folks' home, I suddenly realized that something new and important was being revealed to me by this tottering and crippled friend; I was learning something about freedom in our world today.

Afterwards, thinking about my visit to Ohio, I remembered other experiences with Jerry and saw them in a new light. I recognized that, a few years earlier, Jerry had taken a decisive step toward becoming free. In the early 1990s, I had not seen him for a year or two and heard he had retired and moved to a remote Indian fishing village in the South of the state of Oaxaca, after having worked for some thirty years in Mexico.

After leaving CIDOC and Cuernavaca, he was employed by the Mexican Indigenous Institute in the city of Oaxaca, training young people to teach Spanish to the Indians. Not having received a letter from him, and worried, I got on a bus in Cuernavaca and after three days' travel, the last few kilometers on the open bed of a racing truck, bouncing over a non-existent road, reached the village, San Mateo del Mar. The trip took an extra day because I got lost along the way. After getting off the truck, I asked for "Maestro Jerry," and was directed to the government-built kindergarten, a wholly nondescript concrete block building. There I found Jerry, on his knees, pulling weeds or crab grass out of a lawn he had seeded in front of the kindergarten while the children were on vacation.

Surprised to see me—he did not know I was coming—he greeted me joyfully, and took me around the village to introduce me to his friends. The people lived in what could most accurately be called extreme modesty. Since it was warm the year round, some houses were made completely of thatch. One more affluent family made an extra room in their concrete block house, put a mattress on the floor, and invited me to share their home for the few days of my visit. The Indigenous Institute had given Jerry a one-room apartment for the teacher at the end of the kindergarten building, but it was so cluttered and dirty that no empty space could be found for a guest.

Talking with the hospitable family and his other friends, many of them mestizo former students in Oaxaca, I tried to find out something about Jerry and his living conditions, for I did not fully trust him when he said that everything in his place of retirement was ideal. I knew he would not complain, and would assure me that all was well, no matter what the actuality might be. So I was relieved and happy to learn that his friends faithfully but unobtrusively kept an eye on him. They had offered to give him his meals each day but Jerry, with his independent spirit, refused. He preferred to eat his one daily meal at the public market, a kind of open warehouse building with a dirt floor and a tin roof that shaded people from the strong sun. Cooling ocean breezes circulated freely through the interior, since there were no walls.

There was a "restaurant" in the market, run by a woman with a primitive gas burner, an extremely limited menu, a rough table and one plank on which the few customers sat. Accompanying Jerry each day for lunch, I saw that the routine never varied. Jerry arrived, sat down, greeted the woman, inquired about her family, and learned the latest news. He never asked for anything to eat or drink. The woman always served him exactly the same meal: fresh fish and beans and whatever vegetable she had that day. At the beginning and halfway through the meal, she placed a bottle of soda pop before him, always the same kind. After finishing, he put the fish bone scraps in a rather filthy plastic sack for his cat, and paid for his lunch.

Almost all the people in the village were Indian, not mestizo. The women wore only traditional dress, a white, embroidered blouse and a long, full and colorful skirt, but never any shoes. They always seemed to have something to carry, and balanced it on their heads. As they walked down the unpaved streets of sand, they talked to one another, but would never look at me or greet me. The men usually wore blue jeans and white T-shirts, and almost always shoes; their principal occupation was fishing. It appeared that many families had pigs, who roamed freely through the village. Jerry said the people knew which pig belonged to whom, but I could see no distinguishing mark on them. Both men and women rode the open truck to Salina Cruz, a neighboring city, to sell their fish and make household purchases. Only the truck and electric power lines connected the village to the farther outside world of Oaxaca and Mexico.

About a year later, I received calls in the States and Mexico that something was wrong with Brother Jerry. No one was clear about what actually was the problem. The most coherent conclusion I could reach was that Jerry had gone "crazy." But no one had been to San Mateo del Mar, no one had seen him, all was rumor. In earlier years, Jerry had often traveled from Oaxaca to Cuernavaca when he knew I was coming to Mexico. I decided it was time to visit him again. On my earlier trip, I had found the village and its people fascinating. For example, I could eat fish fresh from the ocean, and I met a man who made fishnets by hand. The fishermen formerly went out to sea in huge dugout canoes with sails. I saw several of them beached, but the men appeared to use only fiberglass boats with motors today.

When I arrived—again, without notifying him by letter—I found him somewhat changed; definitely, he had aged. He was not working in the yard, but sitting quietly in the shade of a large tree, one of two that nicely graced the government-issue building. When he stood to greet me, I was taken aback, although I knew him well and had seen his living quarters a year earlier. I suppose many Americans, coming upon him, would exclaim to themselves, "This guy is a mess!" He wore old, dilapidated sneakers; they required a good deal of heavy string both to hold them together and to keep them attached to his feet. The zipper on his pants was broken, and the fly was held shut with a safety pin. His ragged shirt and pants, torn in several places, looked as if they had not been washed in weeks.

I had forgotten the disorder, the clutter, the dirt of his room. In the bathroom I again found a bucket under the sink, to catch the water after he washed. This was then thrown into the toilet to flush it. I found some old, dusty soap to take a shower, but could only locate one much-used, greasy towel. I took it to the outside laundry sink and scrubbed it, that I might have a cleaner towel for a shower. The sub-tropical sun soon dried it for use.

I wanted to stay with Jerry at the kindergarten, and found I could sleep on a table in one of the classrooms, thinking that that would be more comfortable than the concrete floor. I folded up an old blanket and used it as a mattress.

Simone Weil has a good deal to say about attachment, for example, "Attachment is a manufacturer of illusions, and whoever wants reality ought to be detached."[4] In Jerry, I was beginning to grasp what she wrote, for I find most of her writing striking but unintelligible. Jerry's way of thinking and living made sense of these words:

---

[4] Weil, *Gravity and Grace*, 59.

Always beyond the particular object whatever it may be, we have to fix our will on the void, to will the void. For the good which we can neither picture nor define is a void for us. But this void is fuller than all fullnesses.

If we get as far as this we shall come through all right, for God fills the void. It has nothing to do with an intellectual process in the present-day sense. The intelligence has nothing to discover, it has only to clear the ground. It is only good for servile tasks.

The good seems to us as a nothingness, since there is no *thing* that is good. But this nothingness is not unreal. Compared with it everything in existence is unreal.[5]

What I met in San Mateo del Mar was not a man who had become senile and mentally unbalanced, but someone who had advanced toward living in a spirit of detachment, the genuine detachment Jesus talks about in the Gospels. Jerry had found out that "there is no *thing* that is good." I came to a man whose happiness was almost childlike, thrilled to see an old friend arrive unexpectedly, and who accepted the visit as a gratuitous grace. He had never written me, inviting me to come to this remote village in the South of Mexico. In the last two or three years, he did not come up to Cuernavaca when I was in Mexico for he was getting older, feebler. Somehow, I was moved to make a journey to see *him*. Our friendship then achieved a certain rhythmic balance.

After seeing Jerry, I returned to the States and called his Marianist superiors to report that he was neither crazy nor offending the people of the village with his filthy habits—two rumors I had heard. The only thing "wrong" with Jerry was that he was progressively conforming himself more and more closely to the Gospel. For some, of course, this meant that he became a scandal, a stumbling block. Not long after my visit to San Mateo del Mar, Jerry returned to Dayton, the headquarters of his religious congregation, and entered the retirement home.

When Jerry and I worked together in Cuernavaca during the 1960s, we would sometimes sit down to share a drink after the day's work. We enjoyed the conversation and the sense pleasure of the evening's treat. And, although I'm nearly as old as Jerry, I continue in my attachment to such indulgences. But I found, at the St. Leonard Center, that Jerry had left me, had moved beyond me, had learned how to grow old, how to prepare for death. It's true that he enjoyed certain luxuries at the Center,

---

[5] Ibid., 58.

the perquisites of an affluent society. But these had to be seen in the context of his contentment and happiness in San Mateo del Mar. Few if any persons in the United States could put up with the wretched simplicity of Jerry's existence in that fishing village. I needed a Simone Weil to reveal Jerry to me. He had internalized the truth of her statement: "The reality of the world is the result of our attachment. It is the reality of the self which we transfer into things."[6]

As the bus took me away from Jerry, I discovered that my thoughts had again been turned inside out, that I was again surprised. When I had planned to visit him, which I would do by public transportation, I was pleased with myself for making some effort to give my old friend something before he died, a visit. But I found everything reversed: *He* gave me something, the example of a life lived well, a life of startling paradoxes, a life of obedience to the Gospel. To me, his daily routine, always the same, appeared totally circumscribed. But he took time each day to pray before that cheap image, to open himself to prayer, to seek God in quiet.

When I saw how Jerry lived in San Mateo del Mar, and how he acted in the retirement home, I initially thought he had gotten to the essence of Illich's ideas on modern needs, that he had penetrated to the heart of Illich's thought. But after some reflection, I decided that was not exactly true. Jerry had gone far beyond the social surface of Illich's critical statements. The ideas on needs had to be understood in a context of faith, in the reality of Illich's belief. Then I could really see Jerry, a man reaching the end of his life, a life of fidelity, fidelity to his vows out of love for God, a love that manifested itself for so many years in his work with students: Europeans, North Americans, Latins, Indians. I've sometimes wondered about the vocation of a teaching brother. Who are these people in the Church? Since I've never read anything about them, and Jerry is the only one I've known, my understanding comes from him.

In view of my death, I want to live well. But, assuming faith, there remains one condition *sine qua non*: I must be free; I cannot continue to embrace the world, to hang on to any of its wiles. As well as I could see, Jerry ended up where every person of faith would like to be—free to take the final step, the step into death. The paradox shines out: The rules and structures of a religious congregation of teachers provided Jerry with

---

[6] Weil, *Gravity and Grace*, 59.

the possibility of a radical freedom.[7] Jerry received a fitting framework to live out his personal, intimate, oftentimes idiosyncratic vocation.

[7] Jerry lived and died as a faithful member of the Society of Mary (SM), a congregation popularly known as the Marianists. The work of the brothers and priests is principally teaching. For example, they operate the University of Dayton.

5

Walking with My Dead

I think it is good, maybe necessary, to experience strangeness, to feel myself as a foreigner, some kind of alien. I've been fortunate in this respect for I've been a stranger several times, having lived in at least six countries and traveled in a dozen more: military assignments, friendship and work called me to many places. When I was eighteen, I joined the Marine Corps, partly to "see the world." In 1946, they sent me to China. My first taste of foreignness there left a powerful impression on me that has marked my life to this day. Many years later I lived in Latin America, and stayed in a Gandhi ashram in India. In 1978, a trip to Europe introduced me to an unfamiliarity which, marvelously, opened me up and suggested yet another way of being on the earth. I, thoroughly confirmed in my sedentary habits, learned something new about walking. Eventually this led me to disturbing insights about myself and the world in which I live. I was brought to ask fundamental questions about how I think and act.

When I arrived in Germany, many customs and procedures struck me as unusual or odd. One very common practice surprised me: people taking a walk. In Bremen, where I lived for more than ten years, people regularly walked up and down beside the river Weser at all times of day and into the early hours of night. In small towns or at the edges of cities, one always saw people walking on Sunday afternoons. I was unexpectedly startled by friends who suggested we take a walk in order to discuss something, even serious matters of literature, theology, or how one lives well. Again and again I found myself rejoicing as I came to like and esteem this novel and rewarding addition to my life.

I had never thought about the time before history, the time before the creation of humans, when our near relatives used their own limbs to move across the earth. I had never thought about the history of walking, or even reflexively about the reality of walking. Like many Americans of my generation and social background, my experience of walking was almost exclusively utilitarian. In Marxist language, walking had no use-value for me.

However, I never questioned walking across town to grammar school. Then, when I was old enough, I rode a bike. That was convenient, and there was no need for a lock since people in that town seldom stole bikes in those days. There were also no school buses, except for the farm kids who were driven to the community high school. In that school, only one young man had a car, which he used for a part-time job to help support his widowed mother and younger brother. In college, I knew only one student who owned a car, which he parked on campus, and the college enforced strict rules on when he could drive it. Today the landscape of my youth has become unrecognizable. This was a time before hiking, backpacking and jogging had become widely fashionable; they didn't exist in my social circle. I suspect, though, that extended hikes, especially a trek around Europe, were beginning to be popular among more affluent young people. The romance of being transported captured peoples' imaginations and massive traffic had not yet tightened its grip, braking the nation's wheels.

A first-year college class suggested an idea I had not considered and did not see practiced until thirty years later. In 1948 it appeared a quaint but long-lost historical curiosity. Abstractly, however, I started thinking about walking and its place in a reflective life. We studied and wrote a weekly essay on a text from ancient Greece: I remember Homer, Thucydides, Plato, Aristophanes, Sophocles, and Aeschylus. After reading the *Phaedrus*, I wondered about the relationship between walking and thinking, between conversation and an examined life. Like the Germans I later came to know and respect, Socrates and Phaedrus take a walk in the country along the river Ilisus, come to a plane-tree, to a place "full of summer sounds and scents," and sit on the grass. They discuss love, the immortal nature and temporal actions of the human soul, rhetoric, philosophy, and language. In a passage that still inspires thinkers today, Socrates relates a myth about the origin of the alphabet. The god, Theuth, the inventor of many arts, tries to convince Thamus, king of Egypt, to adopt the use of letters. After listening to Theuth, Thamus replies:

> O most ingenious Theuth, the parent or inventor of an art is not
> always the best judge of the utility or inutility of his own inven-
> tions in the users of them. And in this instance, you who are the

father of letters, from a paternal love of your own children have been led to attribute to them a quality which they cannot have; for this discovery of yours will create forgetfulness in the learners' souls, because they will not use their memories; they will trust to the external written characters and not remember of themselves. The specific which you have discovered is an aid not to memory, but to reminiscence, and you give your disciples not truth, but only the semblance of truth; they will appear to be omniscient and will generally know nothing; they will be tiresome company, having the show of wisdom without the reality.[1]

From the example of Socrates I began to think about serious discussion accompanied by walking, but was soon distracted by the excitement of reading.

My experiences of strangeness were not brought about through geographical movement alone, though. I have also been caught, surprised, sometimes shocked, by certain books, by what occurs in prayer, and by meeting people. Some of these were extraordinary personalities who lived in the realm of notables, others were among the lowly, invisible people, the ones never noticed.

Looking further into questions concerned with living a graceful life, I reread Plato's *Symposium*. To get at the contrast between pre- and post-Christian views, I compared the ideas on friendship struggling for clarity in the *Symposium* with those more fluidly and concretely described in chapters 14–17 of St. John's Gospel. Reflecting on these two visions, I wanted to learn about the love of friendship from two different but somehow related sources of our tradition. In spite of the great distance I discerned between the two expressions of what it means to hold a friend in one's heart, and my strong pull toward the example of Jesus, I continue to believe I can learn from the Greeks, whom I regard as occupying a privileged path to truth. So, when I read the *Phaedrus* I ask myself: What is the relationship between the character of Socrates' thinking and the activity of walking?

I remembered, then, that Aristotle walked while teaching at the Lyceum. Because of this practice, followers of the Stagirite are called Peripatetics, the Greek word meaning to discourse while walking about. Today, however, students are generally expected to remain seated, often at precisely the same desk. What advances? What regresses? Further, do such practices disclose reality?

[1] Plato, *The Dialogues*, vol. 1, 277–78.

Wealthy people, moved by vanity and other "loftier" motives, endow, not a walk along the river, but a chair in a college or university. Institutions eagerly run after money given for this. Prestigious teachers feel honored to be selected to occupy such chairs. In the academic world, the closest approximation to teaching and walking I've seen is the occasional practice, usually on the first warm day of Spring, of taking a class of students out of the building to sit on the grass! I wonder. Is there an inverse relationship between the quality of thought and lack of both literal and figurative movement?

Except for walking to school, occasional short hikes as a Boy Scout, and a good deal of close order drill in the Marine Corps, I have done no regular walking in my life. Given this limited personal background, I was therefore rather astonished to find myself in Spain on the Camino de Santiago, a backpack riding securely on my hips, walking across the country to Compostela. Even more surprising, I was sixty-five years old! Why was I engaged in what could be characterized fairly as a foolhardy adventure?

In early 1993, a friend, Carl Mitcham, offered me the opportunity to give several lectures at the University of Oviedo. As I was walking out the door from our house in Germany to catch the train for my first trip to Spain, Ivan Illich, another friend with whom I lived, called out, "If you're going to Spain, you must visit Compostela." I had heard the name, and vaguely associated it with the practice of pilgrimage in the Middle Ages. I seemed to recall that Illich had written an essay on the subject but knew nothing else about it.

I had been asked to speak in Oviedo about living with technology today. My orientation tends toward a decidedly critical stance, but the faculty and students appeared interested in my perspective and presentation.[2] When I finished what I had to say, there were still two full days before I was scheduled to return to Germany, enough time to act on Illich's suggestion and briefly visit Compostela.

It was dark when our train reached the most famous city in Galicia. Several men waiting outside the station offered to take the passengers to a good hotel. Having some experience of travel, and being fluent in Spanish, I declined their offer, walked a block or two, and asked a local person for directions to the "old city." I felt certain I could find my own way to decent accommodations and pay only the minimum required.

---

[2] See Hoinacki, *Stumbling Toward Justice: Stories of Place*, especially chs. 7 and 8.

After about twenty minutes, I located a cheap pension on an attractive side street near a small plaza. After registering for a room, I immediately went to bed. I wanted to arise early the next day, Sunday, the one full day I would have to explore Compostela.

While darkness and quiet still enveloped the city, I rose, washed and dressed, and quickly covered the short distance to the cathedral, walking on narrow, stone-paved streets. The doors were just being opened; I entered and investigated the interior, a cavernous emptiness of a huge temple with only one person wandering about. Since I am rather unlettered in the study of church architecture, almost nothing caught my attention except the large statue of St. James the Greater, Santiago, dominating the high altar. The church was, after all, the centuries-old shrine dedicated to the Apostle whose bones, some believe, are buried there.

My principal notion of a place of pilgrimage was taken from photographs I had seen of Lourdes, visits I had made to la Villa, the church of our Lady of Guadalupe in Mexico City, and one trip to Czestochowa in Poland. I was therefore puzzled to see no evidence of the sick visiting the shrine; there were no crutches hanging, nor *ofrendas* fastened to the walls. I had seen these in la Villa, and many more in a museum at the site—small thanksgiving images left at the church for an obtained cure or favor. My first impression was a series of questions: What's the attraction? Why does Compostela's fame extend over a thousand years? Why do people come to this place? The questions were especially pressing, because no one was in the church, kneeling in prayer, as I had seen in Mexico City and Czestochowa.

Puzzled, I left the cathedral, stepped out into the enormous Plaza del Obradoiro, and looked across at a magnificent façade of twenty-five graceful arches stretching across the front of the Palacio de Rajoy. Turning right, I saw another impressive monument, the splendor of the restored Hostal de los Reyes Católicos, originally built as a hostel for pilgrims by Ferdinand and Isabella when they finally conquered the last stronghold of Islam on the Peninsula in 1492. Today it's an elegant and expensive hotel, and the only "pilgrims" who stay there are those who can afford first-class accommodations.

Wandering through the old city that clusters around the cathedral, I again felt what I had first come to experience in a visit to Assisi: lots of stone, quaint old buildings, and narrow, winding streets—an artificially restored "medieval" town. As in Italy, I again felt a certain uneasiness. What I saw about me was pleasant to the eyes; most tourists and foreign visitors would be charmed. But Compostela, like Assisi, is a famous shrine—it looks to the past, to the tradition of faith in Jesus Christ. This tradition includes the meaning discussed by Chesterton:

> Tradition may be defined as an extension of the franchise. Tradition means giving votes to the most obscure of all classes, our ancestors. It is the democracy of the dead. Tradition refuses to submit to the small and arrogant oligarchy of those who merely happen to be walking about. All democrats object to men being disqualified by the accident of birth, tradition objects to their being disqualified by the accident of death.[3]

The tradition enshrined in this place must also embrace the many dead who walked here from all over of what is now called Europe during the last thousand years.

The principal reason, I believe, for looking at the dead is to recover them; through them I can come to know the tradition. I assume that in some sense I need the past and the dead. But where are they? I see the stones; they're obviously ancient. But are they real? What is the relation between attractive reconstructions and the truth of the past?

I came back to the cathedral at the hour of Sunday High Mass. The great church was full and animated, but many gave off the flavor of being vacationers. Their attention to the ceremonies of the altar indicated they were more readily identified as tourists than as pilgrims. Perhaps they were a modern incarnation of pilgrims retrieved from another age. Perhaps my notion of a pilgrim was overly romantic or nostalgic or literal.

Returning outside with the crowd after Mass, I passed through a kind of vestibule. There, in a magazine and book rack, I found a booklet on the pilgrimage to Compostela. After buying it, I continued out and sat at a small sidewalk table for a cup of coffee. The pamphlet said that people still walked to Compostela today. It claimed there was some meaningful continuity between this action and that of others who traveled from all of Europe centuries ago. The author suggested one could relive the experience and faith of the dead—just by walking to Compostela. I wondered if this were true.

I strolled again through the adjoining streets, breathing in and savoring the festive atmosphere created by many people, Spanish and foreign, out for a Sunday airing. The sun-filled early spring morning was

---

[3] Chesterton, *Orthodoxy*, 85–6, quoted in Marlin, *The Quotable Chesterton*, 351.

enlivened by wandering musicians, by aromatic coffee shops whose tables overflowed onto the sidewalks, and by picturesque restaurants, inviting me to sample the cuisine of Galicia. I again felt a vague disquiet. I could not shake off the feeling that I was not participating in the celebration of the Lord's Day in one of the most famous shrines of the West. I had the sensation of a pleasant gadding about made possible and encouraged by leisure and affluence, mine and that of the people who brushed past me. Did the crowd promenading about the Old City of Compostela have anything in their minds and hearts beyond the intention of enjoying an amusing diversion, a local variation of "to see and be seen"?

Unable to form a consistently coherent thought or reach a conclusion about this place as the crowning consummation of pilgrim dreams for hundreds of years, I returned to the cathedral. In an alcove inside, I found a Blessed Sacrament chapel with heavy glass doors to shut out the noise of the nave; occasionally, people went in and came out. I, too, went through the door. As in other such chapels I had visited in great churches, I was stirred by the evident piety of the worshippers. They entered and silently knelt, stood, or sat, all their attention focused on the large Host in the elaborate monstrance. As in other chapels, too, flowers and lighted candles filled the altar and much of the surrounding floor. Each person appeared absorbed in his or her world of mysterious communion with the Lord present in the Eucharist on the altar. Each time I enter such a sanctuary, I again ask myself: How can I find a way into the region of these peoples' faith? How can I be a living part of *this* community?

That day, however, I had come to the chapel with another question: Why have large numbers of people, for more than a thousand years, continued to visit this church, some traversing hundreds of miles on foot? I sat there quietly for an hour or two, thinking first about my question, then attempting to empty my imagination and mind completely. I knew this was necessary, for I could not hope to learn about the Beyond if I remained attached to my own thoughts.

I was not disappointed. At one moment, a clear notion came to me: If you want to know why people come, you must yourself come.

I understood the thought exactly: I had to retrace the steps, live through the daily experiences, feel the same air and sun and rain, look up at the stars that thousands, maybe millions, have known over several hundred years. I had to follow the path of the dead, I had to become a pilgrim.

I picked up my small backpack at the pension, hurried to the station, boarded the train, and dreamed about pilgrims in the Middle Ages. But I had no idea where one started walking, whether there was a fixed route, how one ate and slept while getting to Galicia, the time one needed . . . but I was certain about the one essential decision: I was walking to Compostela.

Back in Germany, many details were rapidly revealed. Ivan Illich, the friend who had suggested I visit the city, gave me a pair of old hiking shoes he had bought in 1973. Amazingly, they seemed to fit. A student friend, Sebastian Trapp, lent me a modern backpack, and showed me how to adjust it to my body. Another friend, Barbara Duden, gave me a sleeping bag. A Spanish friend, Alfons Garrigós, wrote me that a traditional starting point was on the French side of the Pyrenees in a town called St. Jean Pied de Port. Beginning there, and following the *camino francés,* a trail marked with yellow arrows painted on trees, rocks, curbs, and buildings, one could hope to arrive in Compostela in about a month.

Since I had never seriously hiked, I put some books in the backpack to give it weight and walked up and down alongside the Weser early each morning. After about a week I grew so excited about this possibly hazardous undertaking that I could waste no more time getting in shape. I boarded a train and finally arrived in St. Jean Pied de Port, near the French-Spanish border.

While in the train, I thought about my experiences in two places of pilgrimage, la Villa in Mexico City, and the Black Virgin in Poland. The Polish image is clearly an Eastern icon, the Mexican one more ambiguous. But the people who kneel before the two images, so far apart physically and culturally, are united in the manner of their devotion. They act in accord with the ancient tradition of Orthodox prayer before an icon. They recognize that the image on which they fix their gaze is theology in visible form. I noticed, however, that the two images are rather different. Viewed as icons, their epiphanic faces are not the same. Figurative, but not naturalistic (a characteristic more pronounced in Czestochowa), the images portray a symbolic realism.

Following the genius of Giotto, Western religious art became more descriptive, more didactic, ending in the blind alley of sweet and sentimental caricature one sees so often today. The East has somehow maintained its rigorous austerity, providing an entrance to the infinite for the simple believer through the opening of the icon. The people I saw in la Villa and Czestochowa, staring beyond the icon, are carried into the Beyond. How else account for the hours they kneel before the images?[4]

In both shrines, the people are uniform in their devotional practice. Many make sacrifices to get to the churches. In each place, faces shine with the same radiance, their attention fixed on the images. In Poland, the chapel containing the image or icon filled up each evening and the people did not depart until the following morning. At that time, others arrived for daytime devotions. What pulled them to these places? How do I think about the evident trust or faith of those kneeling before the image? Is there any relation between those people and what I intend to do now? In both Mexico City and Czestochowa, I had knelt before the icon and attempted to pray. But I was always uncertain. How do I prepare myself to come before such an image? Physically, how do I get there? For example, must I imitate believers of the Middle Ages and walk? If so, how far? Once there, what kind of prayer should I recite? Are recited prayers the proper action? And I could not help but think of the dead. Is it necessary to establish some connection with them? If that is true, what is the precise relationship?

I had read nothing about Compostela except for the booklet I found in the entryway to the cathedral. I had no clear idea of what I was looking for on this journey, nor did I have a definite notion of what I hoped to achieve by carrying a backpack about a thousand kilometers across the Pyrenees and Spain. But, like the initial idea that I had to do it, two others had somehow taken shape inside me: I would read nothing during the time required to reach Compostela, and I would walk with no one. I felt I had to act as I did that Sunday afternoon in the Blessed Sacrament chapel. I needed to avoid all distractions, to empty myself of everything so that I might enter the ancient step-by-step experience of reaching Compostela on foot.[5] My other resolution also turned out to be singular. While walking, I met only one other person who proceeded alone. At night, when I stopped in one of the shelters to bathe and sleep, I sometimes met other pilgrims. They always traveled with friends or in a group. I felt that the insights available under the sky of Spain would more certainly be vouchsafed to someone whose attention was fully focused on the *camino*, the Spanish word for "way," a term resonant with overtones from the words of Jesus Christ. The effort to experience the

---

[4] See Zibawi, *The Icon: Its Meaning and History.*

[5] When I returned to Germany I learned there are thousands of books and articles about pilgrimage on the *camino* and the arrival in Compostela.

camino is similar to the effort to reach the Beyond: In addition to being free from distractions, one needs silence and solitude.

While crossing the Pyrenees on the first day of my undertaking, I came to feel I had to accept a certain truth in order to reach Compostela: the journey was not principally about walking, but about the disposition of my soul. I saw more clearly that I had to touch the dead in my tradition, somehow experience them, hold them tightly, and hope to be identified with them. Briefly, I wanted to become a living member of my tradition.

How did I reach these truths? I don't know; but I experienced them with an absolute certainty that first day and every day for a month. Perhaps the action of putting one foot in front of the other while my mind "wandered" revealed certain insights to me. Perhaps I discovered another route to knowledge, one with affinities to the ways of Socrates, Aristotle, and other walker-thinkers throughout history. Walking on this specific route, guided by the Spirit that moved me, carried by the dead who accompanied me, revealed notions hitherto hidden from me.

For example, I came to see, more vividly than ever before, why Germany, where I then lived, appeared more and more foreign to me. As I walked, I began to reflect on the country from the perspective of the love that united Dietrich Bonhoeffer and Maria Von Wedemeyer, as revealed in their letters to one another during the two years before his execution on April 10, 1945.[6]

These two people, after having seen one another on several occasions, realized they were deeply in love and planned to marry. At this moment Bonhoeffer, suspected of being a part of the plot to assassinate Hitler, was arrested and put in prison, emerging only for his execution. A month later, the war in Europe was over. We know about the reality and depth of their love because their letters were published nearly fifteen years after Maria's death in 1977. A beautiful and tender aspect of Dietrich's person, hitherto hidden, was suddenly seen. The amazing maturity and fidelity of Maria, eighteen years old when they met, brilliantly illumined her letters.

The Barman Declaration, whose principal author was Karl Barth, appeared on May 31, 1934, the same year the Vatican signed a Concordat with Hitler. The Declaration, with which Bonhoeffer identified, was unequivocal: No believing Christian could support National Socialism, the

---

[6] Bismarck, *Love Letters from Cell 92: The Correspondence Between Dietrich Bonhoeffer and Maria Von Wedemeyer, 1943-45.*

Nazi party. As one sees from his life and writing, Bonhoeffer went far beyond this statement. His contribution to the conundrums facing a Christian today is richly rewarding to the person who reflects on its meaning and implication. For example, he died, not for the church, but for a political cause: resistance to Hitler. He was a new kind of martyr to the faith, thereby participating in the sufferings of God in a godless world. In a remarkable affinity with Simone Weil, who died in 1943, Bonhoeffer believed that the God who is absent is the true God. This God did *not* come to help Christ on the Cross.[7]

Bonhoeffer refused to conceive of a God beyond Christ; in a sense, he believed in non-metaphysical transcendence. God is in the nearest Thou. Bonhoeffer wanted to live in the midst of his/our world. Among other things, this meant to oppose the evil that was poisoning his people, his land. Given the nature of National Socialism, Hitler, and those who obeyed him, on one side, and the faith of Bonhoeffer on the other, one can see why he had to die. From the Von Wedemeyer-Bonhoeffer letters, I think Bonhoeffer believed he would eventually be executed. He wrote to Maria assuring her he would be set free, perhaps out of delicacy for her feelings, the disingenuousness of a man in love.

In that first week of April 1945, Bonhoeffer's last week on earth, all of Germany was collapsing. Many cities were wastes of rubble; everyone could see that the end of the Third Reich was only days away, yet the machinery of execution continued to function well; nothing broke down, nothing failed. In a country where events like this could happen, I felt myself a complete stranger; I could never be anything but a confused foreigner. Years later, after studying the lives of Hans and Sophie Scholl, Nazi Germany became more understandable, but no less repulsive.[8]

One aspect of these final months of Bonhoeffer's life especially stands out for me: his love for Maria, his *worldly*—as he clearly and explicitly understood—particularistic love for her. This love appears infinitely lovely. As I walked under the sun of Spain I came to think that the

---

[7] Nichols, *Systematic and Philosophical Theology,* 109–231. See also Simone Weil who wrote, "God can only be present in creation under the form of absence." *Gravity and Grace,* 162.

[8] I learned about one of countless ironic cruelties. Harald Dohrn, father-in-law of Christoph Probst, who was executed by the Nazis with Hans and Sophie Scholl on February 22, 1943, was shot by the Nazis in the Perlacher Forest on April 25, 1945, only hours before Germany surrendered. Jens, *At the Heart of the White Rose. Letters and Diaries of Hans and Sophie Scholl,* 321.

evil of National Socialism can best be seen in the Nazis' destruction of this love. But it also seemed true that their love for one another reached its beautiful height, in some sense, only *because* of National Socialism. This good could only come out of such depths of evil. In Dietrich and Maria, I could understand something of Germany's Third Reich; further, I could begin to look into the mystery of good and evil.

In America, however, we may be too naïve, too crudely "innocent," too young historically, for this kind of evil. Americans could not plan and carry out a "final solution." Some have said, and maybe believed, that "the only good Indian is a dead Indian." But there was no defined, systematic attempt to carry out a direct national policy of extermination. Analogous arguments can be made for attacks on blacks, Catholics, Jews, and foreigners generally. Perhaps Americans have not entered so deeply into the mystery of good and evil.

There is a further difficulty for Americans: Evil today is increasingly abstract. Consider, for example, the more than decade-long wars against Iraq. Before each began in earnest, before the invasions, the wars were designed to succeed without American casualties as state-of-the-art technological wars. In judging American foreign policy adversely, how many turn aside with revulsion similar to what is felt for Hitler, Stalin, Mao, or Pol Pot? Many feel more ambivalent, even if they are deeply disturbed.

There's a further step in the question of evil today, an evil that reaches out and penetrates not only one society, but all nations. An altogether new species of evil stalks the world: the attempts by those entranced with technological magic to supplant Creation. Not only Americans, but many from other nations, too, enthusiastically populate the world with modern sorcerer's apprentices. At the moment, no single nation is the undisputed leader. In fact, almost every nation strives to participate as vigorously as possible; no one wants to be left behind. No nation on earth, in a society-wide effort or policy, acts to repudiate the technological project: the attempt to produce a new, man-made creation to replace what is widely regarded as a multi-flawed hodge-podge of imperfect creatures and their artifacts.

The Nazis committed a sin against Christianity; men such as Franz Jägerstätter clearly and courageously recognized this. He and other heroic witnesses, such as the Jesuit Alfred Delp, understood the nature of the Nazi sin, therefore, they acted to oppose it even though such action inevitably merited execution when they were caught.[9] The Nazi sin came out of a Christian society, that is, what was left of one, a society in which you needed to be a kind of Christian to hate a Jew.

Our world is partly defined by the way we, individually and socially, conceptualize and confront good and evil. In the West, this was generally done in terms derived from Christianity. Repeatedly, however, the Gospel is both used and abused. Therefore, today's task is to search for truth in a world where, paradoxically, believers must live *etsi deus non daretur* (as if God does not exist). The Latin phrase is a key to Bonhoeffer's thought and life and may be more applicable to our time than his.[10]

Thinking about both then and now I can approach the darkness through the notion of sin. What is, ultimately, the contemporary sin? I reflected on this question during the month-long tramp through Spain and concluded that sin today, in both its personal and societal essence perhaps is, again paradoxically, post-Christian. Many, in their thought and action, in their dreams and desires, deny Christianity in the sense that they ignore the reality of the Incarnation. But Christianity is defined as a belief in the Incarnation, in the belief that God became a man and rose from the dead.

In several places, St. Paul emphasizes faith in the Resurrection from the dead. For example,

> And if Christ has not been raised, your faith is futile; you are still in your sins. . . . If only for this life we have hope in Christ, we are to be pitied more than all men (1 Cor 15:17–19).

Creation, therefore, is doubly sacred. Its fundamental character and goodness is revealed in Genesis; its new participation in divinity is seen in the Christ. Sins against Creation, then, are especially heinous. One can see how today's sin comes out of a profoundly post-Christian world. This is what most precisely characterizes our world, not all the pseudo-posts one reads about: post-ideological, post-industrial, post-historical, post-modern, post-human. Our world is militantly ideological, increas-

---

[9] Zahn, *In Solitary Witness: The Life and Death of Franz Jägerstätter*; Coady, *With Bound Hands: A Jesuit in Nazi Germany: The Life and Selected Letters of Alfred Delp*.

[10] Bonhoeffer wrote: "And we cannot be honest unless we recognize that we have to live in the world *etsi deus non daretur*. And this is just what we do recognize—before God!" Bonhoeffer, *Letters and Papers from Prison*, 196. The phrase comes from the seventeenth-century legal philosopher, Grotius.

ingly industrial in the production of all "goods" and services, ever more dedicated to a necrophiliac historical commitment, subscribing to a hubristic modernity that ignores the wisdom of the past. To ignore the past is no longer to be condemned to repeat it; to ignore the past today is to fixate oneself on death.

Through the technological project, individuals, institutions and nations have gone "beyond" Christianity to sin against the truth of Genesis. Believing Christians, Jews, and Moslems can recognize the truth of this statement. The sin is committed most directly in areas developed out of applied chemistry, biology and physics. These sciences, especially, have tended to serve the ends of industrial technology. For that reason, it is often more proper to conceptualize them, not as sciences, but as branches of technology.

For scientists, technocrats, and the "ordinary" citizen, killing Jews, Gypsies, Jehovah's Witnesses, some believing Christians, and homosexuals could be acknowledged as evil. If one retained a modicum of consistency in his or her thought and life, one could not have some contact with Hebrew and Christian Scripture and approve the killing of these groups of people. But today, terrifyingly, there is an obscurity that affects everyone.

Attacking Creation through chemical and biological manipulation is recognized by almost no one—believer, agnostic, atheist, pagan, humanist—for what it is: the most serious sin individuals, institutions, and entire societies have yet dared to commit in the history of the world. I judge the gravity of the sin by the fact that Creation is the first gift, the original gift coming from the Infinite, from the Beyond, from what many people call God.

Bonhoeffer could not follow the advice of his American friends and stay in New York. He had to catch that last ship in 1939 and return to his land, to his people, to his act of witness, and to his death. Just as Bonhoeffer saw the evil in his place, Germany, so I must try to see the evil in my place, America.

In the 1930s and early 1940s, the Nazis were world leaders inflicting evil on the other, on their neighbors. Today, the USA is a similar kind of leader. But there are many differences, perhaps the principal one being how the infection of evil affects the minds and hearts of individuals. There is a new, devilish attractiveness in evil today. Technological wizards, through knowledge and control of the genetic code, assure vain parents that they can program a body and mind made to order for their children according to whatever fashion and human depravity dictate. Married persons desperate to have a child are vulnerable to the promises of high tech medical manipulation of their bodies—as a good! Some older people, regarding their bodies not as temples of the Holy Spirit but as a kind of used car, will sometimes seek technical remaking of their bodies through organ transplants.[11] The most prevalent sin today, the violation of Creation, is a sin extremely difficult to perceive because it is named "progress" and "improvement."

For believing Christians, Bonhoeffer's insight is more necessary than ever: "Christ is only Christ in the midst of the world." But it's difficult to see Christ in our world. Two generations after Bonhoeffer, the denial of Christ's presence, a *Christian* sin, appears easy to recognize in the Nazis and their collaborators. But judging our world today is difficult. The opaqueness is illustrated by an event I witnessed in Germany. I went to our local Catholic church for Good Friday services and saw a choir standing on the sanctuary steps, dressed in black, facing the congregation; they sang the "Glasshütter Passion" from 1680. There was no organ, of course . . . all was artistically correct. It was a formal, dignified, even majestic performance. Sitting there, I asked myself: Where is Christ in his shame? Pascal says that "Jesus will be in agony until the end of the world."[12] If the Incarnation is real, should a believer not want to *see* this: the abandonment of Jesus on the Cross?

In the Gospels of Matthew (27:46) and Mark (15:34), the first words of Psalm 22 are reported as the cry of Jesus from the cross: "My God, my God, why have you forsaken me?" Simone Weil, commenting on these words, says that "There we see the real proof that Christianity is something divine." She adds:

> Christ healing the sick, raising the dead, etc., that is the humble, human, almost low part of his mission. The supernatural part is the sweat of blood, the unsatisfied longing for human consolation, the supplication that he might be spared [all three in the Garden of Gethsemane], the sense of being abandoned by God.[13]

---

[11] See the arguments of Ivan Illich in: Hoinacki, *The Challenges of Ivan Illich*, ch. 19; Illich, *In the Mirror of the Past*, 218–31; Cayley, *Ivan Illich in Conversation*, 256–8, 279–287.

[12] Pascal, *Pensées*, 313.

[13] Weil, *Gravity and Grace*, 139.

If I understand anything of Pascal and Simone Weil, should not the liturgy help us see the bitterness of his suffering, his accursed affliction? I think the magnificent music on that Good Friday precisely symbolized the absence of perceived sin in our world. As a living belief in the Incarnation has diminished, so has Christian sin. As the world is doubly blessed, so is sin doubly heinous.

Reflection during thirty-two days of walking in silent solitude brought me to understand that I need my dead. Because I was living in Germany, I realized that Dietrich Bonhoeffer is one of the principal participants in this community; I must try to associate myself with him. But even more important for me are the dead of my own country. The Incarnation means that I, too, must be incarnate. That can occur only in my proper place, my own land. To live as a foreigner, for me, is to live an abstract life, to participate in the technological world, not in the fleshly world of my dead.

I now recognize that *the* crucial questions today are these: Who are my dead? How do I come to know them intimately? How do I identify myself with them? These are the essential questions for philosophy, religion, and thought itself.

Walking over the mountains and plains of Spain, I felt a peculiar oneness with those who had preceded me in the past thousand years. They asserted themselves as living members of my tradition; they constitute my tradition—*if* I share their faith. I came to understand that if I am to be something other than a straw blown about by the wind, I need to find my tradition and insert myself in it. I now believe this is a primary task for each person who wants to live a *human* life, who wants *to be* human. Animal instinct is not sufficient; the passions often mislead. Because I think and desire, I need to learn how to live. Ultimately, there is only one way: to enter my tradition and follow in the footsteps of my ancestors. I was not so much in need of historical scholarship, textual accuracy, and an overly cautious mind with regard to received tradition. Rather, I needed to walk, to *feel* the truth of the imperfect and variously-motivated people who trod the plains and mountains before me.

Walking under the sun or through the rain on the *camino*, I saw that the truth of tradition is known most certainly and accurately through its dead, through those who have most fully tested and lived it. Each day I was reminded that they are alive! The history of thought and ideas is not. The dead of my tradition can be known because they reveal themselves to me. I learned this out there in that sacred space in Spain, the places where I set my feet, the path established and sanctified by so many dead who walked before me.[14]

Each person must ask this question: Who are my dead? For each, the answer will be different, for many traditions have contributed to where people stand today. Traditions are not abstract but are of flesh and blood. They are made up of those who have "kept the faith," those who have lived honorably, those who have sought to supersede self, who have reached out in love to the other. Every tradition on earth is peopled by such saints or witnesses. One need only look for them and, finding them, hold them tightly.

I have used the concepts good and evil, God, the Incarnation, sin, beauty and ugliness, without any attempt to establish their truth or existence by rational argument. Nor have I defended the ontological character of truth. I have proceeded in this way because I believe those who have ears to hear will hear, and those who do not will not. I judge that we, those living in the midst of an advanced technological society, are inundated with evidence. The most certain way *to see* the evidence is to go through an experience like my month in Spain. Obviously, not many can do this. Hence, I ask the reader to stop, reflect on the world and its evidence, found especially in the dead, and what, from my peculiar journey, I have written about them.

Not everyone can walk a thousand kilometers across Spain. But each person can find his or her *place* in the world, in the cosmos, and in the Beyond. It is my firm belief that one's place is primarily in Creation; everyone is incarnate, and each can explore the nature of her or his particular incarnation, find the essence of creaturely existence: Am I my own raison d'être, or part of some larger reality? The dead know.

---

[14] Hoinacki, *El Camino: Walking to Santiago de Compostela.*

6

An Art of Suffering

A REPORTER, CALLING the house in Bremen, Germany, where Ivan Illich had recently died, asked Silja Samerski the cause of his death. "We don't know," she answered. A friend of mine, referring to Illich's death, asked me, "What did he die of?" Others, too, have asked me and those who were close to Illich while he lived. Depending on who the person is questioning me, I answer with some variation of: "That's the wrong question; it doesn't make any sense. Illich did not die of *something*, as he was not living *with* something, that is, he didn't have a disease, he didn't suffer an illness." He himself was quite clear about this when people asked him about the bump on the side of his face. They assumed that the swelling, about the size of a large grapefruit in the last years of his life, was an indication of some disease, most probably the result of cancer.

Illich, in *Medical Nemesis*, pointed out the historical contingency of the notion that people experience an entitative reality called disease.[1] Strictly speaking, even today, to talk about a disease may be no more than a way of speaking; it may not refer to an identifiable reality at all. The expression I have heard, "Oh, it's all in your head," may be more inclusive than many suspect. But that was not Illich's point. He wanted to question the very idea of illness or disease as entitative, and as being a specific, sensible reality that one could define.

However, he did not want to deny the existence of pain or human suffering. Rather, he strongly suggested that today's practice of allopathic medicine, with its emphasis on instruments for diagnosis, does not lead to the truth of what occurs in the human condition. Years ago, he spelled out his thought in *Medical Nemesis* and later essays.[2] One

[1] Illich, *Medical Nemesis,* 159–60.
[2] See Duden, "The Quest for Past Somatics," in Hoinacki, *The Challenges of Ivan Illich*, 219–30. See also Cayley, *Ivan Illich in Conversation.*

can read these writings and find an unequivocal exposition of his position. But much stronger evidence is given us in his personal example.
Looking at him, people were shocked to see what he did not disguise or
hide: a huge, lumpy growth on the side of his face.

When *Medical Nemesis* was first published, Illich gave lectures to
audiences of doctors at leading medical research centers in America and
Europe. The book, and Illich in his talks, was strongly critical of the
institution of mainstream medicine. The first sentence of the book's
Introduction accurately expressed his view: "The medical establishment
has become a major threat to health." Among the comments by physicians who heard him, one was especially memorable: "We'll wait to see
what you do, Professor Illich, when you are seriously ill."[3]

Ivan Illich died on December 2, 2002. For some years preceding
his death, the collection of small tumors, making one large swelling on
the side of his face, slowly continued to become larger. He assumed the
growth was also inward, since the jaw on that side of his face did not
function well and his hearing in that ear was blocked. But he sought no
treatment, indeed, refused it. He believed each person should work out
and practice his or her own art of suffering . . . He answered the question
of the doctors. In fact, he was a living, walking example of his ideas on
pain and allopathic medicine. As someone like José Bergamín might say,
he violently threw down a gauntlet for the world by quietly suffering an
intensity of pain that no one could possibly fathom.[4] Once I came across
William Stringfellow's description of the terrible pain he suffered:

> Part of the ambiguity attending pain is attributable to ignorance
> and some of it to prejudice, but much of that ambiguity has to
> do with the sentimentalization of pain in the experience of a
> particular person. I found that so myself. To maintain lucidity
> in the midst of pain requires an effort at once enormous and re-
> sourceful. In pain, as much or more than physical health, sanity
> itself is always at issue. The issue is present, subtly, even where
> pain is minimal and transient; it is there blatantly where pain is
> ferocious and obstinate. In the latter circumstances, the tempta-

[3] Conversation with Ivan Illich. All subsequent Illich quotes and reports of his
experiences and opinions, if not referenced by published or unpublished material, come
from my conversations with him.

[4] Bergamín's paradoxical way of expressing himself is nicely caught in the title of
one of his books of essays: José Bergamín, *La importancia del demonio y otras cosas sin
importancia*. For an appreciation of Bergamín's thought and person, see: Arana Palacios,
"José Bergamín, un hombre de su siglo," *Revista de Occidente*, 29–52.

tion of delusion and, beyond that, the danger of hallucination have no ruth.[5]

I gave the pages to Illich and, after reading them, he said, "He [Stringfellow] knows what he's talking about."

In 1998, a mutual friend, Father John McNamee, asked me about Illich's growth. McNamee knew a doctor who had a malignant brain tumor. She expressed the opinion that Illich did not have cancer, that his tumor was benign. If it were cancerous, she reasoned, he would have been dead long ago. She assumed that if it were malignant, the cancerous cells would metastasize and eventually kill him.[6] Referring to Illich's bump, she asked, "Has he ever had a diagnosis?"

McNamee and another friend, Joe Ferry, both close to Illich, drove from Philadelphia to State College and asked me the question. I said I didn't know, but I was leaving for Mexico in a day or two, and would ask Illich. A diagnosis would presumably answer the question of whether he had cancer. In our conversation, however, I pointed out that Illich did not have an illness. To have an illness, is to assume that disease is entitative, is *aliquid* (some-thing). Illich insisted that "disease as an entity" is an historical construction, not an Aristotelian universal, referring directly to a reality as, for example, the term, tree, can mean this specific organic growth in front of me. If disease or illness is not in fact entitative, then it may be true that modern medicine does *not* deal with the reality of the body.[7] One needs to emphasize that Illich *was* someone, a certain kind of person; he lived in a certain way. It seemed to me that for Illich a diagnosis might be meaningless. If it were done and made known, it would only reveal a distorted aspect of the whole man, his life and ultimate purpose for living. Nevertheless, I promised to ask Illich about his situation, and to let McNamee and Ferry know what I learned.

After getting a diagnosis from a doctor, many are radically changed in their very being. I have seen that in its effect on some people; a diagnosis can be devastating, destructive of their spirit. After receiving this contingent judgment many are pushed further into medicalization or sucked up into the medical system. This may include the identification of oneself with medical procedures, thereby alienating oneself from

---

[5] Kellermann, *A Keeper of the Word: Selected Writings of William Stringfellow*, 63.

[6] Some believe one can have a malignant tumor without metastasis. Illich believed metastasis had occurred.

[7] A good friend, Gene Burkart, suggested this opinion.

one's own body, from one's very self.[8] Living close to Illich, I had never noticed any evidence of such an effect on him, however.

Illich had studied and thought much about the history of diagnosis in the West. Following Webster's, he knew that the word comes from the Greek and means to know by distinguishing. Today, its more usual sense is: the art or act of identifying a disease from its signs and symptoms. But Illich recognized the word's power. He pointed out how the term, sex, as distinct from vernacular gender, "is the result of a diagnosing (in Greek, 'discrimination') of deviations from the abstract genderless norm of the 'human'."[9]

I knew, however, that his fundamental thinking about the notion was distinctly colored by his own youthful experience. He was twelve years old and living in Vienna at the time of the *Anschluss*, the annexation of Austria by Hitler. If one accepts Hitler's criteria, Illich was a Jew. In one moment, as Illich pointed out years later, he was transformed from a half-Aryan to a half-Jew—through the Nazi diagnosis. Among the assaults on his person was the action of a school official. The young Ivan, not yet a teenager, was paraded before the other children with the official pointing to his nose: "A typical Jewish profile. That is the blight we must erase from our land!"

Physicians might quibble about Illich's sense of the Nazis' action as being a diagnosis. But his judgments and reflections on them were often startling in their revelatory uniqueness; one could easily be thrown off by rigid, conventional thought. In terms of Illich's later work, two aspects of the traumatic Vienna episode were important: The experience itself did not destroy the young boy's image of himself and, secondly, it gave him an insight into the reality of modern medical definitions and procedures. As with other occurrences in his life, he turned a personally painful perception into an understanding of how a part of the modern world functions.

When I arrived in Mexico, I asked Illich about a diagnosis. "What was the growth?" He described several ways of considering it. Each of them appeared to carry some weight, but I concluded that one had to make distinctions between them. I had to determine the hierarchy of "reasons" to complete the picture, to reach the truth of his thinking, the character of his person and, as it turned out, his irrevocable decision.

[8] See chapter 7 for a detailed description and analysis of how this occurred to someone I knew.

[9] Illich, *Gender*, 4.

He spoke of his mother's brother, Uncle Paul. This man was an accomplished astrologer, closely associated with Rudolf Steiner and quite prominent in European anthroposophic circles. Knowing the date and hour of Illich's birth, he worked out a horoscope. On a visit to Mexico years later Uncle Paul, now an old man, said that Illich would experience some serious trouble, perhaps in or connected with his teeth. Because of this problem, he would be tempted to seek professional help. Uncle Paul strongly advised against such action; it would be a terrible mistake. He should never consult the appropriate professional, for example, a doctor. Uncle Paul said this before any swelling was visible on Illich's face, indeed, long before he experienced any indication of pain.

Illich told me another fact might have some relevance. He had heard that an identifiable group of Jews is supposed to be subject to developing a certain kind of tumor. His mother, whose family was Jewish in origin, was diagnosed as having such a tumor, and it was inoperable. While pregnant with her first child, who would be Ivan, she was X-rayed twice. This was in 1926 when such a procedure was still considered to be unproblematical. He thought that perhaps the exposure to X-rays had some effect many years later. Illich's mother died in the mid-1960s. In his estimation she died, not from the tumor itself, but from the difficulty of carrying its weight; it had become quite large.

In the early 1980s, when the bump was visible on the side of his face, a doctor friend, Quentin Young, wanted to do something about it. But he knew Illich was not really interested in investigating and treating the condition. So he devised a ruse. He arranged to have Illich invited to a social gathering in Chicago at which an oncologist, prepared for the trick, was present. When a group of previously informed people surrounded Illich, the oncologist took out his syringe and quickly withdrew fluid from the swelling for a biopsy. Not wishing to cause a scene, Illich did not resist or create a commotion. Years later, a friend reported what Illich said about the incident: "Now I know what it feels like to be raped."[10]

Later, Dr. Young told Illich the biopsy revealed the presence of a tumor that medical opinion considered dangerous. It was not unequivocally malignant, but the doctors strongly advised surgery to remove it. Illich decided to do nothing.

---

[10] Reported to me in a letter from the friend, Aaron Falbel.

A few years earlier an event occurred which, I believe, carried some weight with Illich. In the late 1970s, he was in India and Pakistan, and had come to know Unani theory and practice through Unani physicians. This tradition has its origins in Pythagorian, Hippocratic, and Galenic thought, and is widely followed in India, Pakistan, and Bangladesh. Through the commentaries of Avicenna (980–1037), the views acquired many elements of Aristotelian philosophy. A principal idea, still strongly held in Unani reasoning, emphasizes the notion of balance, especially of the four humors.[11]

Illich came to respect one Unani practitioner, Hakim Said Mohammed. After examining Illich, he told him that the still small bump was a part of him, it belonged to his person. If he were to do something about it he would throw himself out of balance. Wearing glasses for reading and submitting to surgery for a hernia were not such invasive procedures as to destroy his balance. He could accept their help. Illich had always placed importance on achieving and maintaining a balance, and toward the end of his life concentrated more and more on the idea of balance contained in the notion of proportion. Interested in the history of medicine, Illich pointed out that "hakim" means one person who is a scientist, philosopher, and healer.[12]

I began to wonder . . . What if the Philadelphia physician, who had died with her inoperable brain tumor, were correct in thinking that Illich's protuberance was benign? What if no metastasis were going to occur? What if, acting on the advice of the Unani physician, he chose to live with this expanding mass of tissue? He might continue to live for many years.

The lump was progressively causing him more and more pain, always greater interference with his jaw, his hearing, his speech, and his ability read and think. He continued and perhaps intensified his lifelong practice of yoga and its controlled breathing. I was amazed, for example, to see how easily he put himself in the position of what looked to me like standing on one's head when he was over seventy![13]

---

[11] The four are: sanguine, choleric or irascible, phlegmatic, and melancholic. Their delicate balance determines one's temperament and health. Information on Unani medicine can be obtained from The Indian Institute of the History of Medicine in Hyderabad, India.

[12] Illich, "Do Not Let Us Succumb to Diagnosis, But Deliver Us from the Evils of Health," unpublished speech.

[13] He usually did special yoga exercises before giving a lecture. I remember once, at

Through Robert Duggan, Dr. Beate Zimmermann, and others, he attempted to get some relief from the pain through the needles of acupuncture. He always carried a few needles with him, knew the points where they should be put, and asked us to insert them now and then. Friends who had "the touch," for example, Sajay Samuel, would massage his feet when they were with him, especially at night before he tried to sleep.[14]

Illich also smoked raw opium and strictly limited the amount smoked for he did not want to become addicted. In his last years he increased the use of opium. He said that smoking did not eliminate the pain, it was not a pain-killer, but it moved the pain to one side, allowing him "to distance" (his expression) himself from the pain. He was then better able to converse and read. He once told a friend that the pain made him more aware of his body, it heightened his sensual awareness. For example, colors appeared brighter, more vivid.[15]

In various ways, he had to adjust to the pain. He continued to meet with friends, to travel, to lecture and teach. People, including doctors, seeing the enlargement of the outgrowth, expressed their amazement and questioned me about his health. They were afraid to confront Illich himself.

In my own thought, I always returned to one fact: the pain. From many indications I noticed, and from candid remarks he felt he could make to an intimate friend, I had some notion of what he suffered and I realized that the torment increased with time. It always got worse; there was no reversing the unremitting agony; he had to live with it.

I sometimes asked myself, "Why didn't he have the bump removed years earlier?" Now, apparently, it was too late. But he could have submitted to surgery when the excrescence started to grow, as the Chicago oncologist advised. I know he was not ideologically opposed to all medical intervention. For some years he wore a truss. But when he experienced great difficulty sitting and walking, he submitted to a hernia operation.

Berea College in Kentucky, I asked for a private room next to the lecture hall for Illich to do his yoga for some minutes immediately before speaking.

[14] Robert Duggan, an old friend of Illich, is one of the founders of the Tai Sophia Institute for the Healing Arts in Columbia, MD. At the institution, one can learn acupuncture, botanical healing, and applied healing arts. See: www.tai.edu.

[15] Aaron Falbel, the friend, wrote me these comments (July 2003). Falbel was surprised to hear Illich extolling the benefits of pain!

When an infected tooth was causing various kinds of anguish, he had it removed. Why had he done nothing about the facial tumor?

I think the opinion of the Unani practitioner was important. Illich would sometimes lose his balance and fall over, perhaps because of the tumor's growth into his inner ear. This occurred, for example, in the 1980s when he was teaching at Penn State University. Beginning a lecture, and referring to the falling, he once told the students that if he were to do something about the tumor he would throw himself out of balance!

Illich was a Christian, a man deeply imbued with the traditions of the Church. Among these, the most important is that derived from Scripture. Living with him, I came to sense the nature and depth of his insertion in these traditions. For example, from the way he prayed the psalms in the Divine Office with me each day, I picked up a glimpse of his understanding of these words and his faith in the reality behind them. From his casual but repeated remarks, I could infer something of the essence of this faith, namely, its childlike character. Although he never explicitly spoke of this, I have good evidence that he embraced the words of St. Paul's second letter to the Corinthians: "We always carry around in our body the death of Jesus, so that the life of Jesus may also be revealed in our body" (2 Cor 4:10).

Ultimately, Illich lived as a man of deep faith, a faith focused principally on his belief in the Incarnation. Partly because of this centrality, he was terribly upset one day in the 1980s. We were in Chicago at the invitation of David Ramage, that Illich might initiate some lecture/discussions with clergymen who came to the Presbyterian Theological School, an institution directed by Ramage, and located on the campus at the University of Chicago. We did not pay attention to the denominations to which the audience belonged, but I guess it was made up mostly of Presbyterian and Lutheran pastors. After one session, Illich stopped me, roughly gripped my arm, and exclaimed, "Do you realize that these men don't believe in the divinity of Christ?" He was visibly shocked, profoundly upset.

Because of his belief, he was passionately interested in all aspects of technological artifacts. He thought these devices, taken together, are not only desensitizing people, not only cutting people off from elementary sense experiences, not only deforming the sensible world beyond recognition, but they are also, definitively, disembodying the human condition. They affect all of us, turning us into abstract ciphers, and this distortion has invaded the consciousness of many. He argued that this removal of the self from one's body achieving, in effect, disembodiment, makes it extremely difficult to conceive of the reality of the Incarnation and, thus, perhaps impossible to believe in the body of Christ.

He first developed a similar argument in his book on water, *H₂O and the Waters of Forgetfulness*.[16] Basing his thinking on a phenomenological analysis, he questioned whether "purified" water from the tap is any longer water. If it is not, one faces a theological difficulty with the matter of baptism, interpreting the sacrament in terms of the hylomorphic Aristotelian thesis about matter and form. In his apophatic mode of procedure, Illich suggested the existence of a serious theological doubt. Phenomenologically, he was quite explicit about the dire effect of treated water on the imagination. Both myth and history point to the importance of water on the life of the imagination and, therefore, on the possibility of a human manner of living. But what if H_2O, the stuff that passes for water today, is not real water? Further, what if the absence of true water indicates a transcendent vacuum? Similarly, what if I need a palpable, deeply sensible experience of my own body to believe in it? Illich strongly felt that one needs the experience of the senses, inner and outer, in order to believe in one's own body.[17] He further suspected that one could not believe in the total reality of the Word's Incarnation without this vital experience of one's body. The fear that many today do not know this experience progressively tormented Illich more and more in the latter part of his life.

The pain he suffered from his lump made him acutely aware of his body . . . he could never forget it. Because of the heightened experience of his own body, he may have sensed an essential truth, a truth needed by every believer: I, too, need to feel my body in order to believe in Christ's body. Every artifact that removes me from an available sensation of direct touch, seeing, hearing, tasting, and smelling must be regarded with suspicion; it might be dangerous in a hidden way difficult to discern. As a Christian, needing the physical experience of my body, I can never know when I cross the threshold dividing my self from my body, leaving me a helpless time-bound hypothesis. According to one tradition, my self, made up of body, soul, and spirit, is a composite, not a unified whole. Only God is simple, not made up of parts; everything in

---

[16] Illich, *H₂O and the Waters of Forgetfulness.*

[17] The principal inner sense is the imagination. According to some, the common sense is also included. Illich lectured on the inner senses at Penn State University in the 1980s.

creation is a composite. If through technological artifacts I have become disembodied, that is, effectively losing my body, I am left as an abstraction but am still absolutely mortal. The immortality of a Christian rests on belief in the resurrection—of the *body*. Without sensing the reality of one's body, the believer exists only as a rational subject doomed to despair.

For many years, I have read and reread the writings of Simone Weil. Although I don't understand very well, or at all, what she writes, I cannot leave her books untouched on my shelf. Now and then a flashing penetration into the Truth strikes my dulled sensibility. Then, after the death of Illich, I read her with new eyes. I saw what I had not previously seen. Here I'll mention only one truth of that seeing, the truth of suffering. Reading Simone Weil in the days since Illich's death on December 2, 2002, I may have come close to realizing what Illich suffered.

Her essay, "The Love of God and Affliction," filling about twenty pages, goes further into the question of suffering as experienced by a believer than anything else I have read. Reflecting on her words, relative to what I saw and felt in Illich, I have reached a more acute awareness of what she wrote and what Illich suffered.

> The great enigma of human life is not suffering but affliction. It is not surprising that the innocent are killed, tortured, driven from their country, made destitute, or reduced to slavery, imprisoned in camps or cells, since there are criminals to perform such actions. It is not surprising either that disease is the cause of long sufferings, which paralyze life and make it into an image of death, since nature is at the mercy of the blind play of mechanical necessities. But it is surprising that God should have given affliction the power to seize the very souls of the innocent and to take possession of them as their sovereign lord. At the very best, he who is branded by affliction will keep only half his soul.[18]

Until now, I found these words incomprehensible. That was principally because I myself experienced nothing of affliction. And knew no one who had. Thinking about Illich's life in the light of what I've glimpsed in Simone Weil, I have come to feel a greater affinity with both these persons.

In his or her person every Christian must somehow approach the Cross. Therefore, I did not place any special importance on the fact

---

[18] Weil, *Waiting for God,* 119–20.

that Illich sometimes referred to the essential character of the Cross in every believer's life; that was only to be expected. Now, however, I see an altogether new aspect of this truth in Simone Weil and Illich, and for myself, too. Several of her remarks reach directly into the mystery of the Cross, for example:

> In order that the imitation of God should not be a mere matter of words, it is necessary that there should be a just man to imitate, but in order that we should be carried beyond the will, it is necessary that we should not be able to choose to imitate him. One cannot choose the cross.
>
> One might choose no matter what degree of asceticism or heroism, but not the cross, that is to say penal suffering.
>
> It is the most purely bitter suffering, penal suffering. This is the guarantee of its authenticity.
>
> Christ healing the sick, raising the dead, etc., that is the humble, human, almost low part of his mission. The supernatural part is the sweat of blood, the unsatisfied longing for human consolation, the supplication that he might be spared, the sense of being abandoned by God.[19]

She takes the initial words of the psalm spoken by the Lord on the Cross: "My God, my God, why have you forsaken me?" (Matt 27:46), and writes, "There we have the real proof that Christianity is something divine."[20]

For Illich, the pain from the tumor led to his experience of affliction. As with the humiliating encounter with the schoolmaster in Vienna, Illich did not turn the hurt back on himself. Rather, he found its meaning outside himself, in this case, in the Cross. Hence, his words about the centrality of the Cross in the Incarnation were not mere words, but came out of his terrible and essentially lonely suffering. Further, this connection between him and the Lord gave him the grace, the strength, to endure the pain.

Because of his faith in the words of St. Paul, Illich could not but feel it a great privilege to carry around in his body the death of Jesus. It is in this sense that he accepted the swelling, the pain. If he refused to believe in the Cross, all the hours, days, weeks, months, years of suffering would be meaningless, lost. This is true because otherwise he would

---

[19] Weil, *Gravity and Grace,* 139–40.
[20] Ibid., 119.

be a walking contradiction: a believer who did not believe! As many Christians have pointed out: It *costs* to believe. Years ago Illich noted:

> Traditional cultures made everyone responsible for his own performance under the impact of bodily harm or grief. Pain was recognized as an inevitable part of the subjective reality of one's own body in which everyone constantly finds himself, and which is constantly being shaped by his conscious reactions to it. People knew that they had to heal on their own, to deal on their own with their migraine, their lameness, or their grief.[21]

I was with him in all the years of the tumor's growth. Although he would sometimes groan aloud and express a mild complaint, I never noticed any rebellion and, of course, never any rage. Reflecting on Simone Weil's remarks about the struggle of Christ in the Garden, I now feel that Illich's agonized questioning occurred when he was alone and I asleep . . . as with the Lord and his friends.

He had also read, and found enlightening, the words St. Paul wrote in his letter to the Colossians:

> At this moment I find my joy in the suffering I endure for you, and I complete in my flesh what is lacking in the afflictions of Christ for his body, the church (Col 1:24).[22]

Illich saw these words as an unveiling, for they revealed to him something of the mystery of *his* suffering. He knew, as every Christian knows, that it is necessary to participate in the "afflictions of Christ," that this is an integral part of faith in the Lord. The believer might cry out, as Christ did in the Garden of Gethsemane, "'My soul is overwhelmed with sorrow to the point of death'" (Matt 26:38). But the person of faith always ends his lament with the prayer: "'My Father, if it is not possible for this cup to be taken away unless I drink it, may your will be done'" (Matt 26:42).

St. Paul could say that he experienced joy in the sufferings he endured because he underwent them *for* someone. Illich, knowing this text, believed that he also was called to bear with the pain . . . *for* someone. That is what it means to be a member of Christ's body, the Church, to believe in the Communion of Saints, to embrace the truth of the vine and branches parable (John 15:1–17). Illich further believed he could

---

[21] Illich, *Medical Nemesis*, 134.

[22] My translation from the French of the original Jerusalem Bible (1961).

identify some of the persons for whom he suffered. In this he might have been mistaken; as a fallible creature, he could not look into the "heart" of God to discern there what is called the economy of salvation. But the possibility that he did know contributed to his strength and courage in the face of great pain. I wrote McNamee and Ferry what I had learned, and my reflections on Illich's report.

An analogical reading of Graham Green's remarkable book, *The Heart of the Matter*, opens up further unsuspected aspects of Illich's life, suffering, and death.[23] Greene's portrayal of Scobie's love enlarges a conventional notion of what it is to love another, to love the unattractive, to love in a way that appears to deny the teaching of the Church. Out of his singular love for two women, Scobie mysteriously enters the realm of suicide. As this happens, Greene's genius forces the reader to embrace the teaching of Jesus: Do not judge.

Scobie offers his life out of love for others in a way that defies rational explanations. Given the complexity of his circumstances, dreams, interior musings, and motivations, he appears to have been a "pilgrim of the absolute." He definitely demonstrates that love is not a univocal concept, that love encompasses more than a gross reading of the medieval abstraction of universals. Greene portrays various theological realities in a strikingly singular way, for example, prayer, the sacraments, the crucifix, and other aspects of the Catholic faith.

In Scobie, three experiences increased together: knowledge, love, and pain. Greene finely delineates the persons directly affected by Scobie, but does not fall into a false wisdom that would attempt to say what was prior and what posterior in Scobie's awareness and sentiments. With our inadequate way of speaking, we can say that knowledge, love, and mercy are one in God.[24] In creatures, they can go together, but no one can discern the intensities, nor the direction of the respective relationships. Further, in Scobie I see there are kinds of love, knowledge and pain beyond anything I had imagined.

Reading this book, I was continually thrown back into the life of Illich. Imagining those years, I was reminded of some offhand remarks he made. Several times he spoke about St. Alexis. According to the story, Alexis came from a patrician Roman family and lived in the fifth cen-

---

[23] Greene, *The Heart of the Matter*.

[24] In this context, Greene also includes the pain of God. Because of his imaginative power as a writer, he can speak of seeming impossibilities in ways that make one stop and reflect.

tury. After having been in the Holy Land for over a decade, he returned to Rome and lived as an unknown beggar under the outside stairs of his parents' house.[25] Illich praised the invisibility and holiness of his secret life, and seemed to suggest that he, too, lived a hidden life. I now believe these obscure hints revealed an infinite truth.

One can say that the suffering of Illich was necessary for the persons affected. If persons of faith believe that Christ's sufferings are in some way incomplete, then each of us is called, each of us literally has a vocation, to share in the suffering of Christ. Each of us must do "our part" in making up "what is lacking in the afflictions of Christ." If we refuse to do this, we fail as persons of faith, as persons who believe in the Church; we reject the Lord.

Can I say something about the persons for whom Illich suffered? Yes, but what I say has more to do with speculation than with fact. It would seem that if Illich was afflicted, and if he assented to this as a participation in the suffering of Christ, and if the overall situation was, as I believe, a genuine expression of Providence, then the persons for whom he suffered could not live without what he endured, they could not live the life that genuinely counts, a life of grace.

What I say about Providence appears to be true, true as a firm belief, because Illich embraced his trials in good faith, he consented to his situation as being within the loving care of a providential God, he simply accepted reality, what is. He did not ask, "Why me, Oh Lord?"

I can say that because, according to the faith, all this has happened, namely: The Word of God, the Second Person of the Blessed Trinity, became man, that is, took on human flesh, and in his flesh suffered, forming a bond of infinite strength with all those who can be united to him by grace. This occurs within a Providence whose nature is the economy of salvation, meaning that individuals can accept the vocation to participate in the suffering of Jesus Christ for another. In this sense, I can say that such participation is necessary for the other's salvation. But this does not mean that the other is absolutely predestined. That person's eternal happiness depends on his or her assent to grace, on whether they accept the Lord's invitation. I cannot know who this person is, nor whether that person welcomes God's grace. I believe the person must really act, must do something vital, something free. A person can also fail,

---

[25] An account with annotated bibliography can be found in: Farmer, *Butler's Lives of the Saints*, vol. 3, 123–4.

can sin against the Holy Spirit. One is not automatically assured a ticket to eternal bliss because Illich suffered for him or her.

Several times, as the progress of the growth advanced, Illich again talked of keeping himself "in balance." From these remarks I saw that the notion of balance was key, crucial. It was his entrance to reality, a means to see and grasp "what is." In a gross sense, his action enabled him to achieve a certain equilibrium in his own life, the polar opposite of what people mean when they say that someone is unbalanced or crazy. For Illich to be balanced in his life meant to be harmonized with the universe, his micro-cosmos was symmetrical with the macro-cosmos. But, for a believer, all mention of a cosmos begins with the realm of grace; any other realm is posterior or secondary.

To strive against this vocation would be to throw himself out of balance, to become sick, for sickness is the absence of a due or fitting balance, as Unani theory also holds. The truth is similar to what St. Augustine taught about the nature of evil: evil is the absence of a due good; it is not a positive reality. If Illich were to seek the intervention of conventional medicine, he would have upset the infinitesimal but, for him, all-important portion of the universe he inhabited. In the "objective" scheme of phenomena, his place was immeasurably small, but in his perspective, from where he stood, illimitably large. The reality with which he was in touch, through his pain, extended infinitely beyond his existence; it reached into the divine life, and through that into the lives of those for whom he suffered.

A question immediately arises: What if Illich's refusal to go the route of conventional allopathic medical practice was the "NO" required of him at this moment in history? What if the grace to say "NO" was given to Illich as his calling, or vocation? What if his friends needed Illich to say, "NO!"? What if the world needed Illich to say, "NO!"? What if someone, perhaps a few, saying "NO" is somehow necessary to destroy the seemingly invincible grip of the medical paradigm, of the modern illusion of "health"? Such a necessity directly touched a person invited to pronounce publicly his "NO." The necessity was, paradoxically, *offered* to him. He could have refused; others, perhaps, do. The necessity weighing on Illich was not physical. No question of cause and effect was involved. The necessity he faced was, rather, moral; it had to do with how he stood before God.

Illich's acceptance reached beyond his neighbors, beyond the society, beyond the universe and the cosmos. The bump on the side of his face allowed him to live two lives simultaneously: the outward living that rejected the ministrations of mainstream medicine, and the inward living that reached into eternity. The example of St. Alexis is a true analogical insight into the reality of Illich's life.

As he emphasized more than twenty years ago in *Medical Nemesis*, many people deeply inserted in the industrial world, the so-called advanced sectors of our societies, unthinkingly live perverse lives in their pain, disabilities, and death. These three constants of the human condition are directly confronted by the institutionalized structure of the medical establishment. The perversity results from the fact that the medical system treats these constants exclusively in terms of the techno-science project. Their transcendental character must be ignored; science demands that.

Many times in both speech and writing, and always in his personal life, Illich simply accepted an important given: the human condition. But one can act to affect what one is born with, a person can practice various possible arts, acquiring a certain *habitus* or habitual mode of acting. For example, one learns to walk well or eat pleasantly with a fork. According to St. Thomas, an art begins with "nothing other than a correct notion of some acts to be performed."[26] The work carrying out these acts is a good, therefore, participation in a transcendental.

One can make a dichotomous division of human arts between those of enjoyment, responding to the sunny side of the human condition, and the arts of suffering, responding to the shady side. Further, Illich believed the human condition has always been "suffered."[27] From his study of history he concluded that the difference between the great traditions can be seen through their respective sets of ideas and practices that deal with the dark side of the human condition. This fact means that to live well each person must first work out an art of suffering. Illich often spoke of this requirement and one could go through his writing documenting and commenting on the different ways he refers to that obligation. Others have also written of this. For example, Graham Greene: "To be a human being one had to drink the cup."[28] Greene refers to the metaphor the Evangelists use to catch the feelings of Jesus in

---

[26] " . . . ars nihil aliud est quam ratio recta aliquorum operum faciendorum." Aquinas, *Summa theologiae*, I II, q. 57, a. 3.

[27] Illich, "Pathogenesis, Immunity and the Quality of Public Health," unpublished talk.

[28] Greene, *Heart of the Matter*, 129.

the Garden of Gethsemane shortly before his final arrest. He said, "'My Father, if it is possible, may this cup be taken from me. Yet not as I will, but as you will'" (Matt 26:39).

Reflecting on these words, and on the more complete accounts of what Jesus felt as recorded in the other synoptic Gospels, the believer comes to *the* exemplary instance of an art of suffering. In the feelings and actions of Jesus Christ, a new tradition was begun. For the past two thousand years, Christians in pain have looked to that night in the garden. There one hopes to find, not only an example to follow, but also the divine strength to bear with one's flesh and affliction. As Illich strongly implied, to ignore this scene and seek instead a pursuit of health is to create "the principal impediment to suffering experienced as a dignified, meaningful, patient, loving, beautiful, resigned and even joyful embodiment."[29] Since Illich was a believer, a Christian, and a Catholic, he went before all to *this* tradition to find his way. He knew other traditions, but he chose his own, the one in which he was born and died.

As many who knew him well could testify, Illich was not a masochist. But he knew, perhaps better than many of his generation, the power of the medical system. For him, medicine was an appropriate "paradigm for any mega-technique that promises to transform the *conditio humana*," that is, to change human nature, to make creatures into something other than what has been recognized as a man or a woman.[30] Therefore, the medical system, with its promise of progress, leads to a rejection of the human condition and an aversion for the art of suffering. For Illich, realism is to subordinate all technological intrusions to the arts of suffering and dying.[31]

As a friend wrote me, Illich's "NO" to diagnosis went much further than many imagine. Speaking of the growth on the side of Illich's face, he wrote:

> That lump, in a way, was a gift, an act of grace, albeit a painful one. It let Ivan "say" what he had been saying in his books in a way that went beyond words. . . . Ivan's "NO!" was more than just a condemnation of the medical system. I used to think, when contemplating Ivan's decision about his tumor, "Well, how can the author of *Medical Nemesis* do otherwise?" . . . I

---

[29] Illich, "Pathogenesis . . ."
[30] Ibid.
[31] Illich, "Do Not Let Us Succumb to Diagnosis," unpublished talk.

now see that Ivan's "NO!" went beyond medicine. It was a NO! to the entire technological project, the whole realm of *la technique*. I see that Ivan's "NO!" was an embodiment of everything he tried to say in *all* his books, not just *Medical Nemesis*. And, ultimately, like all his books, his decision is a reflection of his faith, as you say so convincingly in your essay.[32] His "NO!" was the ultimate apophatic act. So not only does the modern world prevent or discourage what you call "genuine human acts," but it also sabotages, thwarts, usurps the possibility for one to be a good Christian—not entirely, perhaps, but to a very large extent. Is this not the nature of evil, as you and Ivan see it, in the modern world, that this network of systems and institutions eclipses the good? It is as if these systems and institutions are saying: "You don't have to be a good Christian anymore. We have taken over the job. You are relieved of the duty." As I read Ivan, and things you have written, this voice is the voice of evil in the world today.[33]

Illich commented on the fact of powerlessness today, on the fact that most of us are utterly powerless, that actions or movements directed toward empowerment are often illusory. Illich's cup was a distinct powerlessness, a very specific passion and cross. He wished above all to give himself to others, to bless them with his example of saying "NO!" But those "gifted" could not always straightforwardly face him, could not live with this present, could not accept the offering. Perhaps one can speak of a final sadness, a personal tragedy.[34]

A truth of our world was prophetically and imaginatively seen in the nineteenth century by Fyodor Dostoievsky with his story of The Grand Inquisitor.[35] Many eagerly run to hand over their free will (*liberum arbitrium*, in the expression of St. Thomas) to the promises of high-tech wonders.

In his last years, Illich's task was not to write another book on the medical system. After all, his published works, especially *Medical Nemesis*, are clear and conclusive for those still able to see and reflect on their personal experiences. Illich's specific burden was to live his life, to suffer. Albert Camus, speaking in 1948, said:

---

[32] Hoinacki, "Why *Philia*?" unpublished essay.

[33] Aaron Falbel, in a letter to Lee Hoinacki (July 2003).

[34] Silja Samerski and Matthias Rieger in a letter to Lee Hoinacki (February 2004).

[35] The poem is found in his novel, *The Brothers Karamasov*.

> What the world expects of Christians is that Christians should
> speak out, loud and clear, and that they should voice their con-
> demnation in such a way that never a doubt, never the slightest
> doubt, could rise in the heart of the simplest man. That they
> should get away from abstraction and confront the blood-
> stained face history has taken on today. The grouping we need
> is a grouping of men resolved to speak out clearly and to pay up
> personally.[36]

No speech or writing, no action could be more evident, more dramatic,
than Illich's appearance. His judgment on the medical system was voiced
anew whenever anyone looked at his face. He had studied the history of
medicine, he was familiar with the record; he concluded that his final
word would be his personal witness.

Today conventional allopathic medicine is in retreat. But it remains
one of the mainstays of the techno-science project. That project may
ultimately fail, but no one is going to destroy it. Illich's final teaching is
that the project is dissolved only in the mind and heart of individuals.
By his suffering, his life, Illich "bought," in the realm of grace, our freedom. Because he lived the way he did, each of us is free to imitate him
in denying our allegiance to the system. My act of faith can bring about
the collapse of medical hubris.

---

[36] Camus, *Resistance, Rebellion, and Death*, 25.

7

The Moral Beauty of No

THE STAMP said Eire. In a moment while opening the envelope my imagination ran through several Irish friends. Which one was sending me news? Reading the letter, my emotions became troubled; I was surprised by their vehemence; I thought my beliefs were stronger, more able to withstand shocks.

Dara had noticed a small bump on his back. Somewhere, every day, a lump on someone's body is found, and all know what to do, immediately . . . that is, everyone living in those areas of the world strongly influenced by one of the principal modern projects: Use science and technology to bring everything under control. Without any unnecessary delay, you go see the appropriate professional, a competent oncologist.

Dara, too, decided to act. He called together his friends, members of a small community, and they discussed the bump: What should Dara do about it? After a long, searching conversation, Dara decided to notify the local priest and ask to be anointed. There is a specific ritual for the anointing, and the affected person sometimes calls the family and friends to participate in the ceremony. With their hearts all are attentive, with their voices they respond to the prayers at specified times. The priest came, and anointed Dara with the oil, the *oleum infirmorum*, an oil specially blessed by the bishop each year on Holy Thursday, just before Easter. Dara and his friends believed that the effectiveness of the touching is dependent on the faith of the participants:

> I tell you the truth, if you have faith as small as a mustard seed, you can say to this mountain, "Move from here to there" and it will move. Nothing will be impossible for you (Matt 17:20–21).

An ancient rite was again repeated, an action which, in the minds and hearts of the people gathered together, contravened the usual, accepted, normal, reasonable practice of a modern person. Dara and his friends were believers, perhaps a rarity today. Curiously, after some weeks, the bump disappeared.

At about the same time another friend discovered a lump near his neck while shaving. He was on vacation in a foreign country, and his scheduled return flight left in a few days. So he decided to wait until then before acting. As soon as he arrived home, he called a colleague and friend who knew the medical personnel of the city. Indeed, beginning a couple of years earlier, she had been in direct contract with them, since she had had a mastectomy, after having been diagnosed as suffering from breast cancer. Apparently, she had beaten the cancer.

After talking with her, Christian contacted a well-known and respected oncologist. The doctor wanted to run tests immediately; time was all-important, he explained. Christian decided to follow the recommendation. After examining the test findings, the oncologist was quite frank with Christian: he had cancer. The doctor gave his diagnosis, strongly urging surgery—to be done two days later. It should be a relatively simple procedure, he claimed, and that would probably take care of the matter. Before consenting to the physician's imperative prescription, Christian spoke with a close friend, Ivan Illich.

Illich expressed strong reservations, a frankly skeptical attitude toward the contemplated procedure; he was not ready to accept the medical opinion so easily. In fact, he discussed the possibility of rejecting the diagnosis altogether, and not just this test result and the concomitant professional judgment, but the very idea of a diagnosis. He talked about two radically different modes of life, one that emphasized the autonomy of the person, and the other, the heteronomy demanded by advanced medical technology. Perhaps Christian was faced with the possibility, and necessity, of choosing one or the other. Perhaps these opposed paths, patently extreme and clear-cut, were nevertheless the most truthful statement of his dilemma. Perhaps he was given a rare grace, the opportunity to glimpse the final outline of his life, together with the power to shape his personal story into a purposeful order through one decisive action. Illich argued in terms of an ultimate, the kind of finality that one rarely finds in this world. Christian could definitively direct his life from that day until his death.

At that moment, Christian was blessed with genuine freedom: Real choices lay before him, one presented by the concerned and competent technical expert, the other suggested by his critical friend. He was still his own person, he could decide the direction, the very character of his life. After making the irrevocable step into the medical system, he would not be able to go back. Setting out on the alternative course, he would have to learn to live with his lump, as he now lived with ten fingers, or near-sightedness. As every person must—for him, perhaps earlier than for some others—he would have to learn the art of suffering. Taking the conventional course, he had only to submit himself to the best available medical knowledge and practice, and . . . what? hope? relax? expect a cure?

Christian faced, in a situation of heightened intensity and compressed time, what everyone faces except that, for most, the reality of the options is never so dramatically seen. They are often much more commonplace, or are seemingly lost in a pattern of living hardened by earlier choices made over many years. One does not become addicted to eating or drinking too much by today's or yesterday's indulgences. To form a character takes time and an infinite number of actions. Further, there are endless distractions today, a profusion of beguiling chimeras, myriad insane delusions. Christian dimly recognized that, whatever his judgment, he would have little control over tomorrow. Perhaps he did not see that, as never before, he was being shown that one cannot live a completely rational life; such is not possible in this world. One must choose a faith: Christian could decide to rest in an ancient tradition surrounded by the love and support of friends, or to submit himself to the promises and marvels of modern medicine.

Christian, a professional himself, a university professor, believed in the competence of physicians. Did not their expertise rest on the claims of science? Did not the history of medicine show a marked and evident progress? Does not the modern faith vitiate all superstition? In one sense, he felt he had no choice. He had lived an orderly life. The decisions making that life evidenced a real consistency; they formed his character and colored the situation he faced. He decided to undergo what was promised to be a simple operation.

The hospital was not far away and I went to visit him the day after the surgery. But I couldn't find his room; they had no record of him in the building where he was supposed to be. Finally, I located the central administrative office in another building of the sprawling complex and learned that he was in the urology section. I don't know much about physiology and anatomy, but I was certain a lump on one's neck had nothing to do with urology. He was there, however, and explained that the operation was not exactly as the physician had predicted, nor quite so simple. It turned out that he needed a second operation, immediately; they had to remove one of his testicles. He was told that after recovering from the two surgical interventions, he would have to undergo a series of chemo-therapy treatments.

I could sense that he was somewhat dismayed by what had happened and by what was yet to come. Fear irregularly flickered in his eyes and face, independently of the more confident meaning of his words. I had the impression that he was on the verge of teetering into a simultaneous schizophrenia, one part of him clinging to belief in the power of high-tech medicine, another part fearing a dark, unknown terror ahead.

Shortly after the chemo-therapy started, his thick black hair began to fall out. He shaved his head, wore a hat when he went out, and attempted to resume his accustomed life. I saw that with only a few steps he was firmly stuck in a medical miasma that would progressively tighten its grip on him. I feared he was caught in a malevolent quicksand. It would become ever more impossible to get out.

He, however, struggled to maintain his usual good cheer. He told me how impressed he was with the chief doctor—quite an intelligent and articulate fellow. He spoke to Christian as to an equal; no condescension at all. He explained the details of everything, holding back nothing. Christian felt he had a comprehensive view of the cancer and the complexities of the obligatory treatment. Over and over again, he emphasized the need for the procedures he had agreed to; he *understood* their urgency.

Over the weeks, in the different hospitals or at home, I sat many hours with him. Each time we met, I asked about his health. I tried first to see where he was, that I might know how to speak, what to say. I wanted to be guided by who he began to be, not by my own ideological position. I did not want to offer some jarring opinion to a man weakened by both illness and treatment. Having seen that he was securely in the chambers of modern alchemy, I judged it best to confine myself mostly to listening. It was far too late to discuss candidly what I saw happening.

Two men, two stories. One had chosen to live outside, the other inside, the medical system. But there is much more. Some years earlier Dara had decided to live outside the employment system, the insurance system, and the entertainment system. Except for a tenuous connection to the monetary system, mostly through writing and picking up odd jobs now and then, he would seem to have almost no contact at all with the normal social systems. He also chose to live in an out-of-the-way place, one of the Aran Islands in the Atlantic, off the coast of Galway. He thinks that the place itself is important for him and for contemporary society, important for someone seeking to learn how to live in time. He once told me that, per square yard, there are more historically significant ruins on Aran than any other place in Ireland. Vigorous and exciting forms of monastic community life, eventually affecting much of Europe, once flourished on the three tiny islands, the largest of which measures about eleven by six miles. Dara believes that people today can find insight and strength, direction and goals, through living in the place where these ancient and mysterious flowerings once broke through the crusts of self-interest and vanity. So, together with a few others, he has chosen to leave his comfortable urban home, build a simple house for protection against the harsh winter winds and rain, and seek a precarious and near-subsistence living in that place.

Each of the three islands is an irregular rock, roughly protruding above the surface of the ocean. Over the centuries, the people have leveled the porous rock in many places, creating small, roughly flat surfaces fenced in by stone walls. They continue to bring up seaweed and sand from the ocean, compost them, and create a soil. This growing medium is continually replenished with new compost. It is not deep, and one sees almost no trees, only the bright green grass, the stone fences, an occasional stone cottage, and oddly-shaped, small rocky mountains. Here and there, in the 14,000 patches of grass—average size, just under one-half acre—cattle, sheep, goats, a donkey or horse. The local people—now just under a thousand native-born—say that if one extended the stone fences in a straight line across the Atlantic they would reach Boston. If you insist on a wooden literalness, however, the fence would only reach about (!) a thousand miles into the ocean.

Life on the islands today is quite different from that evoked in John Millington Synge's beautifully sensitive diary that he kept while living here at the turn of the nineteenth century; and from that described in Liam O'Flaherty's powerful stories begun a generation later; and from that presented in Robert Flaherty's stark, classic documentary, *Man of Aran* (1934).[1] But one can still climb the mountain Dún Aengus on Inishmore, and find, at the top, a perfectly flat rock surface, high

[1] Synge, *The Aran Islands*; O'Flaherty, *Short Stories*; Griffith, *The World of Robert Flaherty,* 83–106.

above the Atlantic, with the ocean crashing and swirling hundreds of feet below under the sheer cliff. From archeological evidence, we know that people gathered up here thousands of years ago, but no one knows with certitude why. Some believe this was a fortress; others, a place of worship. To me, the enigma is not so puzzling. One has only to stand there in the resounding silences of the place, with the awful power of the ocean pounding far below, with the ominous ever-metamorphosing black clouds in all shades of gray scudding overhead—I have only been there in winter—with the wind whipping the rain into one's face, and then be startled by a warm and bright sun awakening one to a new place, surely not in heaven, but only scantily still on earth, to know why people would come here. I was compelled to keep silent, so as not to disturb the sacred space, to await the epiphany that breaks through in such pure wildness.

No matter how many people ascend the mountain to stand there alone absorbed by the elements, the place will always remain a wilderness—if no tourist development destroys it. Except for a ring of stones piled all around the edge at the summit, there is no evidence of a human violation of the rock platform. In this setting Dara finds the contemporaneity of his ancestors, here all notion of linear time collapses. Standing under the swiftly-moving sky, I felt I could understand something of the statement of an islander at the time Synge was here: "We send for the priest before the doctor if a man has a pain in his heart."

Christian inhabits a very different world. Time still runs in a line for him, yesterday was yesterday; the past is past. Knowing classical languages well, he finds a translation of *Winnie the Pooh* into Latin to be amusing, fun to read, a pleasant diversion in today's high culture. Christian holds a prestigious high profile job that entails regular international travel and contacts. He moves easily in this world, the world of sophisticated connections and glamorous cocktail parties. He is a leading member in several of the organizations and institutions to which he belongs, and actively participates in various civic programs. He lives very much inside the systems rejected by Dara. All these allegiances and activities strongly incline him to accept unquestioningly the various institutional forms that shape and support his life. When he told me of the initial diagnosis, the day after he received it, I immediately thought of the good that could come of it: The shock appeared powerful enough to be unsettling, perhaps salutary. Finally, he would now be inclined to question many of the assumptions that imprisoned him. But I was wrong. The modern world had too great a hold on him. His substance had become weak-souled, his rootedness shallow. He saw no brightly-lit space in the diagnosis, only a frightening dilemma.

Whenever he returned to the hospital for more chemo-therapy or radiation—the cancer had metastasized to other organs—I visited him. He always had the most detailed clinical report to give me. To my untutored ear, he sounded like a scholarly academic delivering an impressive lecture. What more was there to know? What other course of action could one reasonably follow? The cancer was an especially aggressive kind. One had to respond with equally aggressive counterattacks, using the great array of high-tech scientific medicine available today. But underneath all the learned therapeutic eloquence and ingenious antiseptic jargon, I discerned only the crude and already timeworn formula: Cut it out, burn it out, poison it.

The respective development of the two stories—whether Christian ever recovers, whether Dara discovers another lump—is not so important. Whatever happens, each man will die. There is a long tradition in the West, to which many witnesses have strongly and imaginatively contributed, which holds that the crucial question is not when I die but how. One of the early persons I meet in this history is found in a tragic drama of fifth-century Greece, the young Antigone.[2] The king, Creon, had forbidden the burial of her brother, with death prescribed for disobedience. In the king's judgment, Polyneices had forfeited any claim to an honorable burial because of his treasonous actions. Antigone believed that the virtue of piety required that she disobey, although the punishment for her act would be instant death. A young woman deeply in love, betrothed to the king's son, who also loved her passionately, she nevertheless acted. Her stated reason: There is nothing so awful as an ignoble death. That is, if she failed to act, her own death, whenever it might come, could never be a noble death, a good death.

The story Sophocles bequeaths us is instructive today, in spite of the fact that Antigone, as so many other steadfast figures in this tradition, seems to belong to a world very different from ours. She faced an apparently clear-cut choice: to follow her inner voice, or to obey the king. The good act was to bury her brother. She would then die well because she had lived well. It might seem to some today that the principal virtue she exercised was courage: she was not afraid to risk death. But

[2] Sophocles, *The Three Theban Plays*, 159–212.

her courage served her in terms of another virtue, piety. She clearly recognized the debt in justice she owed her family, the nation and the gods, a loyalty that could, on occasion, supersede obedience to the reigning authority. She was a faithful daughter and sister, a patriotic citizen and a pious child of God, that is, a person who acted out of the traditional sense of the virtue of piety.

The people of Thebes were of one mind in their moral judgment: Antigone had acted well, Creon badly. This very unanimity well illustrates the conundrum many face today: Agreement on the moral character of specific acts is rarely found in contemporary society. Further, I do not often hear that the primary consideration in any possible action is to ask oneself the question: What is the good, the virtuous thing to do? I do not often find that someone strongly believes it is necessary to act out of pure principle, no matter what the consequences. Do I think about the possibility that situations similar to Antigone's might arise today, too? Do I seek to reflect on my world in order to recognize such situations? And then pray for the strength to act with courage, as she acted?

There are huge empty spaces in both public and private life where, formerly, perhaps, one found moral intelligence. I once noticed an especially sad example of this while working at the university. There suddenly appeared a campus-wide program, with much publicity, many meetings, discussions, lectures, audio-visual presentations, all kinds of leaflets and pamphlets, special library and book store displays, all referring to an action called "sex." That is, everything was designed to enable the students to protect their bodies from a malady called "disease" when engaged in genital contact with other persons. There was no mention of the larger drama in which such contact might occur, no suggestion that, for persons who professed to be literate, there are classic and powerful portrayals of the joy and pain to be found in the passionate love of one for another, such as the exciting and richly-textured story of Sigrid Undset's *Kristin Lavransdatter*,[3] or that the philosophy and religious thought of the West contain clear but subtle and nuanced comment to help one make sense of such tragedies as those that consumed Romeo and Juliet, Othello and Desdemona. In short, I was appalled by the shallowness and ignorance of the proselytizing presentations, the falsity of the propaganda, the very idea of a campaign.

---

[3] Undset, *Kristin Lavransdatter*.

I was angered by the lies preached in this blitz of pop scientific pap. The students, considered by many of their elders to be altogether too hip, too sophisticated, appeared to me as innocent lambs being led to one of our peculiarly modern forms of slaughter: the stupid excision of traditional wisdom. They were being prepared for the narrow and parochial tunnel-vision of Christian's physicians, prepped for the latest quack's prescription.

Sitting quietly at my desk, reflecting on that cynically thin campaign, I came to think that my shock and disappointment resulted from the fact that I had not yet understood the university, as a modern institution. It now appears to me that the design and thrust of modern institutions is such as to prevent, insofar as such is possible, the practice of what has been known traditionally as to seek the good. The idea of protecting one's body from the other, in those actions that in former times were associated with love, is to deny the very possibility of virtue, of acting well, honestly, generously. It is to condemn one to selfishness and meanness. I suspect that the character of the campus program was not accidental or fortuitous; it was necessary; it came out of the institution as water comes out of a faucet. The young people were encouraged to act viciously, that is, to live a life of moral turpitude, because this is the very mode of living modern institutions are designed to initiate and foster.

To make a moral judgment is an intellectual act; it is to be able to recognize the difference between worthy and unworthy, beautiful and repulsive. All societies, as in the Greece of Sophocles, have worked out ways for their members to learn the distinction. These societies have also encouraged their members to act out of a moral intelligence, that is, as good men and women. The modern university is the one place in a secular society where a self-selected and trained group of people are paid to study, reflect on, and speak about the moral heritage of historical time. But this very activity, of its nature, is itself a moral enterprise; it can be done well or badly as a *human* act.

Given the conditions of contemporary society—emptiness, boredom, despair, mindless consumption, the various varieties of disorder and violence—the university is a most fitting institution, that is, as an institution, to search for ways to act well. But an ethics course offered by the philosophy department is probably little more than a palliative. Academic philosophy has become increasingly marginal to university life and public discourse. Further, with such a course listed in the catalog, all other faculty can relax and quietly continue to pursue their pet research interests in the belief that something is being done. Students will not set out on a lifetime of denying self and acting for the other by reading a textbook, listening to a lecture or participating in a "Socratic" dialogue.

In the past, there have been discussions, arguments and wars over conflicting perceptions of the good. Today, pandemonium reigns, with occasional outbursts of strident position-taking, usually in a highly non-rational manner. In the meantime, I suspect people have been bludgeoned into insensibility so that a general moral paralysis affects many.

For example, a particularly bizarre illustration nicely reveals the matter. I was offered a brief teaching job in Spain, a week or two of seminars and meetings with students. Coming down from my room on a Sunday morning, I noticed the day's newspaper on the counter, and the words over a photograph caught my attention. Translated: "He can be a father again," with the picture of a young man in a hospital bed, smiling. I picked up the paper and read the extended caption under the photo. This fellow, named and clearly identifiable in the picture, was celebrated as the first man in Asturias to have his vasectomy successfully—it was claimed—reversed!

My gut reaction was, "That's sick!"—a total obliteration of the traditional distinction between public and private. Yes, but what did I see there? I concluded that it was a contemporary expression of the grotesque, not in the rich and subtle meanings evoked by the figures in medieval manuscripts, but more in the sense of my children's remark about something which disgusts them, "Yu . . . uck!"

But this was the leading daily newspaper of the region, regarded as a thoroughly respectable journal. I then remembered that I have increasingly seen such public displays, in both America and Europe. The young man and others involved in this pandering to voyeuristic curiosity have lost all sense of decency; they appear to have no notion of propriety, of modesty, of good and bad taste. Such parading of "private parts"—now an antiquated expression?—has occurred before, of course. And one can find worse historical examples. But what is new today is that few or none were outraged or nauseated that Sunday morning when they picked up their paper. That is, they didn't *feel* the incongruity of such shamelessness—(shame . . . another lost experience?).

The newspaper that published the picture and caption is part of a communications system or, in terms of mainstream news and information, *the* communications system; one could argue that there is only one today, worldwide. The university that promoted safe sex is part of the educational system; there is only one of these today, too. And so it goes with all the various services in modern society. Each one is organized in what is called a system. Indeed, the planning, production and marketing of all goods and services are carried out, insofar as possible, in systemic terms. This has come about, descriptively, through the wedding of rational control and the appropriate machines, principally computers.

More and more, the modern person—like my friend, Christian— lives in the institutions that make our kind of society possible. That is, they have little or no independent life apart from an institutional life. When they seek "to escape," they use the transportation industry to move them to a spot designed by the travel and tourist industries. This means that they live *in* systems. They never escape; they are never free.

The results, in terms of the possibilities for growth into a moral being, into what traditionally has been understood as a person, can be seen in a small electronic innovation. In the last few years, first in Germany, later in America, a change occurred in those buildings to which the public has regular access, whether it be a post office, bank, train station, or supermarket. The door is more and more frequently fitted with an almost invisible and seemingly innocent device: an electronic eye that opens and closes the door for you. I once had a teacher who insisted that the act of opening and closing a door was either virtuous or not. Virtuous, if one was respectful of the door itself, that is, if one did not jerk it open or slam it shut; it had a certain materiality that invited one's sensitive awareness, that allowed a good sense experience. One could appreciate and honor a well-made door, because one thereby honored both oneself and the door maker, by the manner of opening and closing it.

Further, one could look back, going out a door, to see if someone else followed; one could hold the door open for another; thank a stranger for opening the door. That is, something genuinely human and personal can take place at a door, the possible exchange of a smile and friendly word could accompany that simple act. Or, one could treat the door and the other viciously. In either direction, a *human* act. Often, this is no longer possible. And, I would argue, all modern institutions are organized in this way. As systems, they are designed to eliminate human acts, to deny the exercise of virtue, to prevent the growth of moral beauty in the society.

These designs are sometimes rationalized by saying that the goal is to cut out human error and increase convenience. True, people still make mistakes and some are lazy. And if someone in a wheelchair depends on a spontaneous helping gesture to get up the curb or down the stairs, he or she might have to wait, might be disappointed when another thoughtlessly (perhaps viciously) passes by. But ramps, electric eyes and all the variety of built-in safeguards and automatic activators in our institutions, which themselves are all-pervasive, remove countless possibilities for goodness, for the flowering of lovely actions.

The students at the university, the people at the newspaper office, the employees at Christian's hospital, all who are inserted in a modern institution, to that extent cease to be free to act in a human fashion, lose the opportunity to experience goodness. The overall institutional effect is seen in the dramatic difference between two contrasting situations. For some years, I had to travel on trains in Germany. At first I marveled at the system. Everything is designed for convenience and comfort, schedules are clearly printed and posted in many places in the stations, the locations and times of trains plainly written out and announced. And, if all these helps were still not enough, information counters are staffed with knowledgeable bureaucrats. I do not remember ever needing to ask anyone—fellow traveler or official—for directions or information, and I was a foreigner, a stranger.

Then some work with disciples and followers of Gandhi took me to India. While in the country, I had to travel by train several times. There were some signs and indications, but they were few, hard to find and usually subject to numerous changes and exceptions. But every time I needed help, someone was there to take excellent care of me, that is, another friendly passenger. I remember people helping me figure out schedules, guiding me to the right track, assuring me that I did not miss my train—it was only several hours late that day. One person even shared the simple breakfast he had brought with him—how good it tasted after an all-night train trip! Another bought me a cup of coffee when we stopped at a station. Once, a fellow passenger showed me where to find good drinking water on the platform when the train stopped at a station on a hot day.

On a journey from the interior to Bombay, I grew increasingly nervous as I imagined the crowds of people and the probably complicated connection I would have to make to reach some friends in a distant suburb. I asked a passenger in my compartment if he could give me any general directions. "Don't worry, I'll take care of you," he assured me. When the train stopped, he accompanied me through the thick and noisy crowds, led me to the nearby station for local commuter trains, bought me a ticket (!), and put me on the correct train, with careful directions about recognizing the station where I wanted to get off. I shall never forget these experiences, these people.

As I looked out the train window, I would sometimes see scenes that were truly foreign to a person coming from Germany: people living squashed together in sordid, makeshift shelters on the outskirts of every city. Then I realized that my repeated experiences in the trains and stations were equally foreign: the warmth, openness, friendliness and beauty found there are largely unknown in Germany; it has been institutionalized out of the people. They have been impoverished and diminished by efficient laundry systems. One must fight through years of administrative accumulation of impersonal institutional care and the now-ingrained cultural indifference to the other to reach out and give the stranger a hand.

An up-to-date society's institutions, highly developed, are designed and operated in such a way that no one senses another, no one need ever reach out to another, no one has to touch another. From this, I can make an inference: To the extent a society has perfected its institutional systems, to that extent beauty has been erased, wiped out; to that extent, the society is monstrous; to that extent, goodness is not to be found. Those who formerly were people are on the way to becoming something other.

The memory of my friends, Dara and Christian, returned; their differences appeared clearer—and, important. I recalled that Dara, when he spoke about what he was doing, how he was living, the concepts and judgments came out of *him*. He was standing in a unique place, *his* place. On the contrary, Christian's language, when he spoke about his specific situation, came out of the mouths or books of experts. He was precariously perched on an institutional shelf and repeated what he had picked up. I wondered—Am I seeing the birth of a new historical creature? If so, the reality was much more terrifying than the fantasies of science-fiction . . . because real.

The world of modern institutions, of interlocked systems, is every day being extended farther and being perfected more. This means the annihilation of the moral beauty formerly shining out from lives illumined by the lifelong practice of justice, fortitude, temperance and prudence, the four traditional cardinal virtues. I have asked college students to name these virtues, described and honored in our tradition for over two thousand years, and they were unable to do so; they had never heard of them!

It seems necessary, then, to ask the question: Is a virtuous mode of living still possible? I am inclined to argue that the world of systems constitutes a kind of bottomless evil for, finally, it makes society be the kind of place where one is discouraged or prevented from reaching out to another, from loving another, whether that other be one's "intimate" or a complete stranger. In place of numberless opportunities to make goodness be and joy felt, there is only the scheduled delivery of programmed goods and services. Each time I have the opportunity or necessity to submit to these faceless public servants, I feel more confined, more restricted, more a prisoner. So much of that which supposedly establishes a high quality of life actually sickens me to death. A price must be paid for convenience, control, service, security, rights. And modern persons pay it—daily, hourly.

Now it is clear that as institutions, qua institutions, are perfected, no one is actually in control. Originally, much of the thrust and character of modern institutions came from the desire to establish control—over nature and over recalcitrant humans. But as control is perfected, no one stands behind it, no one is there. Modern institutions have eliminated the need for a Wizard of Oz. The contemporary situation, then, is one of overriding helplessness. Those persons today who speak about the powerlessness of certain groups in the society, and the reverse, empowerment, are perhaps missing the deeper engulfing poverty and weakness that affects all. This can be seen if one examines social, economic, political or cultural reform efforts proposed today. These proposals, if enacted, will serve, first of all, to further legitimate and strengthen the existing institutional systems, along with the corresponding Weltanschauung that gives them meaning. The more rational and efficient the reform, the worse the result. That is, what has traditionally been celebrated and suffered as the conflict between good and evil is further eliminated, with the consequent emptying out of human experience.

In the past, one can see that the course of human affairs changed—through ideas, war-making, law-giving, social and religious movements, usually in some combination. But perhaps this time has ended; perhaps another threshold has been passed, dimly noted, especially by those who, on their own claim, are the persons dedicated to the practices of a critical intelligence. For is this not one of the principal claims of the university: to be the place where these persons are enabled to make their unique contribution to the common good?

The modern university finds its origins in the twelfth century. It was at this very time that the practice of monastic reading ceased and a new approach to letters was developed, what is sometimes called "scholastic reading." In this kind of exercise, one could imagine an abstract text, independent of both the page and oneself.[4] Very quickly, powerful thinkers such as Peter Lombard and Thomas Aquinas produced their great works, a very different kind of writing than that seen in the previous one thousand years. But the subsequent history of Scholasticism, as a mode of reading, suggests that something was missing. Great subtlety was matched by great controversy between competing groups of thinkers, while overall a kind of creeping irrelevance became the common attribute of philosophical thought.[5]

In the West, commerce and science, colonial power and technology, came to dominate both the world and peoples' interests. Through these centuries, the idea of a moral intelligence came to be replaced by that of a critical intelligence as the governing concept in the academy. And universities are defended today on the ground that they are the unique host and nurturer of the ideal. This attitude, in its most extreme form, finds its ultimate end in the critique itself, not in an original text, nor in the person of the reader. Institutionally, such a practice takes place in the fragmented structure of academic specialization where everyone vigorously competes for the available money and honors, thereby becoming more and more narrow, more deeply frozen. This was the world of Christian, whose humanistic patina could not protect him from the cold.

Thinkers in the academy were thus freed, cut loose to pursue their respective interests. These included the construction of various new institutions as responses to modern human "needs." With the state as sponsor and a growth economy as provider, a new era of well-being was promised by leftist ideology. People would no longer have to depend on their neighbor, on the virtuous action of a friend or stranger. Social progress would be automatic, just like the seeing-eye doors. Thinking

---

[4] For a remarkable interpretation of such reading and insights into today's "reading" world, see: Illich, *In the Vineyard of the Text.*

[5] The modern indictment reaches from Benda, *The Treason of the Intellectuals,* to Lasch, *The Revolt of the Elites.*

about the results of such progress, both within and without the academy, those devoted to study face a pressing task today: How can one see? Has seeing largely departed the academy, to be found in the pseudo-sight of technological devices like satellites, cameras and those doors, or in the penetrating, prophetic insights of independent spirits like Flannery O'Connor, Mark Rothko or Simone Weil?

But to be able *to know* what Antigone faced, to enter her world and have her world enter oneself, is to reach a kind of awareness, a kind of experiential knowing quite outside the parameters of a critical intelligence, as this is generally understood in the university today. One also needs certain graces or gifts. Thinkers in the early Middle Ages were unanimous in recognizing that the perfection of knowledge only occurred through these gifts, which they attributed to the Third Person of the Trinity, the Holy Spirit. One of the seven gifts they named "understanding." [6] Through this grace, one knows, apprehending spiritual goods, subtly penetrating their intimate character. When one sees sensible reality, one sees *into* it. In a pure, piercing vision, one sees . . . what is there. All good poetry is filled with examples of this; it is common to say that a certain poet or artist is particularly gifted. That is precisely true. How else could he or she have seen, having access only to the same sense sensations available to all? When I read poetry, I immediately learn how much I have been missing, how much I do not see. Such a realization moves me to ask: May I seek to obtain the same gifts? Yes, but the tradition teaches that one must first undergo preliminary disciplines which, while necessary, may not be sufficient. For the gifts are mysterious, gratuitous—they are truly gifts.

According to Aquinas, the gift of understanding is opposed to blindness of mind and dullness of sense. He believed that these obstacles originate in the personal distortion resulting from inordinate or disordered sensual delights found in venereal and food/drink pleasures, respectively. That is, these pleasures, as human, can be enjoyed either virtuously or viciously. But today, one must add additional powerful distractions that are specific to our age. The traditional vices of *luxuria* and *gula*, although still vigorously present among us, do not nearly exhaust contemporary obstructions to seeing.

Historically, two kinds of experience contributed to the sharpening of one's vision: the very precariousness of existence, and the various

---

[6] According to the tradition, the gifts are understanding, counsel, wisdom, knowledge (*scientia*), piety, fortitude, and fear. See Aquinas, *Summa theologiae*, I II, q. 68, a. 4.

ascetical exercises practiced throughout one's lifetime in order to purify one's external and internal senses, the passions, one's mind and spirit. But today's religious personnel and secular academics are among society's most protected and privileged persons. They are the very ones who most benefit from the rights, securities, honors and perquisites that the various social systems offer. Further, they often seen to be singularly unaware of the need for a *moral* askesis, that is, the lifetime practice of that complex of disciplines traditionally designed to affect and transform the various aspects of one's faculties or powers and being with a view toward reaching an unclouded vision, a crystalline insight. In this sense, one can recognize that the goods and services of modernity, the up-to-date, state-of-the-art institutions or systems are poisonous, sickening one, making one blind; they are ersatz substitutes for acting well. In a strange irony of history, many of those things men and women of the labor movement ostensibly fought and died for over so many years must now be recognized as producing enervating obtuseness . . . worse, if one hopes to live by faith.

One day when I arrived at Christian's room in the hospital, I found the corridor cluttered with stacks of clothing-like paper and a sign on his door: Enter only after donning the sterile clothes. I put on the paper gown, cap, mask, shoes and gloves . . . and knocked. Christian's voice invited me in. From all the treatments, he was in an extremely weakened condition, and the medical people were afraid he might pick up some bug, which would finish him off quickly!

Christian gave me the usual medical up-date on the latest treatments, his reactions, and the scientific background or basis. He then started describing the next procedures that were to take place on the following days. As he spoke, an inner shudder racked my spirit. He no longer used the first person singular, only the first person plural. I realized he had thoroughly changed beyond anything I could have imagined. He had lost any capacity to view himself as a self, as a person independent of the system that had embraced him more intensely this year. The only subject of predication and action now was the complex of medical personnel, together with their belief system and technological tools. Christian, the person, was subsumed under, inside . . . but where? My friend had ceased to exist.

During about twelve months, before my eyes, I had watched the death of Christian. I had seen, in an extreme and exaggerated form, what a modern institution can do to a person. Step by inevitable step, always under the guise of care, motivated only by the desire to help, acting out of the assurance of impeccable scientific credentials, the medical system inexorably replaced his person with an abstract hollowness parading as a we. The white-robed priesthood sacrificed him on the altar of knowledge, of progress, or perhaps only of hubris. Apparently no one learned anything from this horror. The doctors and their scientific technological tools killed him before he could die. I would not have believed that such a monstrous murder could occur if I had not witnessed it myself slowly taking place before my eyes . . . week after week. Now, Christian was no longer able to die.

I was deeply disturbed after leaving the hospital. In this state, I searched back through my reading and experiences to find some suggestion, some insight, a lead to understand what I had witnessed. Finally, I reread Dostoievsky's "The Grand Inquisitor," the prose poem related to Alyosha by his brother Ivan Karamazov.[7] At first, the fit appeared frighteningly perfect . . . if I looked at the doctors' project as an unconscious secular vulgarization of the Inquisitor's acknowledged transcendental sophistication. But the more I reflected on the two situations, the more convinced I became that the Inquisitor and the doctors served the same master . . . the one definitively rejected by Christ in the desert. There remained one major difference, however: The doctors lacked the finely honed intelligence of the Grand Inquisitor; they were unaware of the full import of their employment. In a sense, they did not know what they were doing.

Do Christian and Dara really exist? Yes. I have known them; I have been blessed by their friendship; they are important to me. But they are critical for others, also, not as individual persons, but as stories. Each has a story to tell, a story about the possibility and impossibility of freedom today. And as freedom is different for each of us—for example, all cannot accept or handle equal amounts of freedom—so each will interpret the stories differently. Each can learn something about his or her unique truth in the two stories. For me, it is a question of faith: In what, ultimately, do I place my faith?

An immediate objection arises: Not everyone can cut himself or herself off from modern systems and flee to an island that has an especially rich cultural heritage. But this is to misunderstand the nature of story in human cultures; stories are not literal photos, nor laboratory

---

[7] Dostoievsky, *The Brothers Karamasov*, 292–312.

models. The objection is completely beside the point. What to think and do then? I assume that I cannot exercise control over, or change, the world of systems. It is there, apparently firmly in place, demanding acquiescence if not universal allegiance. I refuse, however, to accept my helplessness; I refuse to submit myself as a kind of powerless non-entity; I refuse to accept the world as it is today. I, too, want to experience the friendship of the saints, the sense pleasures and painful dramas celebrated by poets, the precariousness of creaturely existence.

The one action clearly open to me is to say, "NO." No, I will not go along quietly. No, I will not obey. I will not make myself compatible with the program. This may be a necessary absolute today to begin to live humanly and, to the degree possible, autonomously and virtuously. This decision must be clearly spoken, and spoken daily. To be real, it requires a regular reflection, a quiet time when I enter into myself to look out at what I have rejected, what I still accept and what I grudgingly put up with. Some believe that a good place to begin is with the contemporary notion of health. Recognizing that health today is an illusion, actually only survival in a technical system, I say, "No," no to the health system, no to the fantasies it fosters and promotes. But this demands acts of renunciation. And these actions will be different for each person, the NO spoken in each one's unique voice, place and time. For me, it might begin with the refusal to take an aspirin for a headache; for another, the rejection of a bypass operation. For yet another, with something as complex as the struggle to define oneself over against the diagnosis of a physician . . . or the decision to die one's own death.

For the person of faith in the transcendent, this NO is an initial step in leaving the world of blasphemy. Blasphemy is predicating something of the divine goodness that does not belong there, or denying something that does, usually accompanied by contempt. But that which is constitutive of the contemporary world—reality conceptualized and manipulated as a system—is just such a predication and denial, colored by a peculiarly modern arrogance.

Ultimately, blasphemy is a sin against faith. Through faith, what I see and feel I *know* to be creation; I know that I, as much as all the universe, am in God's hands. What I believe to be real exists only by participation, by sharing in the being of the divine goodness. Through faith, I know that the world is, that it exists, only contingently. Nothing has independent existence—except what I call God. But the "everyday" world in which I find myself acting is more and more an artificial world, a manufactured "reality" ever further removed from Creation. Through this construct, men—and today, women, too—deny Creation, accepting without question the pronouncements of professionals and the hype of publicists, handing themselves over to the inventiveness and manipulation of the more clever and unscrupulous among us. In an efflorescence of vanity, the more enlightened, viewing Creation as a system or set of systems, claim they understand something called an "ecological problem." Rather than beginning with Creation on one hand, and the fact of vicious behavior, individual and social, on the other, they look to political fixes guided by current views of science and implemented by technological ingenuity.

Formerly, men humbly or arrogantly, trustingly or fearfully accepted Creation as a gift, as the primary gift, the original expression of the divine goodness, the outpouring of divine love. But the world viewed as a global system, and humans seen as immune systems, deny this ancient belief. Aquinas teaches that blasphemy is a most serious sin because it attacks what basically establishes one in what is—through faith I place myself *in* Creation.[8] Accepting the placement of myself *in* systems is to deny this, to be blasphemous. And this is why, for the person of faith, the most fundamental question today is: How do I act, vis-à-vis the systems construct? For this is precisely where the denial of faith occurs.

As my friend Dara found, a free life requires a certain self-denial. For some in the affluent sectors of society, those who are most distant from the possibilities of good behavior, such renunciation may seem too drastic, too frightening. It definitely means withdrawal, in some way, from the embrace of institutional supports that act as blindfolds and straitjackets. I firmly believe that one aspect of Dara's behavior is directly and necessarily imitable: to join with one's friends in the search for the places and times to say, NO.

---

[8] Aquinas, *Summa theologiae,* II II, q. 13, a. 3, corp.

8

Timeo Dominum Transeuntem:
Might I Miss the Lord's Passing?

REFLECTING ON what I see in a child, I realize that humans manifest a built-in desire to know. Perhaps it is correct to say, with Aristotle, that I am a creature made to know.[1] But along with everyone else I must face death, *the* most unknown and unknowable event. No matter how intensely I think about "what comes after," how many others I accompany in their dying, how many books I read on the subject, if I am honest with myself I have to admit that, ultimately, I know nothing. Further, death seems so final; it is the end. Therefore, I cannot help but feel fearful.

As a confused participant of society, our current experiment in living together, I find little comfort in the paradoxes surrounding death. For example, in many sectors an important specific historical anomaly reigns: When the more pampered affluent approach death, a life-cycle curve of complex and expensive interventions of technological wonders shoots up off the chart. In the precise moment of death, the medical system often devotes more societal resources to the dying person than at any earlier period in peoples' lives. If I cooperate with or demand this treatment, such a commitment to the end time may actually evidence an obsession with death, or indicate a disguised dedication to necrophilia. One begins to see the darker aspects of a modern benefit.

I also see a seemingly contrary phenomenon, a great emphasis on life and lives. This can mean that one regards life exclusively as a noun, a substantive standing by itself. In the daily paper, I read about a life saved or lives lost. The media are always careful to provide the exact body count. Sensitive people are generally dismayed by the loss of life through untoward death, "accidents," and the disasters of weather or

---

[1] Aristotle, in the first line of the *Metaphysics*, wrote: "All men by nature desire to know."

war. But, I wonder, I sometimes have the suspicion that many have effectively substituted a life for a person. In a seemingly secular society, the notion of living has taken on a new meaning for many believers and most agnostics. People of a faith community often mix up life with Life, in spite of the fact that their belief in life is principally in the one promised by God. Many of all persuasions seek to surround living with every possible safeguard, from nutritional labels to bureaucratic security measures. Some frantically pursue the protection and preservation of life through high-tech procedures and instruments, finally with costly and bizarre therapies. However, the latest marvel associated with life may, in reality, be a strong enticement to become even more credulous, an open invitation to embrace yet another superstitious illusion. For example, I can believe that life insurance has something to do with protecting my life.

To begin to reach reality I need, first of all, an explanatory concept, a notion that opens the world to me, an idea that brings intelligibility out of deceiving appearances and disparate experiences. Jacques Ellul, a witness who dared to thrust himself deep into the maelstrom of the twentieth century, came out with a clear insight: The principal concept to break open and reveal the macro and micro pictures, and the contradictions and delusions of our age is that of *la technique*, often translated by the term, technology.[2] What he meant was the overall dominance of rational efficiency. The modern emphasis is on the means. Everyone is pushed to instrumentalize everything in his or her daily living. The means become the only end for which I act.

For example, I show up regularly at a place of employment in order to be paid. I want the money to finance my house, car, and kids' education. I go to the ball game or theater or on vacation to relax, to unwind . . . to escape. Ellul claims that in each of these instances the reality is shot through, structured, by *la technique*. Perhaps it is most accurate to say that, overall, our society is organized into a technological project. Rational techniques determine what occurs in the media, government, commerce, entertainment, in how I am born, how I die. In the rites surrounding dying, the all-inclusiveness of *la technique* is especially gripping. But people do not generally look upon death as an end, or as *the* end. Their emphasis is on death's contrary, life, imagined by many as health. But among these, a disturbing configuration occurs.

[2] See, for example, Ellul, *Perspectives On Our Age*, ix–x; 33–4; 44–8. One can also see Ellul's other books, such as: *The Technological Bluff*.

In many sectors all over the world, immediately affecting greater numbers of people in the North than in the South, a flagrant impropriety of increasing enormity confronts the angel of history: Privileged persons are proselytized to become members of an interest group that demands as a civil right high-tech medical services. Within this gathering, a proportion generally holds true: Those with more education and greater access to information demand more services; they attempt to obtain the most sophisticated specialists, equipment and drugs, and to be treated in up-to-date cathedrals of care. Because of the character of the doctrines this multi-million-member mass accepts as true, and these persons' mostly unquestioned individual faith in the principal propositions of the creed, it would not be amiss to speak of a new international church. The members worship an abstraction, health. They believe, they have a religious faith in the scientific-technological medical system as the principal means to obtain health, although some have begun to supplement this obeisance with occasional recourse to so-called alternative medicine. In reality, most unconventional remedies are used as complementary medicine; people combine allopathic with other nostrums, such as herbal treatments.

Those who bow before the idol, health, also assist the medical system to achieve its presumed ends. They might be vegetarians, only eat food uncontaminated by chemicals, hormones or GMOs, exercise regularly, commit themselves to the regimen of a health club, and look for a less polluted living area. Most of those concerned with health have a set of criteria on which they want to base their living. The standards for judgment are derived from the science and practice of medicine, currently exercised in such acts of faith as regular check-ups and tests for the early detection of cancer or other threats to health.

The apparently favored ones of our world present a great stumbling block to the ordinary person's need to live, not a religious, but a human life. A human life minimally requires a certain autonomy or independence. For example, most now accept the position that the life of a slave is a mode of existence radically other than human. A slave's life is utterly at the call of another; he manifestly cannot live his own life. In the contemporary world, every person working for or involved in an institution recognizes that she gives up some measure of her independence in return for the many securities of a job. The planners and designers of most institutions attempt to make them as regularized and efficient as possible: they want to create systems. But to be human means to be wary of systems.[3]

One can arrange systems on a continuum. At one extreme, for example, I might place the postal system, as a means of encouraging me to express myself clearly through a letter to friends. At the other, the energy-use system that contributes to global warming. Somewhere in the middle, I can place the school and 911 systems. I am tempted to conceive of and order my life in terms of the medical system. Doing this, I can reach a grotesque situation where I tend to forfeit the possibility to live my own life; I can even become little more than an adjunct of the personnel and machines, the dreams and therapies, of medical entrepreneurship.

Because of the influence of mainline medicine's propagandistic thrust and its evident achievements, many do not think about *their* death; they cannot see death as a necessary step in living. Many practitioners and participants in the medical system, insanely at war with the invincibility of death, desecrate the last moments of living; the drama then becomes deeply religious, paradoxically, sacrilegious; the patient stumbles and falls at the end time, at the precise moment when one is destined to rise and enter eternity.

The contributions of Western-minded persons to the history of the earth and its peoples are decidedly ambiguous. The benefits of our scientific, artistic, and social inventions are not only two-edged, but "progress" can mean that the negative may increase more rapidly than the positive. For example, many travel faster and farther, but the earth's atmosphere cannot sustain the exhaust; large parts of the world are overrun with even middle-income vacationers, while ever more people are turned into waiters, chambermaids, tour guides and sex workers; I have access to an infinite quantity of information through the Internet, but I'm losing the ability to form my own questions, to ask good questions.

Our world is inundated with physical, anthropological, economic and social evils, such as pollution, mass man and now mass woman, poverty, torture, and war. But here and there, a still small voice is heard: Perhaps many acted precipitously and foolishly in denying the existence of theological evil, evil in terms of a transcendent God. Further, perhaps the medical system is tainted with this specific evil; perhaps God-fearing

---

[3] Illich, conversations with me, 1980–1992.

persons need to ask disturbing questions; perhaps agnostics need to be much more skeptical.

Almost every day in America, the person in touch with the media is treated with another touted breakthrough actual or, more often, prospective, which promises to repair an additional area of the human condition, to remove yet one more malady. It would appear that people are weaker, sicker, in short, more wounded and crippled than at any time since a creature first moved itself, Aristotle's notion of life, an event lost in the beginnings of time.

I can be thankful, however, that common sense still exists: Some experience a flicker of distrust hearing the confident or hedged promises of the hucksters associated with the body and mind business. Doubt leading to questions suggests an exciting possibility: Perhaps there are traditions in our past that express truths one can still recover. For example, for several millennia, physicians were trained to recognize the "face of death," the *facies hippocratica*.[4] Seeing that configuration on the patient's face the doctor withdrew for the person was no longer a patient, no longer a fitting subject for curative procedures. Rather, the weakened person was a creature directly faced with mortality, definitely beyond the cure or care of medicine.

Informed by modern diagnostic and prognostic procedures, today's physician is even better equipped to make that crucial judgment, to distinguish between curative and palliative care. But more than a doctor's conventional training is required. Although based on empirical evidence, the judgment is prudential, comprehensively moral rather than simplistically scientific; it's immediately directed to an individual person, not to an abstract truth. As with science, however, perceptive seeing and clarity of mind are necessary. What is more difficult to face is the fact that the situation demands personal courage, a kind of stance generally possible only after a lifetime of actions or practices leading to the acquisition of the cardinal virtue of fortitude.

People still die; all must pass through that threshold. But, all too often, a modern chaos rules the scene in a medical center. Apparently, everything is extremely clean and well ordered, generally to a greater degree than at any previous time in a person's life, especially when visitors are welcome to see the patient in a hospital. Chaos is defined as a state of utter confusion. The ideal, to live one's humanity, obviously admits a

---

[4] The source of the description is found in the Hippocratic corpus, printed in: Hippocrates, *The Theory and Practice of Medicine*, 43.

more and less. At times, one was said to be less human if he or she exhibited animal-like behavior. Today, however, there may be a new kind of
the non-human: one gains in humanness as one is more free of sophisticated technologies. Consider: What if there is an inverse relationship
between the naked human on one side, and invasive technological procedures and artifacts on the other? Experience and literature agree that
the more human is beautiful. But human beauty, too, may consist in a
proportion: The more beautiful person is the one requiring less artifice,
less adornment. In reality, high-tech treatments for many extremely ill
patients may be only a prelude to death, a new variety of chaos.

Intensity of technological medicalization extends one's life but,
simultaneously, one's suffering, too. Can that be thought of as a new
kind of darkness? One may live longer, but to what end? A doctor may
be tempted to participate in the creation of yet more cruel illusions by
acting in a way that encourages the person to die in a final orgy of pain
and delusion, or in a drug-induced coma. A patient is led or forced into
a dark man-made night, one of the worst imaginable on earth. Because
of the superstitious nature of the beliefs demanded for participation in
such a ceremony, it appears to be an antiseptic version of a Witches'
Sabbath. The medical system regresses to promoting embarrassing cre-
dulities historically reactionary and physically irrational. The underlying
reality, however, may be non-rational rather than irrational. Doctors,
perhaps unconsciously queasy about the possibility of demonic rituals,
are usually not there. One seldom or never sees them at the "last" moments.

To be prepared to distinguish between a human and a non-human
death today one is greatly helped through some knowledge of the history of death; such is available. What if a bit of the time and money,
energy and resources, expended on disease and health were devoted to
learning about human experiences of death in the past?[5] True, such individual or institutional study would not reveal death as finally knowable.
For example, I can know the abstract concept, triangle, or a concrete
artifact, a house in front of me. But a human death is totally different,
an individual person's death will remain mysterious forever. For that I
can be grateful.

As doctors today often know nothing about the *facies hippocratica*,
so they are not educated or prepared to make a supremely important

[5] Illich, *Medical Nemesis*, 174–208.

judgment: This way of dying is inhuman! Further, they are manifestly unqualified and generally uncalled, that is, they have no vocation for it, to assist a person stepping into the antechamber of eternity. What are they actually in charge of? What can they hope to do for a dying person, except to extend the suffering a few hours, days, weeks longer? Is time/number the bottom line, to which vanity, prestige, profit, and a technological imperative contribute? In the reversal of a more than two thousand-year-old tradition at the heart of Galenic-Hippocratic practice, doctors are more and more forced to be the agents of medicide. Because of the omnipresence and predominance of technologization in the medical system, passing over and forming the Weltanschauung of the doctors themselves, they, too, become infected with a modern version of necrophilia.

A doctor sensitive to questions and doubts about human and inhuman, technology and dying, time and eternity, is sometimes pushed to an extreme and objectionable position by relatives and friends of a sufferer who is obviously near death. These persons may be guilt-ridden, vis-à-vis the dying patient. Or the doctor has reason to fear their avariciousness; they might sue. The doctor is also under the pressure of colleagues who cling to a principle of our age's conventional medical ethos: Do everything feasible to postpone death. He or she is put in a very difficult place.

In general, the more a person undergoes the interventions of medical treatments, from aspirins to the latest specialized drug, from tonsillectomies to the most sophisticated laser-surgery, extending over the course of a life-time, the less able and prepared is that person to face suffering and dying. In spite of all the advances in therapy, pain, physical and spiritual, remains universal. All animals experience it. Humans, however, can also suffer. Therefore, to be human is to work out and practice one's own art of suffering. But the medical system substitutes mechanical and drug fixes for the continual struggle needed to exercise an art. The sad and depressing reality is that many in the North today, to a greater or lesser degree, often face a predominantly technological death. Such a person is necessarily deprived of dying his or her *own* death.

Is there a way out? Yes, I think so. Glimpses of the path can be found four thousand years ago in the story of Gilgamesh and his sorrow at the death of Enkidu, in many ancient accounts of the Hebrew Scriptures, for example, the bond between David and Jonathan (1 Sam 18:1ff), and later in such works as Plato's *Lysis*.[6] Aristotle, who modified and systematized the thought of his teacher, Plato, held that friendship is "most necessary for living" (*Ethics*, VIII, i). But the furthest he would take this way of life was to say that " . . . it is probably the proper course to visit friends in misfortune readily, and without waiting to be invited . . . " (*Ethics*, IX, xi). For me, all these stories and philosophical arguments are like faint *praenotamina*, struggles of the human spirit to reach the truth, the truth of friendship.

Historically, the full and most perfect realization of friendship shines out in the exemplary standard established by the life and death of Jesus, and is expressed in the words, "Greater love has no one than this, that he lay down his life for his friends" (John 15:13). Especially in St. John (chs. 14–16) and St. Paul (1 Cor 13), I find the most eloquent and moving expression of what I can know and say about being a friend. In the New Testament, I see a wondrous teaching joined to a terrible yet resplendent example. In the ages since the time of Jesus Christ, the notion and its realization are repeated and renewed, over and over. Both hagiographic accounts and the radiant examples of converted or struggling sinners are there to instruct and inspire us.

The friendship of Christ is altogether different from what the Greeks understood and some tried to practice. Simply and briefly, it is a participation in God's very life, an infused grace; it is not, strictly speaking, an Aristotelian habit I acquire through repeated acts. If I believe in the Gospel, then I also believe in the possibility of conversion; I can radically change or, more strictly speaking, *be* changed. The life and magnificent testimony of St. Augustine is perhaps the best known Western account of countless persons in a two thousand-year-old tradition. Christian example and teaching tell us that one can become a friend, form a friendship, in the most unpromising circumstances, and at almost any time in one's life; for example, one can come late to friendship. In St. Augustine's lovely expression, "Too late have I loved you, O Beauty so ancient and so new, too late have I loved you!"[7]

The importance of friendship when one is confronted with the medical system today has been emphatically pointed out with particular incisiveness by Ivan Illich.[8] A genuine friend becomes supremely im-

---

[6] Foster, *The Epic of Gilgamesh*, 60–2. Gilgamesh laments his dead friend, Enkidu.

[7] St. Augustine, *Confessions*, Bk. 10, ch. 27.

[8] Illich, "Death Undefeated," 1652–3.

portant, in many instances, necessary, to avoid a technological death, to die my own death. Illich calls this person an *amicus mortis*, a friend of death, that is, one who out of love for me is able and willing to help me die. This means a many-faceted ability and willingness to stand by me. To start, the love my friend has for me must be disinterested . . . he loves me out of the goodness of his heart. He accompanies me from the very beginning of our friendship. He unites an awareness of the ambiguity and problematic character of modern techniques in their many manifestations to an intimate knowledge of my person. In the course of true friendship, our souls are mutually revealed to one another. He accepts the truth that an art of suffering is necessary to live well and, ideally, possesses the imagination to help me work out such an art. When the hour approaches, he strengthens me in all the doubts and fears that assail me in the circumstances of death. Other friends and family can be great obstacles, as bad or worse than many doctors and the false promises of medical ideology. A genuine *amicus mortis* inspires and strengthens my courage that I might refuse hubristic medical treatments. He helps me make my own the words of Robert Southey, "My name is DEATH: the last best friend am I!"[9]

In early modern times some thoughtful Catholics developed the retreat. Often the participants isolate themselves from their everyday activities and plans, ideally close themselves up in a monastery or convent located in a rural setting, and follow ordered exercises of short presentations, prayers, reflection and silence. Today, business and academic groups, among others, adapt the idea and structure of a retreat for a secular end. Some of the great retreat masters in the Catholic tradition have emphasized quite another end, nothing less than a knowledge of God's will for the individual retreatant. This means that, relying on faith and trust in God, I hope to discern my particular calling or vocation (*vocatio*): how, specifically, to live my life . . . as a child of God. Given the qualitative change effected in society through the spreading systems of techniques and the hype of medical profiteers, such vocations especially need a perennial component: the firm desire to work out one's own art of suffering.[10]

Almost everywhere I turn today, I am assaulted by news, appeals, inducements, and demands centered on the abstraction called health.

[9] Enright and Rawlinson, eds., *The Oxford Book of Friendship*, 352.
[10] On the notion of qualitative change, see Ellul, *Perspectives On Our Age*, 36.

Much of the propaganda is derived from some aspect of various medical systems and appeals to my fear and vanity. I am told of health "needs" which, on examination, often appear to be little more than hard- or soft-sell inducements to become even further mired down in consumption. Most of this flashy publicity, with greater or lesser explicitness, also provides a technological answer to a presumed question: How can I achieve health? Simple. Buy this inclusive package, that new product designed for my particular problem, or the latest physician-tested remedy. *Every* such claim is tinged with an unspoken deception: More is promised than can be delivered. If, on the one hand, I consider this massive onslaught of the technogenic world and, on the other, my ignorance and weaknesses, doubts and fears, I see the necessity of having a good friend before whom I can be open and candid, one who, standing on his own feet, can be perspicaciously strong.

No matter how rigorous and brutal I am with myself in a retreat, the danger of self-illusion is always present. In such a matter as death, the possibility of delusion, too, lurks. I have known people who, suffering the encroaching destruction of an aggressive cancer for weeks and days, immediately before lapsing into unconsciousness, through a habit of living by illusions, have become, as far as I could tell, fully delusionary. Perhaps a friend could have helped them escape this demonic terror. To go through such an experience, to witness such a death as an onlooker, is to know the extreme agony of helplessness. One then lives with a heartfelt pain that does not go away.

Some philosophers have maintained that we are social animals. That's an abstraction and, for many, unintelligible. But the truth of the proposition is seen in the concrete and can be known, felt, deeply and irrevocably experienced by anyone through sitting at the bedside of a dying person. Following the two lines of argument I suggested above, technological and personal, such an action is of an immeasurable importance today. Fighting for and with a dying friend, I can come to realize, in the mutual heart to heart exchange, the importance of friendship, of having the gift of a good friend, one who can be an *amicus mortis*.

There is another aspect of a technological death to which I have alluded several times, the possible presence of the demonic. At times dramatically, at times more quietly, universalistic religions have spread far from a modest beginning in the Mideast. With their diffusion, more virulent conflicts also appeared. Religious inspiration, as not only skeptics but believers also point out, necessarily bears within its heart the possibilities of corruption; if evil there be it would find an attractive home here. The history of animosity and hostility, torture and war in the Western world, partly inspired and sustained by clashing religious views, seems to argue for the mysterious presence of evil and to support a demonic source. Personally, I have been brought to think about this possibility every day. Ivan Illich and I, when we were together, tried to pray the canonical hour of Compline at night before going to bed. Each of the "hours" is a mixture of psalms and prayers, some of which never vary while others change with the feast or season. In the old Dominican breviaries written in the Latin of the Vulgate, a reality that goes far beyond the earthly is named each day. This name, establishing the character of the prayer, occurs right at the beginning:[11]

> Be sober and watch because your adversary the devil circles around like a roaring lion, seeking whom he may devour. Be strong, resist him in the faith!

Part way through the hour, which actually takes about twenty minutes to say, we prayed a poem that includes this verse (the words refer to celibate monks and friars):

> May strange dreams depart,
> And fantasies of the night, too.
> Restrain our enemy,
> Lest our bodies be polluted.

Toward the end, we recited this petition:

> We beseech you, Lord, to visit this house, and drive far from it all the wiles of the foe. May your holy angels keep us in peace, and may your blessing always fall on us.

---

[11] *Breviarium Sacri Ordinis Praedicatorum*, 107–10. The Latin texts:
> Sobrii estote et vigilate: quia adversarius vester diabolus
> tamquam leo rugiens circuit, quaerens quem devoret:
> cui resistite fortes in fide.
> Procul recedant somnia
> Et noctium phantasmata;
> Hostemque nostrum comprime,
> Ne polluantur corpora.
> Visita quaesumus, Domine, habitationem istam, et omnes insidias inimici ab ea longe repelle; et Angeli tui sancti habitantes in ea nos in pace custodiant, et benedictio tua sit super nos semper.

The metaphors and meanings of the prayer are multiple. Saying Compline for the last fifty years I have come to feel that sleep is a true image of death; further, the analogy between sleep and death carries me far outside the earthbound, opening into infinity. For over a thousand years, the tradition has maintained that demonic powers hover around us before both sleep and death, a historical constant. But neither we nor our enemy have stood still. Today's technological death is inimical to the immemorial experience of all earlier peoples. Perhaps it is also infected by the demonic; and perhaps I can look to tradition to find my way. Tradition is somewhere in the past; it's found in history. But how do I proceed?

I've heard that from the time of Herodotus (d. 425? B.C.), sometimes called the father of history, until today, people in the West have more and more emphasized the importance of history. Often, this means that scholars who write historical works continually seek greater refinement in their approach and methods. For example, although we already possess many good books on Miguel de Unamuno, a study that appears to offer innovative and new insights is greeted with attention and respect by the scholarly community.[12] But, as Simone Weil noted,

> . . . there is a right and a wrong way of making use of history. We can either seek therein something to exalt the imagination; or else we can seek therein something that is purer than ourselves.[13]

Simone Weil, along with St. Thomas Aquinas and others, is aware of the dangers; the imagination sometimes fosters deformations and falsehoods. Her caution can help me reach the specific kind of knowledge derived from history that I need in order to penetrate and critically judge the assumptions underpinning the contemporary medical system. As she suggests, truth may lie more in a strict desire for mental purity rather than in imaginative curiosity. There is a series of statements in this section of her *Notebooks* that is a sure guide to help me learn from the past in order to face my future, namely, death. Since I am still alive, death is the future; it may also be eternity.

Simone Weil wrote that

---

[12] For a personal and idiosyncratic war on death very different from that of today's medical system, see: Unamuno, *The Agony of Christianity.*

[13] Weil, *The Notebooks*, vol. 2, 444.

> . . . there is more of eternity in the past than in the present . . .
> [that is,] there is less of the temporal and consequently a greater
> proportion of eternity. . . . the past offers us something which is
> at the same time real and better than ourselves . . . [14]

With these words in mind, I want to look at the Cathari, sometimes called the Albigensians. The name is derived from the city of Albi, in what is today Southern France. Many of this religious faith lived in that city.

A movement of believers whose origins were partly Christian, the Cathari were concentrated in Northern Italy and Southern France, and most active in the two hundred or so years around the twelfth century. By the end of that century, they had established eleven bishoprics. At that time they reached their greatest strength, just as a new European civilization was forming, what today is called the West. Western society, from about the eleventh to the fifteenth century, was characterized by growing economic power. The Cathari benefited from this, for some were cloth merchants and weavers, therefore, mobile.[15] The emerging culture also "exhibited a pronounced militarism, which penetrated all ranks of society in a fashion elsewhere unknown among civilized peoples."[16] This contributed to the destruction of the Cathari through the war waged against them.

In the area of religiosity, the Roman Catholic Church claimed exclusive power and authority. But many of its leaders from both the secular and monastic clergy, departing from the examples and truths of the Gospels, took advantage of the society's riches and amassed considerable wealth; some also sought political power. Records show that the local clergy were lax, both in their moral life and in any knowledge of what St. Thomas (d. 1274) was to call *sacra doctrina*, sacred doctrine. To counter what they considered a heresy, reforming popes tried to emphasize doctrinal orthodoxy for all, and strict celibacy for their clerics.

The Cathari had an underlying belief, although such may have been either unknown or confusedly understood by many who thought of themselves as members, and others who were sympathizers. This was an answer to a question still asked today: What is the source of evil in the world? A mystery every religious thinker must face and attempt to

---

[14] Weil, *The Notebooks*, vol. 2, 444.

[15] Runciman, *The Medieval Manichee*, 13; Kaelber, *Schools of Asceticism*, 214.

[16] McNeill, *A World History*, 256–7.

answer. Among the Hebrews, the book of Job (maybe written in the fifth century B.C.) wrestles with the problem. In Persia, Zoroaster (d.ca. 551 B.C.) held for a permanent war between good and evil, spirit and matter. Such a position is called dualism, and most dualists condemn the material world as evil. At the heart of their beliefs, the Cathari appear to have been dualists, they embraced this ancient and historically ever-present metaphysical idea. With them, visible creation, all matter, is evil; only the spirit is good. Strict Cathari, for example, did not accept the baptism of John the Baptist because it was accomplished with water. They believed in a baptism of the Holy Spirit, a purely spiritual ceremony.

Ultimately, all dualistic theories are an attempt to "explain" sin. They take an absolute form, namely, positing two gods, one evil one good, or a relative form, holding for one God who is in some way responsible for the existence of an evil world. At different periods and places, it seems the Cathari embraced each of these positions.[17]

Theorists, historians, and especially interrogators look for a system of ideas and the subtleties of abstract doctrines. But many believers and supporters were not well versed in Cathar thought; they might have known nothing of the movement's foundational beliefs; they were principally interested in experiences and practices, in short, how to insure one's salvation. Many people at that time and in that area, as in all times and places, were concerned with the question: How do I die? Some also asked: Therefore, how do I live today? Above all, if there is a life after death, how am I saved? The pursuit of salvation may have been more widespread and intense than the pursuit of health among the affluent today. The Cathari also claimed to have certain and clear answers to many practical moral questions concerning salvation. The example set by the *perfecti* (women, *perfectae*, were not so numerous or so public) was patent but, for most people, impossible to realize in one's daily life. Precisely through their renunciation, the leaders of the movement could exercise power over believers not yet ready or disposed to become *perfecti* until near death.[18]

Another large group of religious innovators, the Waldenses, or Waldensians, came to prominence about the same time and in the same area as the Cathari. A Lyonese merchant, Peter Valdes (or, Waldo), ex-

[17] Kaelber, *Schools of Asceticism,* 176–7; Runciman, *The Medieval Manichee,* 171–5; Lambert, *The Cathars,* 314–5.

[18] Lansing, *Power and Purity: Cathar Heresy in Medieval Italy,* 10–11.

perienced a religious conversion around 1173, and began to walk about, exhorting people to live a more simple life in imitation of the Lord and the Apostles.[19] The Waldensians tended to be anti-clerical, probably influenced the Franciscan Spirituals, and were persecuted by the Roman authorities. Some were executed, and their numbers much reduced by the end of the fifteenth century.

Historians have unearthed large amounts of material related to the Cathari.[20] However, the reader today must keep in mind that almost all the information on the Cathari was written by Catholics whose bias was decidedly antithetical and whose records were more or less polemical. The name, Cathar (from the Greek, "pure"), may have originally designated the leaders of the movement, the people interrogators called the *perfecti* (all records of the orthodox were written in Latin, not in the local *langue d'oc*). Catholic commentators ended naming all participants Cathari or, popularly, Manichaeans.[21]

Their historical origins are obscure but, considered dualists, they had to be judged heterodox or, simply, heretical, by the authorities in Rome. The popes, alarmed by a religious movement many of whose members saw themselves as directly opposed to the Catholic Church, mounted a twofold campaign against the Cathari. Innocent III first sent reformist-minded preachers to Languedoc in 1199.[22] In 1205, the bishop of Osma and his prior, Dominic de Guzman, began preaching. When that did not extirpate the heresy, the pope convinced the northern nobles to invade the South in 1208.[23] The bloody war, eventually successful, is called the Albigensian Crusade (1209–1229). The interweaving of secular and religious sentiments, structures, lines of command, and relations of authority is probably too complex for scholars today to unravel with clarity and certitude, although a huge bibliography on the area and period exists, and grows.

In 1234, under the direction of Gregory IX, the work of the preachers came to include interrogations designed to detect unorthodox

---

[19] Kaelber, *Schools of Asceticism,* 135.

[20] See Kaelber, Lambert, Runciman, Lansing, and their bibliographies. Also, Mundy, *The Repression of Catharism at Toulouse*; Oldenbourg, *Massacre at Montségur*; Barber, *The Cathars*; Burl, *God's Heretics: The Albigensian Crusade*; Hamilton, "The Cathars and Christian Perfection," 5–13. Some of these studies print primary documents.

[21] Runciman, *The Medieval Manichee,* 184; Kaelber, *Schools of Asceticism,* 175–6.

[22] Runciman, *The Medieval Manichee,* 136.

[23] Ibid., 140.

opinions or practices. The Dominicans, approved in 1216, were given this task, and their procedures developed into what was later called the Inquisition.[24]

St. Dominic and St. Francis, who had contacts with both Cathari and Waldensians, were probably influenced by these people, Dominic more by the Cathar leaders' way of life, Francis by Cathar beliefs about the body, and the Waldensians' poverty.[25] Both Dominic and Francis founded convents of contemplative nuns. It may be that Cathar *perfectae* (women), before they were eliminated by the interrogations and the crusade, were similarly structured. A fascinating historical question arises: To what extent and in what ways were St. Dominic and St. Francis inspired by the examples of these movements?

As mentioned above, many of the Catholic clergy, following the example of cynical secularization exhibited by their leaders, imitated them or sank into despondent apathy.[26] The Cathar *perfecti*, however, were strongly committed to a rigorous asceticism; they were their own best advertisement.[27]

Catharism, then, was a popular form of religiosity in those areas where the *perfecti* walked, partly because of the contrast between Roman clerics and Cathar *perfecti*: wealth, ignorance and lax sexual mores on one side, poverty, detailed and clear exposition of teaching, and complete celibacy on the other. But the Cathar response and promise to people may have been even more important: an unequivocal answer to the question, How can I be saved? accompanied by an impressive liturgy. Further, the Cathari claimed that their liturgy, contrary to that of the Catholics, was derived from the practices of the early Church. Scholars now admit that they were sometimes more literally exact than the Catholics of their time.[28]

Two ceremonies of the Cathari were especially directed to the question of salvation, seen in terms of how I die. In the Latin of interrogators' scribes, these were called *consolamentum* and *endura*. Generally, one could be admitted to the *consolamentum* only after a long period (usually more than a year) of instruction and reflection in the company

---

[24] Kaelber, *Schools of Asceticism*, 185–6.

[25] Runciman, *The Medieval Manichee*, 130, 174, 179; Kaelber, *Schools of Asceticism*, 191; Mundy, *The Repression of Catharism at Toulouse*, 10.

[26] Runciman, *The Medieval Manichee*, 116, 134–6; Lansing, *Power and Purity*, 11.

[27] Ibid., 147; Lambert, *The Cathars*, 155.

[28] Lambert, *The Cathars*, 344; Oldenbourg, *Massacre at Montségur*, 43.

of the *perfecti*. Therefore, full membership as a Cathar embraced both an elaborate structure of belief and difficult behavioral norms. Then, if the *perfecti* accepted the novice, he or she could receive the *consolamentum*, complete incorporation into the faith of the community through a liturgy, namely, a religious ceremony directed and presided over by the Elders, or *bons hommes* (seemingly the usual term among the Cathari). The liturgy utilized the book of Scriptures and prayers, especially the Lord's Prayer. The *consolamentum* was usually received only by adults, and perhaps most frequently by adults close to death. People in general found it difficult to embrace the extreme asceticism demanded of the *perfecti* in so many dimensions of one's life. After the ceremony, one was a *perfectus* or *perfecta* and bound to certain practices: perfect celibacy; complete abstinence from meat, eggs and cheese; the obligation to observe the three great Fasts—Advent, Lent, and the time between Pentecost and the Feast of Saints Peter and Paul (June 29th).[29] One also agreed to live in poverty, prayer, and study, and not to fear death because of one's belief.[30]

The *perfecti* were quite emphatic in their faith and teaching: Through the *consolamentum*, the person's soul was purified by the Holy Spirit, thereby escaping from the material world, achieving salvation.[31] Considering the power of doxology and personal example, all directed by the *perfecti* toward a question uppermost in many believers' sensibility— How do I reach eternal happiness?—one gets some appreciation for the appeal of Catharism. When this is held up against what people saw in the behavior of many Catholic leaders, namely, wealth and worldliness, one sees the necessity for a bloody crusade combined with a years-long rigorous interrogation accompanied by certain punishment—a painful death by being burned at the stake, fines, or imprisonment—to root out unorthodox beliefs, actions, and rituals.

The historical record on the nature and practice of the *endura* is particularly confusing and uncertain. It is mentioned in later documents, principally of the fourteenth century, but there is no agreement on its exact character or frequency. All investigators appear agreed that the term, the *endura*, refers to a liturgical ceremony that a "consoled" Cathar underwent only when the person was close to death. All are also

---

[29] Lambert, *The Cathars,* 244–5.

[30] Oldenbourg, *Massacre at Montségur,* 47; Lansing, *Power and Purity,* 5.

[31] Lansing, *Power and Purity,* 5.

in accord in thinking that, after the rite, the Cathar would eat and drink less. Some believe there was a certain flexibility in what was permitted. For example, the sick person would abstain from all solid food, but could take some water. Others think that no nourishment, solid or liquid, was taken after the *endura* ceremony. There does not seem to be enough evidence, however, to assert any position with certitude. Historians surmise that the rite was carried out to prevent a relapse: After undergoing the *consolamentum* and *endura*, there was less danger that the person would violate the strict requirements of the *perfecti*; one simply died first.[32] What is clear is that the believing Cathar, through the *endura*, took a further and more decisive step on the path toward eternity.

The testimonies of two women are particularly instructive to interpret the meaning, then and now, of the Cathari. Living in the Rhineland, far to the North of the areas where the Cathari were most numerous, Hildegard of Bingen (1098–1179), a Benedictine nun, was one of the great polymath geniuses in the history of the West. Among her many letters, she wrote two, probably in 1163, in which she spoke about the disastrous conditions of the Church and the appeal of the Cathari.

The flavor of the first letter, in which she excoriated priests, is graphically caught in this judgment: "But just as a snake hides in a cave after it has shed its skin, you walk in filth like disgusting beasts."[33] Without naming them, she wrote of what the Cathari would do to the Catholic clergy:

> When the time comes, ruin will fall upon you at the hands of certain people [the Cathari], you wicked sinners, and they will pursue you relentlessly, and they will not cover up your works, but will lay them bare, and they will say about you: "These are scorpions in their morals and snakes in their works."[34]

A community of brothers wrote to Hildegard, asking her for what she had written "against the heresy of the Cathars."[35] Citing words and images from Daniel, Isaiah, and the Apocalypse, she described what she saw when she "looked from afar and, in the shadow of a true vision," learned something about the Cathari. Her words strike to the heart of

[32] Lambert, *The Cathars*, 240–4.

[33] Hildegard of Bingen, *The Letters of Hildegard of Bingen*, vol. 1, 56.

[34] Ibid., 58.

[35] Hildegard of Bingen, *The Letters of Hildegard of Bingen*, vol. 2, 122.

the movement's beliefs. With singular power and imaginativeness, and with perceptive accuracy, she pointed out that

> These are the people who deny first principles, that is, that God created all things, and commanded them to wax and multiply. These are the people who deny the sovereign principle, that is, that it was clear even before the ancient days that this Word of God was bound to become man. . . . [They] are too blind to see the fiery form that now shines as man in holy divinity.[36]

Hildegard believed that the leaders were directly inspired by the devil:

> These men in whose ears the devil is building towers are like a crab, which moves forward and backward, and they are like scorpions, which furtively sting you with fiery tails and kill you with the terrible poison of cruel unbelief (p. 124).

Toward the end of her letter, articulating the source of her knowledge and judgment, she wrote:

> And soon in that same vision, I heard a resounding voice saying to me: Write these things which you have seen and heard, and send them quickly to those priests of the Church who worship God with the purest faith . . . [to protect the faithful] from these devilish treacheries, lest those evil people put down roots among them, and they perish (p. 125).

She ended the letter, saying:

> I, a poor little form of a woman, languished for many days oppressed by sickness so that I could scarcely walk until I had committed these things to writing (p. 125).

The truth of Hildegard's insights and judgments shines out with particular brilliance because of the character of the age in which she lived. She called it a "squalid, womanish time."[37] Therefore, paradoxically, God called on a "poor little form of a woman" to speak to all, noble and commoner, prelate and cleric, man and woman.[38] However, she saw the clergy as key in that era, and especially addressed them:

---

[36] Hildegard of Bingen, *The Letters of Hildegard of Bingen*, vol. 2, 124–5.

[37] Hildegard of Bingen, *The Letters of Hildegard of Bingen*, vol 1, 13.

[38] Hildegard of Bingen, *The Letters of Hildegard of Bingen*, vol 2, 125.

You ought to be the day, but you are the night. For you will be either the day or the night. Choose, therefore, where you wish to take your stand. You are not the sun and moon and stars in the firmament of God's law and justice. Rather, you are the darkness, in which you lie as if you are already dead.[39]

Our age is both similar and different. Although we experience an awful era, it's not so much a "womanish time," rather, we are suffused with a bourgeois spirit. Persons such as Léon Bloy (1846–1917) loathed this commitment to success, comfort, and the idolatry of money.[40] According to Emmanuel Mounier (1905–1950), both believers and agnostics are infected by the bourgeois ethos.[41] Each of them, devout Catholics like Hildegard, looked to churchmen to take a stand against the established disorder. But so many among the hierarchy and lower clergy, apparently mesmerized by the glitter, are silent today. Hildegard faced a heroic asceticism in the *perfecti*. A contemporary Bloy faces the mediocre egotism of New Age "spirituality." Hildegard was confronted with people who quietly went to the stake rather than deny their beliefs. Where are the modern heretics ready to face the flames? Truly, the times are different.

As Hildegard's visionary letters judged the fundamental source of Cathar faith, so the truth of Catholic *and* humanistic understanding and acceptance of death judges the ultimate notions of the scientific-technological medical system. The analogy clearly holds with respect to truth and falsity. I strongly suspect there is also an equivalence in the two falsities: each is demonic.

The other woman whose testimony is helpful, Simone Weil (1909–1943), was someone whose life and writings, like Hildegard's, continue to move almost anyone who comes into some awareness of them. Her letter to Déodat Roché after reading two of his articles on the Cathari in *Cahiers du Sud* can help us to reach across the centuries to find the truths in a people categorized at the time, and since, as heretics.

In order to cite what Simone Weil wrote in her admiration for the Cathari, it is helpful to point out at least two other opinions of hers. Cathar teaching says that the created world is evil and, therefore, to be contemned. Simone Weil wrote that "For anyone with experience of the transcendent nature of inspiration in the process of artistic creation,

[39] Hildegard of Bingen, *The Letters of Hildegard of Bingen*, vol 1, 58.
[40] See Bloy, *Pilgrim of the Absolute*.
[41] Mounier, *Personalism*.

there is no more manifest proof of God than the beauty of the world."[42] The Cathari also had an insuperable difficulty accepting the reality of the Incarnation, the enfleshment and final suffering of the person, Jesus Christ. Simone Weil wrote much on suffering and on the passion of the Lord. For example, she said,

> . . . my greatest desire is to lose not only all will but all personal being. . . . I hope that this abandonment [leaving France] . . . will finally bring me to the haven. What I call the haven, as you [Father Perrin, her Dominican friend] know, is the Cross. If it cannot be given me to deserve one day to share the Cross of Christ, at least may I share that of the good thief.[43]

In her letter to Roché (January 23, 1941), she began her remarks on the Cathari saying, "I have long been greatly attracted to the Cathars, although knowing little about them."[44] She also expressed her belief in Christianity as embodied in the Catholic Church. Nevertheless, along with many others during the past two thousand years, she thought the Church deeply corrupted, and is quite explicit in the letter: "The influence of the Old Testament and of the Roman Empire, whose tradition was continued by the Papacy, are to my mind the two essential sources of the corruption of Christianity" (p. 83). In what may be an unusual literal mindedness, she wrote,

> I have always been kept away from Christianity by its ranking these stories [of the Old Testament], so full of pitiless cruelty, as sacred texts; and the more so because for twenty centuries these stories have never ceased to influence all the currents of Christian thought (p. 83).

In her most famous essay, "The *Iliad*, Poem of Might," she speaks of force or violence and the soul in the history of the West through her meditation on the Homeric epic. Toward the end of that piece, she wrote:

> But the spirit which is transmitted from the *Iliad* to the Gospels, passed on by the philosophers and tragic poets, has hardly gone beyond the limits of Greek civilization. Of that civilization, since the destruction of Greece, only reflections are left (p. 181).

---

[42] Weil, *The Notebooks*, vol. 2, 412.

[43] Weil, *Waiting for God*, 59.

[44] Weil, *The Simone Weil Reader*, 82.

Simone Weil pointed out that " . . . Plato himself always presents his doctrine as issuing from an ancient tradition . . . " (p. 83). She believed that

> . . . the philosophical and religious traditions of the countries he [Plato] knew were merged in one single stream of thought. It is from this thought that Christianity issued, but only the Gnostics, Manichaeans, and Cathars seem to have kept really faithful to it. They alone really escaped the coarseness of mind and baseness of heart which were disseminated over vast territories by the Roman domination and which still, today, compose the atmosphere of Europe (p. 83).

The historical record is problematical, and some authors more confused than others, but I think it possible to reach a limited degree of truth concerning the Cathar approach to death. The *consolamentum* and *endura*, although not well understood by outsiders then nor by scholars of any age, and named only by the translated Latin words of the Catholic interrogators' scribe, are yet of importance today, especially to persons in the West influenced by the intense medicalization advertised and promoted for the affluent. Such persons, on reflection, might like to avoid a technological death, a death in the grips of the devices and drugs of modern medicine, a death robbed from the dying person.

I want to approach the matter from the perspective of an orthodox Christian, but I think that, making the necessary modifications in the argument, what I write is applicable to other believers and to secular unbelievers, too.

My experience of dying people confirmed, too, by other witnesses to whom I have spoken, is that many at death's door reach a point when they no longer want to eat and drink. This occurs with the breaking of their hold on the human condition. If they can still speak, they resolutely voice their mind; if they cannot speak, they clearly manifest their desire by action, namely, their adamant refusal to eat or drink. Their entire being indicates that they definitely appear *to know*; they know where they are and what they face: a short time and then . . . eternity. Thinking about what I have witnessed, I feel they enjoy a superior comprehension of their total situation, that is, a kind of knowledge unavailable to their relatives, friends or care-givers. If this is true, then those who surround such a person are under a strict obligation to respect and act on the intuition being revealed to them. Perhaps I can say that the departing person possesses a privileged wisdom, a truth in some way already glimpsed from the Other Side.

For years some doctors and nurses associated with Hospice Care programs have pointed out the therapeutic benefits of dehydration in terminally ill patients.[45] The knowledge and conclusions of these caregivers, based on their experience and observation as professionals, coincides perfectly with the inimitable knowledge I have found in gravely ill persons. It is important to emphasize that the absolute propriety I mentioned above is a moral one; it affects me specifically as human, that is, as a moral actor or agent. This moral vocation or calling given me is the expiring person's gift to me, and is supported by the lesser scientific/medical evidence of the professionals. Can the Cathari of the High Middle Ages add anything to these professional, experiential, and moral lines of thought? Yes. In fact, infinitely more.

One of the principal obstacles to knowing the truth is that I live in time. This means that, as Simone Weil stated,

> . . . everything which belongs to the temporal in us secretes lies in order not to die and in proportion to the fear of death. That is why there is no veritable love of truth without a total, an unreserved consent to death.[46]

If what she writes is correct, how is it possible to arrive at "a total, an unreserved consent to death"? I am interested in this thought and her witness in terms of the caution I mentioned earlier; I hope to avoid imaginative flights and wish to seek purity in order to illuminate a basic desire: to die my own death.

There are two aspects to an answer: My inward disposition, and the external realm. As pointed out above, in both respects powerful forces are at work to insure that I never reach such a position. The matter of inner disposition is infinitely variable and must be faced and figured out

---

[45] See, for example, Taylor, "Benefits of Dehydration in Terminally Ill patients," 271–72; Ganzini, "Nurses' Experiences with Hospice Patients Who Refuse Food and Fluids to Hasten Death," 325, 359–65. A growing body of literature discusses the moral aspects of nutrition and hydration for persons gravely ill. Among Catholic spokesmen, one can cite the document prepared for the U.S. Bishops, "Nutrition and Hydration: Moral and Pastoral Reflections," first proposed in 1992, and the statement by Pope John Paul II on March 20, 2004. A short report of the pope's remarks can be found in *America*, April 5, 2004, 4–5. A German friend, Dr. Antje Menk, tells me that the term in that country is *Stiller Suizid* (quiet suicide), but that very little is published about it.

[46] Weil, *Notebooks*, vol. 2, 444.

by each person . . . hopefully, with the help of a faithful *amicus mortis*. The conclusion will be different for each. For believers, the formation of one's heart will be strongly influenced by the teaching of the Church and Tradition, and consent to the infusion of grace. For everyone, namely, all contingent beings, both the fact of existence and the "motion" toward consent result from the creative action of an Unmoved Mover.

Ultimately, the external situation can be easily summed up: If I have stopped eating and drinking, then only the thin screen of death separates me from the joyful fruition of Christ's love in the vision of God. But the Christian community can contribute greatly to the sense or meaning, human and divine, of the ritual surrounding the dying person during the last moments. And it is precisely here that a truth of the Cathari so well illuminates and opposes the perversions of our age.

My first and principal question is this: Is there a specifically Christian way to die? Since I will certainly die, and very much want to be a Christian, I have to believe in a positive answer. Secondarily, I strongly suspect that a believer's way of dying can be true, that is, a participation in the transcendentals. Therefore, I believe this way of death can have meaning for non-believers also.

From what I have written, the reader knows that I regard the radical medicalization of death as an evil, both natural and transcendental. An extremely medicalized death is contrary to and destructive of all traditional ways of dying. Paradoxically, I may also hinder the soul's movement toward eternity. In our world, a medicalized death often means surrendering the spirit to an iatrogenic body, a body created by the medical system, a body I am strongly influenced to internalize, to make my own. That in turn means to be turned into an iatrogenic self.[47] Such medicalization is achieved mostly through a complex of technological instruments. When these are conceptualized, with Jacques Ellul, as *la technique*, they are part of an omnipresent, all-encompassing, totally assimilative system.[48] In other words, many today die, not their own death, but an alienated, a purloined, a technological death. Evidence leads me to believe this is not the way most people want to die.

As I suggested above, one needs to practice an art of suffering to die a Christian death. I strongly believe that everyone today, to die humanly, also needs to practice such an art. What I see in the Cathari is twofold:

---

47 Duden, "The Quest for Past Somatics," 219–30.

48 Ellul, *Perspectives*, 82 and passim.

First, their teaching asked for an ascetic life. Further, they surrounded death with certain actions and ceremonies, symbolized and realized by the *consolamentum* and *endura*, when undergone as one approaches the end time.

Neither the asceticism nor the final liturgy of the Cathari is to be copied literally. Each person today must find his or her proper ascetical practices; one cannot lay these down in general or universal terms. The word (from *askesis*) and practice came to us in a tradition that begins with ancient Greek athletes. Rather than looking for quick-fixes, these men devoted themselves to a daily regimen of appropriate exercises. They invite us to seek a similar discipline. For the final moments of living, however, the Christian community could work out a framework and prayers, what is today called a sacramental. The Cathari give us the spirit of asceticism; for dying, they also provide us with examples of practical liturgical ceremonies.

Every society surrounds dying and death with certain rituals. It's probably safe to say that these are always sacred; they have a sacralizing end or purpose, in themselves and in the minds of the participants. If death does indeed take me outside time that I might enter eternity, then the passage should incarnate a twofold character: be both ceremonial or ritualistic, and sacred. The Cathar practices of *consolamentum* and *endura* speak to both these requirements.[49]

A liturgical form of both the *consolamentum* and *endura* should probably be worked out with an eye turned toward the specific obstacle to a human *and* Christian death: the contemporary tendency toward a totalitarian technological hegemony over the conception and action of dying. A precise response can mine the past. Liturgical authorities have a rich and varied treasure of hymns, prayers, vestments, and movements from which to choose.

Making a distinction derived from the thesis of hylomorphism, one must attend to both the matter and form. The selection of prayers, for example, would constitute the major aspect of the rite's form. The matter, as is fitting at that moment, is an anti-matter, the absence of food and drink. The quasi-substance of the ceremony would be made up of a form and no-matter, symbolizing the end status of the dying person.

The believer wants to be in a place the liturgy can provide, a place where she can meet the Lord. I want to welcome the Lord and, *timeo*

---

[49] Unamuno noted that "all orthodoxies began by being heresies." See his *The Agony of Christianity*, 84.

Dominum transeuntem ("I fear the Lord passing me by," an expression emphasized by Illich), meaning, "I fear to miss the Lord when he comes for me"; which in some way can happen if I have become addicted to technological fantasies.[50] Through participation in this new liturgy, I can find a transcendental meaning in my death, I can escape the high-tech trap. Further, I can thereby contribute to the renewal of the Church's common life; my action reverberates throughout the entire communion.

People in the early Church and the Cathari, too, practiced a liturgical, a holy kiss, in the midst of their ceremonies. Originally, this action was called a *conspiratio*, a "breathing with."[51] Among both the first Christians and the Cathari, the kiss symbolized the infusion of the Holy Spirit; it signified and solidified the community in its common life in the Lord. For the Cathari, their ritual declared a baptism with fire, the fire of the Holy Spirit. That Spirit is still present, patiently waiting; she "broods with warm breast and with ah! bright wings."[52] Because of the power and pervasiveness of the technological project I need, not only protection, but a corresponding "boost," a grace enabling me to stand fast, a strength brilliantly lighted up with a light reaching into the Transcendent, that I might strike through the contemporary claptrap, that I might be drawn to the Other Side.

---

[50] A friend, Gene Burkart, pointed out that Illich feared being distracted by the medical system, namely, being disembodied by it. He might thus miss the Lord passing by.

[51] Illich, "The Cultivation of Conspiracy," 233–42.

[52] Hopkins, "God's Grandeur," 76.

9

The Ice Pick Man

THE HEADLINE of a story in the newspaper stopped me: "Linchan pasajeros a asaltante en un microbús"—"Passengers lynch an assailant in a minibus." In fewer than a dozen short paragraphs, a scene of unspeakable hideousness was described: A young man got on a minibus, paid his fare, and found a seat late on a Friday evening in Mexico City. As the bus darted in and out through heavy urban traffic, the man got up from his seat, pulled out an ordinary ice pick, and threatened the twenty-odd passengers. He demanded their money but could not keep his eye on everyone all the time. One man, watching his chance, judging that he could risk a move, knocked the young man down when his eyes were turned.

Others in the bus immediately jumped on the would-be criminal, punching him with their fists, and violently kicking him. One person got his hands on the ice pick and repeatedly stabbed the felled extortionist. When they saw they had transformed him into a bruised and bloody corpse, all the passengers abandoned the vehicle.

The driver, with his gruesome cargo, meeting a police car, reported the turnabout assault.

Having arrived in Mexico City the day before, May 20, 2000, I picked up *La Jornada* at the breakfast table to see what I could learn of the atmosphere; I needed somehow to orient myself, to place myself again in this country. Various bits of news passed before my eyes, making little impact, until I came to the "ice pick man." The reporter, unable to learn his name, called him an *asaltante*, and a *delincuente*, but he was the only one assaulted and, as the affair ended, some unknown person, plunging the ice pick into his flesh, perhaps completely overcome by the passions of fear and rage, became a material delinquent. If the actual killer were overpowered by his emotions, his act was probably not that of a human, namely, not a *human* act, but that of a thoroughly frightened animal in human form. How could I attribute responsibility to him? The story stuck in my imagination, affected my mind, touched my heart, and may have produced a change in who I was, perhaps my very being.

During the past months, I had been thinking about "the other," for I was confused by what I had heard and read. Some suggested I examine the ideas of Emmanuel Lévinas. It was said that he had gone beyond Martin Buber in exploring one's relationship to another person, to the other. In fact, Lévinas placed this stance, for him an eminently *moral* action, at the origin of one's philosophical thinking.[1]

Critics of the historical development of science in the West, such as Donna Haraway, place great importance on the nefarious consequences of objectifying the other.[2] If the other is objectified, one is led into the anomalous notion of the reification of the person seen; if done habitually, of every person one meets. In the midst of my conversations and reflections, one idea gradually came to dominate my thought: I should pray for each person I meet, whether on the street or in the media. That might be the surest way to avoid making the other an object. On that Sunday morning in Mexico City, after meeting the Ice Pick Man, it seemed that my idea should be turned into a firm resolution.

Praying for him, for his fellow passengers and for the driver, too, I slowly came to see that I had again to challenge the idea of self, of what might be called a modern American self, the self who is encouraged to "realize all your potential," to "be anything you want." Not too long ago, I had come to think that one of the principal tasks facing affluent people in the "advanced" sectors of the world today is to find ways to supercede the self, to get beyond the so-called ego. I had begun to perceive the beauty of a selfless life in the portraits of certain others; I searched for stories of such witnesses, those who challenged a "me first" attitude. In the Christian tradition, a witness is one who attests to the truth through her or his words and life. With renewed interest, I pored over the lives of holy people, reexamining hagiographic records.

But most immediately and directly, my memory gave me images and stories of my father. He was a person I knew, and he was someone who, insofar as I could judge, lived a selfless life. The actions of his life, taken together, made an indelible impression on me. Looking into the

[1] See: *The Lévinas Reader*; Buber, *The Way of Response*.
[2] Haraway, *Modest Witness@Second Millennium*.

narrative of his time on earth more closely, I saw that he ordered his activities and ambitions around his wife and children, family and friends; he never sought out personal perks or self-serving diversions. His life exemplified a modest beauty.[3]

Any prayer for the other would have to be made in terms of what is good for the other, unless I were to succumb to the malevolence of a demon or witch. But to will good to the other is to take a step towards Aristotle's definition of friendship. Apparently I was seeking to ground myself in a tradition reaching into Greek thought. Reflecting on the matter, I saw that I sought something altogether different, quite beyond the philosophy of Aristotle. I wanted to reach into the eternal, there to grasp grace, a participation in God's very life, a gratuitous gift for the other, me. I could then love someone without being a friend, without even knowing the other person. So this kind of willing the good to the other took me to a new "place," seemingly one utterly surpassing the excellence of Greek friendship.

To pray for the Ice Pick Man and his fellow Mexicans was to take an interest in them, to learn about them, to come to know them. For if I turned to them in prayer, I would have to imagine their lives, thereby leaving my self during those moments of thought. This action opened the possibility that I might get better and better at such prayer, that I might be setting out on a path that would take me more and more . . . where? . . . well, into infinity; there can be no limit or end to my concern and love for the other, for each is infinitely knowable and lovable. I've learned that much from my own experience of friendships. So, through entering the life of another in this way, I might come to "know" the unknowable, the inexpressible—infinity!

I returned to the people on the minibus. How often I have taken such buses! Getting on, I usually had to bend over so as not to crack my head; always I had to search for an aisle seat, because my knees stuck out too far for me to fit on the window side. I never counted, but suspect there are no more than twenty seats on one of these buses. That evening, when the passengers realized they had killed the young man, they fled. Perhaps they were still moved mostly by their strongly disordered emotions; as in the killing, they were still unable to act reasonably. Who would dare say they were morally imputable for that death? For running and reporting nothing? But what a scene they left! And what a way for

[3] See chapters 8 and 9 in Hoinacki, *Stumbling Toward Justice,* 133–66; and chapter 1 in this volume.

someone to die! What frightful memories these people may carry until their deaths! What ghastly nightmares may trouble and awaken them when they least expect it.

Generally, the people I have met on minibuses in Mexico have been people from below, those who live at the bottom of the social pyramid. The paper reported that a similar killing had occurred on a city minibus within the previous six months. Is this an example of what people in the lower sectors sometimes, or often, experience? Many years earlier, I had seen some of the early movies the great Buñuel made in Mexico portraying, as caught in one title, *Los Olvidados*—The Forgotten Ones. His films portrayed images and scenes, stories and endings, which were indeed sordid and disturbing. But nothing in Buñuel's genius approached the horror I imagined in that minibus. Perhaps even Buñuel, in spite of his incredible power to conjure bizarre situations, was incapable of dreaming up such a dreadful scene.

The poor, threatening their fellow poor with violence, the poor, living and dying off the poor . . . What must have been the character and degree of desperation that drove the young man to make his foolish threat? The others, acting out of *their* passions—fear, anger, frustration with their life in this crowded and fast-paced city—pounced on him, an instinctive, animal response. How extravagant it would be to speak of guilt! . . . as I have understood the notion. In the face of such extreme destitution, guilt may be a bourgeois luxury. How far removed is my knowledge and experience from so much, from so many, in this world. I need to ask myself: In what sense is their world also my world?

While I'm in Mexico, I'll see hundreds of these buses shooting in and out of the frantic traffic, all of them transporting people from the nether regions, people I'll never meet, never know. I will most certainly never experience the Ice Pick Man's despondency suddenly transformed into terror. I can only imagine his and the other passengers' feelings that Friday night during the few minutes of this tragic drama. Their lives were all twisted into grisly savagery—against one another. Against whom else do they have the power to act?

How can I presume to take such persons into my heart? Reading the newspaper, reflecting on the story, I felt *something*; I believe, too, that I *learned* something. But it is not the kind of learning one generally gets from a book; perhaps it's learning one specifically *cannot* get from the Internet. Because the Ice Pick Man and his fellow city dwellers are in my imagination, running through my mind, stuck in my heart,

I feel I have some knowledge of them. Some piece of them has lodged in my awareness and will stay with me. How does that happen, for an effect demands a cause? Perhaps it is a grace; perhaps I have been blessed with a unique vicarious experience. Perhaps the practice of prayer for the other, and now for these unfortunate people somehow occasioned the grace. Perhaps I've learned something about the character of all prayer: Genuine prayer takes me out of self and gives me the other. If this is true, then I see the absolute importance of the other, but only if I see the other in this way, only if I do not objectify the other, only if I embrace the other as *my* self.

It would seem, then, that my practice is good: My initial thrust toward the other must always be to pray for that person. This action opens the other person to me, to my knowledge and love and, perhaps more importantly, it opens *my* heart, enabling me to escape the widespread contemporary solipsism of self; I can hope to live an honorable life.

From the newspaper I turned to the New Testament, and read the last epistle found there, the one written by Jude. Some editors separate the two verses at the end of the short letter's single chapter and name them what they are, a doxology. They read:

> To him who is able to keep you from falling and to present you before his glorious presence without fault and with great joy—to the only God our Savior be glory, majesty, power and authority, through Jesus Christ our Lord, before all ages, now and forevermore! Amen. (Jude 1:24–25)

The Incarnation establishes a truth partially seen by Socrates, and recorded in the prayer at the end of Plato's *Phaedrus*.[4] Shortly before he is arrested Jesus, in his prayer for the Apostles, says: "And glory has come to me through them" (John 17:10). For those who share the faith of the

---

[4] One of the most lovely passages in *The Dialogues*:

> Beloved Pan, and all ye other gods who haunt this place, give me the beauty in the inward soul; and may the outward and inward man be at one. May I reckon the wise to be the wealthy, and may I have such a quantity of gold as a temperate man and he only can bear and carry.

I never forgot and sometimes return to the prayer for I've always believed that if one is attracted to philosophy, to thought directed toward questions concerning a good life, to the quest for wisdom, Socrates' prayer is one of the best expressions from the Greek pre-Christian past of what it means to live lightly on the earth, in a word, to live well. Plato, *The Dialogues*, vol. 1, 282.

Apostles, a key question is: How do I give glory to God? How do I participate in a doxological life, a life foreshadowed in the faith and action of Abraham and a long stream of Semites?

Plato's *Phaedrus* invites a further argument: That the reality of language, a truth seen more clearly after the Incarnation, is derived from doxology. Doxologic language—words praising God—is the final, ontological source of all language. I can say that language not related to doxology, positively or negatively, does not exist. My speech, if it is doxologic, reaches toward the Beyond, perhaps "touches" the infinite, and thereby achieves existence; the infinite invests my words with reality. I am led to realize that language most truly exists long before writing. I cannot really understand this, but I feel strongly that it's true.[5] Importantly, the Ice Pick Man confirms this truth for me.

The confirmation occurs because of the very repulsive character of his death. Through such a death, he is mysteriously privileged to participate in the *kenosis*—the emptying out—of Jesus. He becomes one with the abandoned Lord of Calvary. Through this participation, he gives glory to God. Of course, only the believer can hope to grasp this. However, Hans Urs von Balthasar, in constructing a "theological aesthetics," points out that

> If the Cross radically puts an end to all worldly aesthetics, then precisely this end marks the decisive emergence of the divine aesthetic, but in saying this we must not forget that even worldly aesthetics cannot exclude the element of the ugly, of the tragically fragmented, of the demonic, but must come to terms with these. Every aesthetic which simply seeks to ignore these nocturnal sides of existence can itself from the outset be ignored as a sort of aestheticism. It is not only the limitation and precariousness of all beautiful form which intimately belongs to the phenomenon of beauty, but also fragmentation itself, because it is only through being fragmented that the beautiful really reveals the meaning of the eschatological promise it contains.[6]

I must come to see "the dialectic of revelation and concealment," in the words of von Balthasar, in order to approach a truth both of the Cross and of the Ice Pick Man.[7] In each instance, the descent into dark-

---

[5] For a recent study of the tradition, explicitly begun by Plato's *Phaedrus*, see Pickstock, *After Writing*.

[6] Balthasar, *The Glory of the Lord*, 460.

[7] Balthasar, 459–69.

ness reveals the reality of sin and, paradoxically, the glory of redemption. The deformity suffered by the Lord is "understandable" *only* as a function of his love. The existence and teaching of the Christ, leading up to the hideous death on the Cross, is conceivable only when I see its rootedness in salvation history; and the Cross shines out with a unique splendor, reaching into that minibus; an eschatological illumination is already present.

All of this is wondrously verified by the historical record in a succession of fools. Among the Greeks, we find Diogenes of Sinope; according to the comic wit of Aristophanes, Socrates, too, fitted the notion.[8] For believers in the Gospel, the archetypical form is definitively realized in the foolishness of the Cross. Although many witnesses have attempted to imitate the example of the Supreme Fool, St. Francis of Assisi is probably the one who most perfectly incarnated the divine example. I sometimes read that holy fools are "explained" by learned psychologizing analysts, and the Ice Pick Man certainly invites the superficiality of academic social theorists. But thinkers who confine themselves to the natural order cannot reach the transcendental and eternal "realm" where the first fool of the new dispensation embraces the latter-day fool of Mexico City.

Johann Georg Hamann writes well of my stance before the *kenosis* of both Jesus and the Ice Pick Man:

> "One and the same proof both of the most glorious majesty and the most radical self-emptying! One and the same wonder exhibits, on the one hand, such infinite stillness that God seems equated with nothingness and one must either conscientiously deny his existence or be no more than a dumb ox. But, on the other hand, this same wonder possesses such infinite power that it fulfills all things and one is at a loss as to how to escape the intimate ardor of its activity."[9]

---

[8] Aristophanes, *Clouds*.

[9] Hamann, *Sämtliche Werke*, vol. 2, 204. Quoted by Balthasar, *Seeing the Form*, 82. Balthasar notes that "Hamann sees glory as *kenosis* being proper not only to the God who became man, but even before that to the Creator who, by creating, penetrates into nothingness—proper, also, to the Holy Spirit, who conceals himself 'under all kinds of rags and tatters,' 'under the rubbish' of the letter of Scripture, in such a way that 'truly enlightened and enthusiastic eyes are needed . . . [to] recognize the rays of heavenly splendour dressed in such a disguise'."

For me to turn from my self-image to the image of God, seen in these two instances of horrendous death, I must become a contrite believer. That demands a conversion, the realization that I, as sinner, am fully revealed or realized only in the concealed essence of the two fools. Then I can reach a truth: The Ice Pick Man suffered and died for me.[10] Reading the paper that Sunday morning, I was slowly beginning to see and understand the hidden purposes of my presence in Mexico City.

Through his silent speech, the Ice Pick Man embodies a truth celebrated by Pseudo-Dionysius; he lives as an apophatic witness. By his very muteness, he reveals to me "the really mystical darkness of unknowing," for he entered "the dark beyond all light."[11] An analogy of proportionality takes me close to the truth of the conundrum alluded to by Pseudo-Dionysius. As I cannot expect to probe the interior dispositions of the Ice Pick Man, so I cannot penetrate the hidden reality of God. Knowledge of these two does not depend on intensity of effort but rather on loving attention. I can hope they reveal themselves to me.

In his short life, did doxologic words ever occur to him? Was he ever moved to raise his eyes heavenward, to the source of all good, all blessedness, and cry out in simple exultation? I wonder how he laughed. Did he ever know any pure and unfettered delights in his life? Did he ever mull over the pleasures of irony? Did he ever stop in awe, savoring the beauty of a poem? Did his eyes ever rest in the glory of a landscape, recognizing the beauty of the world as the tender smile of Jesus coming through matter, as Simone Weil did?[12] Did he ever experience the joys of friendship and love?

The more questions I ask, the more distant and unreal he appears. I know his world is radically foreign to me; I struggle to find some sensible link to him. He disturbs me with the tangible image of a genu-

---

[10] The source of this truth is twofold: First, the Ice Pick Man and I are united in the Communion of Saints, a traditional Christian teaching ultimately based on New Testament texts; and because of the interaction between time and eternity. St. Thomas Aquinas, asking the question whether the knowledge of God includes future contingents ("Utrum scientia Dei sit futurorum contingentium"), for example, that the Ice Pick Man be killed the day before I arrived in Mexico City, notes in his argument that the knowledge of God is measured by eternity, as is his existence. In eternity, however, everything exists simultaneously. ("sua cognitio mensuratur aeternitate, sicut etiam suum esse; aeternitas autem, totum simul existens, ambit totum tempus"). Aquinas, *Summa theologiae* I, q. 14, a. 13, corp. Several concepts in the reasoning are analogical, not univocal.

[11] Pseudo-Dionysius, *The Divine Names*, 214, 215.

[12] Weil, *Waiting for God*, 165.

inely deprived soul; he appears to be one of the truly poor of the world. Perhaps this is most essentially, most fundamentally, to be poor; this is poverty: not ever to raise one's heart and mind and soul in doxological praise and rejoicing.

I have never really known such a man, and it's most likely I never will. But there must be many such in the world, those at the bottom, moving slowly or rapidly toward or away from the edge of despair. I keep thinking that despair is the notion that most accurately captures what he was—desperate. Previously, I had always associated despair with suicide. But suicide may be, for some or many, a kind of cowardice. Perhaps the suicidal person is not suffering from despair at all, but from some other complex of passions or emotions. The young man must have been feeling genuine despair, a despair that drove him to this foolhardy act or threat. Had he actually thought about what it would be like to try to stab someone with an ice pick on a moving minibus? What would all the other passengers do? Remain seated calmly, or be frozen with extreme fright? *Could* he have actually stabbed an uncooperative passenger with an ice pick? If he had tried to stab someone, another would surely seize the opportunity to attack him, which happened even before he could begin to carry out his threat.

From the perspective of himself as actor, and of the others as potential victims who could, however, avoid or thwart his action, there seems no way he could be a successful thief. The entire episode could have only one end: what did in fact occur. The passengers, moved by their frustrations and passions, falling on the poor fellow, hitting and kicking him until someone happened to get the ice pick . . . then stabbing the wretch over and over as he lay there. How long was he conscious? How soon did death mercifully come? It seems impossible to ask the ultimate question: How did a loving God regard the scene?

I returned to the doxology of Jude. I wanted to appropriate it, take it to myself, enter it; I seemed to feel a certain consonance between those words and myself, similar to what I feel when I read the poetry of Gerard Manley Hopkins, or when I try to pray the Psalms. I believe that the world of doxology is one, and includes certain works of imaginative literature. Further, I believe there is a reality to that world, the world of the doxologies of the Sunday liturgy, of Hopkins' poetry, and of the resonances I find in the Psalms. Also, that it is in some way related to the sensible world I see and feel, in which I breathe. This sensible world came to me in a new way that Sunday morning in Mexico City.

However, I did not see and touch the Ice Pick Man. Perhaps through my imagination I could feel him. Finally, I realize I am invited to live in both worlds, that of doxology and that of sense, for they are one.

For Hopkins, there is no opposition between the sense image and the liturgical act, between the perception of God in nature and in the history of salvation. Through the recitation of liturgical words and poetical language, genuine feelings are aroused in my soul. These feelings bear witness to a reality independent of me and my perceptions, a reality infinitely more real than that found in conventional literary estheticism. Then, through my becoming aware of these intimations of eternity, a relationship is solidified between me and what is there—ultimate reality. So, through that contact, I am somehow taken outside my self; I am "lifted up" to a new plane so that, for a moment at least, I am enabled to live outside or beyond my wretched self. If I were able to practice habitually what in the Middle Ages was called a *lectio divina* (sacred reading), I could come to dwell in that world in a kind of permanence. The divinely-inspired words would enter me in such a way that I am carried nearer their source . . . to live *there*. The "natural" fit I vaguely sense between myself and that other world would become real.

But, in the midst of such so-called lofty thoughts, the Ice Pick Man entered my life. He was real, he was outside me, he was something more concrete and living than mere words. Once I learned about him, came to know him somewhat, something was established between us. What was this? What did it do to me? Does this experience relate to that of reciting a Hopkins poem? If so, is one more real than the other? Does one teach me about the other? Which would teach about which? Or is there some kind of dialectical relationship that goes on and on? I go from one to the other, and then back, always getting farther and farther from self in a never-ending movement until death. This may be another experience of the infinite, an opening into eternity.

Perhaps I must hold in my heart the truth of two realities simultaneously: the Ice Pick Man and what lies behind the Psalms. Both are real, but separate from the reality of the table on which I write. I feel that all three are equally real. I also feel that I should attempt to place more importance on my relationship to the Ice Pick Man than to either my immediate surroundings or the splendor of doxology. I suspect that concentration on the experience of liturgy or poetry can lead to a false exaltation of self, and thus to the growth of perilous illusions. How exciting to imagine myself a sojourner in an exalted realm, a *genuine* esthete, an assiduous pray-er! But, on the other hand, thinking I have any connection to the Ice Pick Man seems false, a lie. Even the suggestion of a relationship between him and me appears to be nonsensical, or a perverse presumption. In some sense, however, he came into my life, and now sticks there. As I've seen, he's an important reason why I am in Mexico: Through him, I'm learning who I am, how I am to live. My task now is to search out the sense and extension of this insight.

I have strongly believed there are reasons, there is meaning, for what happens to me; there is no reality in chance happenings; every future contingent, what appears to me as chance, is foreordained in the loving governance of God's providence. This is a belief; obviously, I cannot understand or prove it. But one of the exercises that follow on having a mind is to explore the wonders of this providence, the discernible brushes with divine love in my life.

On a Sunday morning, I picked up the paper at breakfast, ostensibly to get some sense of what is going on in Mexico, the place where I would spend the coming weeks. The only impression the paper made on my sensibilities was to introduce an unknown man to me. Now he does not leave me. Why? Well, I realized anew that I met him—an other—in order to pray for him. Further, I came to see, more forcefully than ever before in my life, that I should be the person who prays for all whom I meet, either in person or through the media. This practice enables me to know who I am. If I realize the practice, continually carry it out, then I will come to be, I will come to exist, for this is the reality of my being, this is my ontological truth. To the extent I fall short of it, in that measure I participate less in existence, I *am* less, I descend into moral nothingness.

All creatures, because they are creatures, enjoy only a participated existence; they are not their own raison d'être. Those who are conscious and reflective, like myself, can exist more, and less, can be more and less real. The Ice Pick Man holds the secret as to why I am in Mexico: The reason has to do with ontology, indeed, with what lies beyond ontology, and *not* with some ephemeral search for self, nor with a vague realization of my destiny.

But I must be careful . . . not to use him! not to instrumentalize him. I believe that what Simone Weil says is true: there is no finality in *this* world; all is a means . . . except for beauty. For her, however, the beauty that is not a means is the beauty of the entire universe, not some particular beauty that catches my attention—this landscape, or that attractive woman. These particular or partial beauties are good as openings to universal beauty. But if I stop at them, they become stumbling blocks, they corrupt my desire. Universal beauty, however, is the good in itself; in the sense of the scholastics, it is a transcendental. I think, though, that the Ice Pick Man has revealed something further about beauty to me. He clearly tells me that beauty is an analogous concept, and that I can begin to intuit what Simone Weil terms universal beauty, I can grasp a bit of the transcendental, here and now.[13]

He came to me in his despair, presenting me with his abominable death and lies before me, a bloody mess. He also presents me with the violence of those who were moved to lunge at him, to pummel, maul, strike, and stab him, until he died from the assault. As I've already re-marked, the scene must have been horribly ugly, grotesque beyond any imagining. Yet it was but a tiny event, hardly to be noticed in a city of millions, occurring on the floor of a minibus, seen by only a handful of people. But these few may see it again and again in their memories and dreams; some may struggle mightily to free themselves from the sight. What perhaps three or four did, what a few more saw, stands at an extreme and opposite pole from the beauty of the universe. Was it not truly ugly?

As noted, Simone Weil maintains that, ultimately, the real beauty to be seen in this world is the beauty of the entire universe. But that's a reality that cannot be sensed, cannot be seen. I think, however, that the Ice Pick Man enlarges on her opinion. With his grisly death, he manifests the most sublime beauty one can see on this earth; but it is an apophatic beauty; a beauty analogous to what cannot be spoken. I can approach the truth of beauty in the minibus, because the event is at such an opposite extreme to what is ordinarily understood as created beauty. In creation, there are many kinds and levels of lesser beauty, for example, that of an infant's smile, of a wild flower, of a sculpture, of a cloud formation, of music. But one cannot see *the* manifestation of cre-ated beauty, the beauty of the universe.

The Ice Pick Man's death may be an icon through which I can see uncreated beauty, the beauty I want to see so that I might reach my proper, my true good. I can't move unless I first see or perceive. Perhaps this is what Pseudo-Dionysius meant when he wrote about knowing God, about naming God's "properties." He said that, when predicat-

---

[13] Weil, 166–67.

ing something of God, one should use metaphors of lowly and common, not of high and sublime things. St. Thomas Aquinas, accepting this teaching, gives some reasons why it is sound. Through these figures, the human spirit is thereby better freed from error, for it is manifestly evident that such tropes cannot be divine. If divine realities were described with the noblest images, one might mistake the figure for the real. Further, such humble or vulgar ways of speaking are more proper to our ways of knowing God in this life: they show what God is *not*, rather than what he *is*.[14]

All knowledge, according to Aristotle and St. Thomas, is based on sense perception. But there can be no sense perception of universal beauty. I have only perceived tiny pieces of beauty: a giant Sequoia, a majestic cathedral, a glorious sunset over the Pacific. I might then be moved to an erroneous belief that I have seen beauty, *tout court*. But that would be illusory. My perception cannot encompass so much, cannot extend so far.

However, I can imagine the Ice Pick Man in his agony. I have seen and held an ice pick. I have seen a person being struck. I have felt fear and anger. I don't have to be there, physically, to know what occurred. I think my imagination can serve me well. And if I see truly, I will see, not ugliness, but beauty. The Ice Pick Man has revealed this truth to me, for the Gospel instructs me on how to understand and interpret the awesome disclosure.

To see beauty is to perceive the true and the good as they simultaneously shine out with a certain splendor. For the believer, Christ is the true image of the Father. Seeing him walking among us, we see the splendor of God. But both darkness and light are contained in Christ. Through his Cross, he enters into the most abysmal ugliness, that of sin. If I can see this, as I know from reflection on my own sins, and heeding the testimony of many witnesses over the past two thousand years, I will in that act of seeing be carried away, pulled outside myself. Such can be the reality of my life. As Balthasar writes, " . . . God's Incarnation perfects the whole ontology and aesthetics of created being."[15] But it's the very loathsomeness of the scene in the minibus that allows me to recognize this truth, the real, the perfection of creation in the Cross.

---

[14] Aquinas, *Summa theologiae*, I, q. 1, a. 4, ad 3. In this place, St. Thomas comments favorably on the opinion of Pseudo-Dionysius. He refers to the writer as Dionysius. Later historical scholarship added the "Pseudo."

[15] Balthasar, *Seeing the Form*, 29.

In Christian tradition, various writers have commented on the *kenosis*, the emptying out of Jesus in his passion and death. Not only did these acts of obedience obtain salvation for humankind, but they tell us something about beauty. There is a consensus among Christian thinkers that the death of Jesus was the most terrible that could occur; no person's death can be worse, because the death on the cross was the death of the God-man. I've learned that the suffering and death of the Ice Pick Man can throw light on the suffering and death of Jesus, and vice versa.

The Lord, the Son of God, reveals, through the mystery of the lowliness of the God-man, most perfectly in his suffering and death, the primal splendor of the love of a God who thus humiliates himself. One sees the most glorious majesty and the most radical self-emptying united in him, in his death. What I see here is (divine) glory as *kenosis*. I am prepared for this seeing by reflecting on the prior action of the Creator penetrating nothingness, and by the Holy Spirit concealing herself under the "rubbish" of the Hebrew and Greek Testaments. One needs the eyes of a lover to recognize the radiance of heavenly splendor shining through such a shaded curtain. Through the folly of the Cross, I can find access to the exemplary beauty of human existence, to the mysterious core of all reality. I am thus permitted to see the truth of the Ice Pick Man.[16] The mystery of faith allows the believer to see the beauty of suffering and death in both persons. But a crucial qualification must be added: Seeing can only occur after a conversion; Jesus demands the complete turning inside out of the person, a transformation, "the movement of man's [*sic*] whole being away from himself and towards God through Christ.[17]

For the believer, the Lord is present in every person, in every person's flesh. That is the meaning taught by St. Paul when he says that we are all members of one body, and that body is Christ, is the Church: "Now you are the body of Christ, and each one of you is a part of it" (1 Cor 12:27). So the Lord was present in all the persons on the minibus in Mexico City that Friday evening; he was present in his agony. If I can arrive at some awareness of the reality of these people, of their pain, of their suffering bodies, I will come close to the Lord in *his* suffering. Then, the awareness should move back and forth in a dialectical fashion, as I remarked above. Each motion will bring me closer to the reality of his love and pain, and at the same time give me greater compassion for

---

[16] Balthasar, *Seeing the Form*, 82.

[17] Balthasar, *The Glory of the Lord*, 121.

the suffering of those whom he loves, for whom he died. *The* reaction, when I see the other, is to see that person in this context, which means that I see the other, every other, in the Lord's agony.

This kind of seeing illuminates and makes meaningful what I have often experienced and remarked. All the persons I have known live in some kind of pain. If I think I meet someone who does not live in pain it may be that I don't know the person very well, or the person has been able to distract and drug herself so that little or nothing is left of a sentient being.

St. Paul says,

> . . . I fill up in my flesh what is still lacking in regard to Christ's afflictions, for the sake of his body, which is the church (Col 1:24).

It must be true that all affliction in the history of the world is in some mysterious way filling up what "is still lacking in . . . Christ's afflictions." After the Incarnation no bodily person is the same: the fact of God taking on human flesh affects *all* flesh; it must be that way. Otherwise Jesus could not have said, "For I was hungry and you gave me something to eat . . . " (Matt 25:31–46). So, he *is* the Ice Pick Man, he *is* the driver and other passengers in the bus, he is the person in pain from the beginning of the world until he comes again in glory. All these persons are making up what is lacking in the affliction of the Christ. Here I enter unintelligible regions, but which, I believe, remain the realm of truth.

The Ice Pick Man also confirms what I understand Shusako Endo to mean in his novel, *Silence*. But, strictly speaking, I cannot accurately state what the story relates; one must read it to see how Endo's talent and skill permit him to show how Christ can be Judas and Judas Christ.[18] In the minibus, the Ice Pick Man was seemingly prepared to kill a fellow passenger. If a Samaritan-figure touches Christ today, then a Judas-figure must do the same. The victim in each case must be the Lord.[19] If the Lord is one, he is also the other, for he is all victims over all time. But as

---

[18] Endo, *Silence*.

[19] At the final judgment, the Son of Man will separate all people "'as a shepherd separates the sheep from the goats'." To those on his right he will say, "'I tell you the truth, whatever you did for one of the least of these brothers of mine, you did for me'." He condemns those on his left, who did not reach out to assist those in trouble. A hard parable. See Matt 25:31–46.

it turned out, the Ice Pick Man became the person stabbed and killed; he passed from being a Christ-killer to being a Christ-victim.

I think I can understand better why I was moved to pray for the Ice Pick Man, and why he sticks in my memory: because of something I read in Simone Weil. She wrote that

> There is a reality outside the world, that is to say, outside space and time, outside man's mental universe, outside any sphere whatsoever that is accessible to human faculties. Corresponding to this reality, at the centre of the human heart, is the longing for an absolute good, a longing which is always there and is never appeased by any object in this world.
>
> Another terrestrial manifestation of this reality lies in the absurd and insoluble contradictions which are always the terminus of human thought when it moves exclusively in this world.[20]

If I remain "exclusively in this world" in my attempt to understand what happened in the minibus that night, that is, if I push thought as far as it can go, I end in "absurd and insoluble contradictions." But if I get beyond this world, I can then approach the meaning of her position:

> The combination of these two facts—the longing in the depth of the heart for absolute good, and the power, though only latent, of directing attention and love to a reality beyond the world and of receiving good from it—constitutes a link which attaches every man without exception to that other reality.
>
> Whoever recognizes that reality recognizes also that link. Because of it, he holds every human being without any exception as something sacred to which he is bound to show respect.[21]

If I see the link that unites me to the Ice Pick Man, I see how I am bound to show him respect, then to love him, for we are one in our longing for absolute good.

This unity is what constitutes the reality of the Church, of Christ's body in time. Once he came, died, and rose from the grave, he made all of us members of his body, the Church. It is highly probably that the Ice Pick Man was baptized, an explicit member of the Church. Once the story of the Samaritan is told, we know that each of us is invited to share in the life of this body through reaching out to the other in the

---

[20] Miles, *Simone Weil*, 201–2. Siân Miles writes an excellent Introduction to the anthology.

[21] Miles, *Simone Weil*, 202–3.

ditch. My action can be the prolongation of the Lord's action. This is the task Jesus gives each of us to do, this is his gift to us: to share in his beneficent action. In every moment, some other stands in front of me, either in the flesh or in my imagination. If this is not true, then it may be that I am locked into regarding self alone. I am trapped in self. The mirror is perhaps a fitting trope; I must fear it; it is an instrument of loss, of getting lost in self.

There are only two ways to look—outwardly or inwardly. To look outwardly can lead to love, to prayer for the other. Actually, this is the way to look; the way I am given to look; morally, there is no other way. But I am free to be perverse, free to violate the truth, free to deny what is. Now I can begin to understand what I read in *The Dialogue* of St. Catherine of Siena. In the past, I have sometimes been critical of certain persons and actions I saw in the Mexican church and in the Vatican. The utter deformity of my complaints now becomes clear. Speaking in the third person for the book she dictated while in ecstasy, Catherine said:

> From her deep knowledge of herself, a holy justice gave birth to hatred and displeasure against herself, ashamed as she was of her imperfection, which seemed to her to be the cause of all the evil in the world. In this knowledge and hatred and justice she washed away the stains of guilt, which it seemed to her were, and which indeed were, in her own soul, saying, "O eternal Father, I accuse myself before you, asking that you punish my sins in this life. And since I by my sins am the cause of the sufferings my neighbors must endure, I beg you in mercy to punish me for them."

The Lord, eternal Truth, answered her, saying:

> True contrition satisfies for sin and its penalty not by virtue of any finite suffering you may bear, but by virtue of your infinite desire. For God, who is infinite, would have infinite love and infinite sorrow. . . . [G]uilt is not atoned for by any suffering simply as suffering, but rather by suffering borne with desire, love, and contrition of heart. The value is not in the suffering but in the soul's desire. Likewise, neither desire nor any other virtue has value or life except through my only-begotten Son, Christ crucified, since the soul has drawn love from him and in virtue follows his footsteps. In this way and in no other is suffering of value.[22]

[22] Catherine of Siena, *The Dialogue*, 27–9.

Catherine, who traveled to the papal court in Avignon in her attempts to reform the Church, saw lucidly, and described vividly, the corruption of the Church's ministers in the fourteenth century. She saw, with the clarity of a purified vision, the *kenosis* of Jesus in his body, the Church. But, and this is her unique contribution to the Western history of faith, she recognized that she herself was responsible for these wounds, because of her lack of love, her imperfections, her sinfulness. The truth of such thoughts and sentiments is not accessible and intelligible unless one is drawn into the realm of faith where she dwelled.

The Ice Pick Man, tortured, killed, deserted on the dirty floor of a minibus, like the bits of discarded garbage one sees on Mexico City streets, invited me to step into this realm. He revealed a new notion of responsibility to me . . . *I* am responsible for him, for the Church, in the sense that I have been greatly gifted, that I have been privileged by nature, by the institutions of society, by the Church. But these graces were not given for adornment, not bestowed for my personal pleasure or to feed my vanity. They were given that I might act as Jesus acted, as he loved. Did he not reach out to the other? Does he not reach out to me today through the presence and impact of the Ice Pick Man? My obligation, my "duty," my responsibility, is to see and act as St. Catherine did, to move both outwardly and inwardly. Looking at self, and considering my advantages and blessings, I can recognize myself as a most lowly wretch because of my serious and repeated infidelities. Looking out, I can embrace the other through compassion and prayer. Thus prepared, I will be moved to act when the opportunity arises.

Picking up the newspaper in Mexico City that Sunday morning was a rather unusual act for me. Generally, I'm not exposed to the media, whether through newspapers or magazines, radio or television, and I seldom use the Internet. Reading the paper that morning, I recognized that the report of the Ice Pick Man was carefully presented as a bit of objective information. No editorial or ideological coloring came through the words. An object was presented to me, and such an achievement is an ideal, the idea of objectivity current in many mainstream intellectual and/or social expressions. To stop and see what I saw in the Ice Pick Man, to embrace him, I had to get beyond the information. As I reflected on this possibility, I saw that I had to fight against objectivity.

The notion of objectivity has a long and complex history in the West. In the Middle Ages, philosophers and, as far as one can know people in general believed in the reality of the represented object. One aspect of the history that helps me understand something of the Ice Pick Man is that of religious images, specifically, in the iconoclastic controversy. In 726, the Byzantine Emperor, Leo III, removed the figure of Christ from the imperial palace gate in Constantinople. His action was the culmination of a many-faceted dispute over the use of images to represent the divine. Jews and Moslems were adamant in their opposition to any representation of God, while Christians were ambivalent. What is called the Iconoclastic Synod condemned John Damascene, a defender of images and their use, declaring that only one image has a divine guarantee and that it presents Christ in his totality, the Eucharist.

A bloody war between the factions was brought to an end in the reign of the Empress Irene when the ecumenical Council of Nicaea II (787) vindicated John Damascene and proclaimed the legitimate use of icons (Greek for "image"), a representation of Christ, Mary, an angel or saint, or an event in the history of salvation.

Three theological arguments in favor of the liturgical use of icons had been elaborated by St. John Damascene, who died around 750, and are based on an analogy. As Christ's human body is to his divinity, so the icon is to the reality behind it. Just as one gets to God through the humanity of Jesus Christ, so the prayerful Christian can reach the saint or the divinity of Christ through a physical image. One's gaze goes through the icon to the "other side," to where the saint or Christ dwells. The icon is the visible expression of the patristic formula, "God became man that man might become God." It is theology in visible form, *and* considered sacred in itself. One might say that an icon is an interactive medium between two worlds. In the Eastern Church, word and image are seen as two aspects of Revelation; both hearing and sight are necessary for the faithful to believe in Revelation.[23]

The Western Church, fundamentally marked by the artistic genius of Giotto (d. 1337), rapidly departed from the icons of the East. The very nature of the image in Western religious art changed. It is possible to trace a continuous development in the portrayal of sacred figures as they became more representational, more "real-looking." One result was that peoples' seeing changed; one's gaze stopped at the image; one had to force oneself to go beyond. The first objects, in a modern sense, were created by the men considered to be the great innovators in Western art.

---

[23] Among the many works on icons, one can usefully begin with Zibawi, *The Icon: Its Meaning and History*. The original arguments are found in St. John Damascene, *Holy Images*.

Because seeing images was transformed, so also seeing the other—in the flesh. The creation of the object was necessary for the advancement of conventional science; it was disastrous for my need to see my neighbor, or any other person, or my own self. The twentieth-century Orthodox nun, Mother Maria Skobtsova, said that "each person is the very icon of God incarnate in the world."[24] It is highly significant that the statement was voiced by an Eastern, not a Western person.

I had to fight my way through the objectivity of the newspaper report to reach the Ice Pick Man hidden behind the words. If I see the other objectively, as an object, then everything is permitted. For example, I can calmly read or see stories in the media like that of the Ice Pick Man, and continue eating breakfast or dinner. I can coolly read about bombs being dropped on an "enemy" because, ultimately, he or she is an object. I can eagerly desire the development of nanotechnology or genetic manipulation, for I'm dealing with objects; atomic particles and genes do not share the same created/participated existence as I; there's a radical distinction between them and me.

It would seem that, through the documented history of the image in the West, I can maintain that objectification, one important example of which is seeing the other as object, came into people's awareness, practice, and very being through a twisting of the presentation of Christian Revelation. The creation of the object begins with Giotto. To look into this history carefully is one of the principal pathways into the mystery of iniquity (the *mysterium iniquitatis*), the presence of evil in our world. If one examines thoroughly the question of the object, one is led into the heart of darkness, into the mystery of evil. The cutting edge of science/technology today is not a threshold on the other side of which unpleasant monstrosities may lurk—the concern of academics—but the lure of terrible temptations to embrace the demonic.

As the horrific death of the Ice Pick Man shows, the evil of which people are capable is truly awful. And it is necessary to conclude that this evil is of a worse character than a similar action carried out before Jesus appeared on earth. Once his teaching about turning the other cheek, about loving the other, entered history, the world was different. I am compelled to ask: Does the sublimity, the exalted character of his love demand, on the other side, a corresponding darkness, a horrid malignancy? If that is true, and I suspect it is, then I do indeed touch on

[24] Quoted in Ellsberg, *All Saints*, 145. For the complete story, see Smith, *The Rebel Nun*.

mystery, on something I cannot understand, on something no one will ever understand. I can only shake my head in wonder.

Earlier, I discussed the possibility of seeing beauty. I think I now understand how to form some idea, some notion, of beauty as a transcendental, although I'm uncertain how to express this truth well. Pushing the insight of Pseudo-Dionysius farther, I think his thought leads to a possible way: One can approach beauty through ugliness. For the most radiant and dazzling beauty, I need to look at the most repulsive thing imaginable. It seems to me that the entire episode of the Ice Pick Man is an example of such a thing. When I take into account his desperation before getting on the bus, the passions and bloody actions provoked in the passengers, the memories that will plague these people until their death, I cannot think of anything worse; I can think of nothing more opposed to the beautiful.

10

The White Rose

Treasonable Actions

EVERY SEAT in the Munich courtroom was filled, mostly by men in the brown or black uniforms of the *Wehrmacht*, the *SS*, *SA*, or the police, all there by invitation. The families of the accused students—Hans Scholl, Sophie Scholl, and Christoph Probst—were not officially informed of the trial which took place on February 22, 1943, and no one of them was present at the beginning.

The judges entered, led by Dr. Roland Freisler, the dreaded president of the Peoples' Court, who had flown down from Berlin to carry out a swift judgment on the impertinent young people who had dared to shock the regime by their condemnation of Hitler and calls for resistance. Freisler has been characterized as "one of the most repellent figures" in the Nazi constellation of power, and he appeared to be a dedicated and fanatical participant in Hitler's crimes.[1] While presiding over trials he would shout at the accused and in his flaming robes gesticulate wildly. With Freisler's performance, there seemed to be no need for a prosecutor.

Unbelievably, the twenty-one-year-old Sophie calmly interrupted his raving during the farcical proceedings: "Somebody had to make a start. What we said and wrote are what many people are thinking. They just don't dare say it out loud!"[2] The young woman spoke out of an inner tranquility, manifesting an amazing boldness in a threatening and hostile setting. She may have been the youngest person and the only woman in the courtroom. Later, Sophie again raised her voice, throwing

---

[1] Domback and Newborn, *Shattering the German Night. The Story of the White Rose*, 201.

[2] Hanser, *A Noble Treason. The Revolt of the Munich Students Against Hitler*, 21.

a defiant judgment into the faces of Freisler and the uniformed men: "You know the war is lost. Why don't you have the courage to face it?"[3] Sophie confronted the National Socialist partisans with an outrageous opinion; almost all of Germany was celebrating the country's military victories on land and sea.

Freisler and the other judges were dressed in blood-red robes, black and red swastika flags blatantly decorated the walls, the colorful accoutrements of nationalistic fervor.[4] All staged events in the country were carefully designed to glorify National Socialism and the Führer, Adolf Hitler. Each such scene appeared cunningly devised for the genius of Leni Riefenstahl to make yet another stirring propaganda film, as she had done with *Triumph of the Will*, a powerful chronicle of the party congress of 1934.

Inge Scholl, Hans and Sophie's sister, in a book first published in 1952, wrote that "some people mocked and vilified them, others described them as heroes of freedom."[5] But no one could deny the utter foolhardiness of their protest. Inge Scholl adds:

> It is perhaps more difficult to stand up for a worthy cause when there is no general enthusiasm, no great idealistic upsurge, no high goal, no supporting organization, and thus no obligation; when, in short, one risks one's life on one's own and in lonely isolation.[6]

Many in Germany were angry and hurt by the vindictive Treaty of Versailles, many demoralized by the Weimar Republic. Into this confused and dispirited people Hitler stepped with his cunning, promises, charisma and occasional brutality. The Nazis appeared as restorers of moral and spiritual values in a nation that, to many, appeared decadent.[7] Hitler assured the people they would achieve greatness and prosperity:

> He would not rest until every German was independent, free and happy in his fatherland. We [Inge Scholl writes] found this good, and we were willing to do all we could to contribute to the common effort. But there was something else that drew us

---

[3] Hanser, *A Noble Treason*, 274.

[4] Hoffmann, *The History of the German Resistance 1933–1945*. Hoffmann writes of Freisler and his death in a bombing raid, 525–27.

[5] Scholl, *The White Rose*, 4.

[6] Ibid.

[7] Nicholls, *Systematic and Philosophical Theology*, 110.

with mysterious power and swept us along: the closed ranks of marching youth with banners waving, eyes fixed straight ahead, keeping tune to drumbeat and song. Was not this sense of fellowship overpowering? It is not surprising that all of us, Hans and Sophie and the others, joined the Hitler Youth.[8]

Hitler, a great populist leader, delivered on his promises to bring the country out of the Great Depression. His government led the nation into a flourishing economy. By the time Germany invaded Poland the Third Reich was generally prosperous. In the belief of some scholars, had Hitler died in 1938, he probably would be regarded as the greatest leader ever to have appeared in German history.[9] Another claims that "the Germans . . . adored the Führer." Around him, a quasi-religious cult arose.[10] But I do not want to propose an "intentionalist" interpretation of the Third Reich, placing great emphasis on the character and genius of Adolf Hitler. Nor do I want to adopt a "functionalist" view, highlighting the structures and direction of German society under the National Socialists within a larger context, namely, in the midst of an industrial mode of production being applied to the goods and services sectors.[11]

The writing of history is neither objective nor scientific. Such concepts are little more than labels. And I don't believe there is a literal historical record that can be retrieved from the documents, what I would term a linguistic reductionism. The deaths of the White Rose people are the principal text. All interpretation centers on this datum and the writer's imagination.[12] The writer, in turn, is a person and to some extent a participant in the material of history. I write from a certain perspective and with a definite purpose.

As Inge Scholl remarks, the Nazi authorities made great efforts to mobilize the youth of Germany, seemingly giving them a higher purpose for living, instilling in them a great pride in their country, fostering an absolute and unquestioning devotion to the Third Reich. Therefore, Freisler and the other officials of the Nazi hierarchy were bewildered. So much was done for German youth, so many of the nation's resources were

---

[8] Scholl, *The White Rose,* 6.

[9] Lukacs, *The Hitler of History,* 95. On page 258 Lukacs also claims that "He [Hitler] was the greatest revolutionary of the twentieth century."

[10] Deák, "Why did they love him?" 4.

[11] See Childers and Caplan, *Reevaluating the Third Reich.*

[12] See Harris, *Lourdes. Body and Spirit in the Secular Age,* xvi–xviii. For an extensive chronology, see Graml, *The German Resistance to Hitler,* xv–xx.

devoted to their future, and yet a handful of attractive and intelligent students directly challenged and cuttingly condemned the regime. Hans and his companions moved when Hitler was at the height of his success and power. They did not wait until the government was definitely failing, heading for defeat, as was the case of the German generals involved in the July 20, 1944 plot.[13] The most famous attempt to kill Hitler, for which many were executed or forced to commit suicide, serves greatly " . . .to fuel the myth of an aristocratic resistance to Hitler."[14]

The German people opposed to the Nazis were caught in a terrible drama that divided them. Some believed they had to endure the National Socialists until the Allies won the war and freed Germany. Others were convinced the Germans themselves had to act. Hans and those participating in or associated with the White Rose judged that the Nazi evil was such that an exorcism could only succeed through the people rising up and rebelling.

In their first distributed flyer, Hans and his friend Alex Schmorell wrote:

> It is certain that today every honest German is ashamed of his government. Who among us has any conception of the dimensions of shame that will befall us and our children when one day the veil has fallen from our eyes and the most horrible of crimes—crimes that infinitely outdistance every human measure—reach the light of day?

The young men spoke with vehemence in their summons to the German people, calling for them to offer resistance " . . . before it is too late . . . before the nation's last young man has given his blood on some battlefield for the *hubris* of a sub-human."

In the second flyer, they toughened their accusation:

> The German people stumble on in their dull, stupid sleep and encourage these fascist criminals; they give them the opportunity to carry on their depredations; and of course they do so.

In the fourth flyer, the daring young resisters reached for the infinite:

> Every word that comes from Hitler's mouth is a lie. When he says peace, he means war, and when he blasphemously uses the name of the Almighty, he means the power of evil, the fallen

[13] See Hanser, *A Noble Treason*, 131, 187.
[14] Smith, "Resistance to Hitler," 19.

angel, Satan. His mouth is the foul-smelling mow of Hell, and
his might is at bottom accursed.

The youngsters were beginning to express the reality of National Socialist
Germany in a theological perspective. But this did not mean to deny or
downplay peoples' complicity. They ended the flyer with: "We will not
be silent. We are your bad conscience. The White Rose will not leave
you in peace!"[15] Hitler, with his cult of the people, was a populist na-
tionalist, standing for and approving only a certain kind of patriotism.
Hans and Sophie Scholl called their fellow Germans back to a more
traditional patriotism that emphasized a love for the land and the good
in its history.[16]

A contemporary, Friedrich Reck-Malleczewen, speaking of Hans
and Sophie Scholl in a secret manuscript, wrote in the month following
their trial:

> The Scholls are the first in Germany to have had the courage to
> witness for the truth. The movement they left at their death will
> go on, and as is always the case with martyrdom, they have sown
> seeds which will raise important fruit in time to come.[17]

Robert Mohr, Sophie's interrogator in the few days before her execution, apparently moved by the simplicity and innocence of the young
woman, attempted to help her find a way out, to avoid death. He suggested she had gone along with her brother, not fully realizing what she
was doing. Sophie let him finish his offer and immediately countered:
she was not misled by Hans; she knew what she was doing; she agreed
completely with her brother. Mohr tried to point out how she was de-
luded. She quickly responded, "It is not I but you, Herr Mohr, who have
the wrong Weltanschauung. I would do the same thing again."[18]

The parents, Robert and Magdalene Scholl, having heard about the
arrest from friends, rushed to Munich, found the courtroom, and forced
their way in after the trial had started. Freisler ordered them ejected.
Before they were thrown out, Robert Scholl shouted, "One day there

---

[15] The quoted words are found in Scholl, *The White Rose*, 73, 74, 79, 85, and 88,
respectively.

[16] See Lukacs, *The Hitler of History*, 260, footnote #9.

[17] Reck-Malleczewen, *Diary of a Man in Despair*, 179.

[18] Hanser, *A Noble Treason*, 264–65; Scholl, *The White Rose*, 143.

will be another kind of justice!" And, as the door was closing, he added. "They will go down in history!"[19]

Because the rules were bent, the parents were able to visit their children briefly in Stadelheim prison after the trial. Hans was the first to be brought out to the visitors' barrier. Among his brief comments, he assured them: "I have no hatred. I have put everything, everything behind me." After Hans was taken back to his cell, Sophie was led in, she entered with a smile. Her mother, distraught, searched for appropriate words. "So now you will never again set foot in our house." Sophie quietly replied, "Oh, what do these few short years matter, mother?" Then, speaking with the same conviction as Hans, she openly declared, "We took all the blame, for everything." Which is exactly what she and Hans did; they revealed the names of no one else; they claimed they alone were responsible for the flyers and inscriptions on the city's walls (for example, "DOWN WITH HITLER!"). To her mother, she expressed her only hope: "That [what we did] is bound to have its effect in time to come." Christoph Probst did not even have the consolation of seeing his family before he died. They did not learn of the students' fate until after the execution.

Else Gebel, a political prisoner, was put in the same cell with Sophie to keep an eye on her. After the war she wrote to the Scholl family, giving them details and impressions of Sophie and Hans, and Christoph. She composed her letter as if speaking to Sophie:

> I begin to be amazed at you. These many hours of interrogation have no effect on your calm, relaxed manner. Your unshakable faith gives you the strength to sacrifice yourself for the sake of others.

On Saturday, two days after their arrest, Sophie again experienced hours and hours of questioning. Else tried to comfort her:

> . . . you will be left in peace until Monday morning . . . [but that] doesn't please you at all. You find the questioning stimulating, interesting. At least you have the good fortune to have one of the few likable investigators [Robert Mohr].

The next day Sophie, "in a soft, calm voice," expressed these reflections:

> It is such a splendid, sunny day, and I have to go [to my death]. But how many have to die on the battlefield in these days, how

[19] Hanser, 276.

many young, promising lives. . . . What does my death matter if by our acts thousands of people are warned and alerted. Among the student body there will certainly be a revolt.[20]

Sophie's hope, expressed by all the members of the White Rose in the weeks before their arrest, and immediately before their death, was not fulfilled. There were only several isolated actions, for example, a few days after the execution a new statement appeared on a wall at the university: "Scholl lives! You can break the body, but never the spirit!" On April 20th, Hitler's birthday, his portrait at the university displayed a defiant judgment: "Germany's Enemy Number One."[21]

Shortly after the trial and executions, the regime scheduled a meeting at the university, a special rally to demonstrate loyalty to the State and its leader. Hundreds of students attended and Jakob Schmied, the building custodian who saw Hans and Sophie scattering flyers from a balcony in the university's principal building and gave the alarm, was greeted with great applause.

In her book, Inge Scholl records the impression Hans, Sophie and Christoph made on the prison guards:

> They bore themselves with marvelous bravery. The whole prison was impressed by them. That is why we risked bringing the three of them together once more—at the last moment before the execution. If our action had become known, the consequences for us would have been serious. We wanted to let them have a cigarette together before the end. It was just a few minutes that they had, but I believe that it meant a great deal to them. "I didn't know that dying can be so easy," said Christl Probst, adding, "In a few minutes we will meet in eternity."
>
> Then they were led off, the girl first. She went without a flicker of an eyelash. None of us understood how this was possible. The executioner said he had never seen anyone meet his end as she did.[22]

Every account of the White Rose story is unanimous: The three young people, not yet thirty, from the moment they were caught until

---

[20] The quoted words are found in Scholl, *The White Rose*, 61, 61–2, 142, 143, 144–5, respectively.

[21] Dombach and Newborn, *Shattering the German Night*, 213–4.

[22] Scholl, *The White Rose*, 62.

the guillotine cut off their heads manifested a calmness and courage before which one must stand in awe.[23] Hearing of their actions and death, Reck-Malleczewen wrote in his secret manuscript that Hans and Sophie, "in the radiance of their courage . . . attained the pinnacle in lives well lived." He wanted these words carved on their tombstones: "Cogi non potest quisquis mori scit" (He who knows how to die can never be enslaved). And added: "We will all of us someday have to make a pilgrimage to their graves and stand before them, ashamed." He, too, hoped they would be "the *first* Germans of a great rebirth of the spirit." But he would not live to see his hope dashed; he was executed on February 23, 1945, shortly before the end of the war, in Dachau, shot in the neck (*Genickschuss*).[24]

Considering their unruffled behavior when arrested, their clarity and single-mindedness during the long interrogations, their composure and forthright declarations during the intimidating trial, their behavior in prison and, finally, their sublime faith as they walked to their death, many questions confront me.[25] For example, Was there a principal source for their stance? What was the meaning of their lives and deaths? Is their witness perhaps more important today than in 1943? Do their insights reveal something at the heart of the contemporary world, a certain spreading rottenness?[26]

The Raison d'Etre

I don't think one should attempt to do the impossible, namely, try to know the motivational factors that impelled the young people to secretly and dangerously risk their lives daily in their rebellion against the Nazis. For a few years they had lived in what some Germans during the twelve years of the Third Reich called "internal migration" or spiritual resistance, a complicated position of outward conformity accompanied

[23] In a letter to the *New York Review*, Sergio Sarri from Turin, Italy, wrote that Hans and Sophie were not guillotined, but beheaded with an ax.

[24] Reck-Malleczewen, *Diary of A Man in Despair*, 180–81. His manuscript was published after the war.

[25] When first apprehended, Hans and Sophie claimed that their empty suitcase, which had held the flyers, was to send laundry home to their parents (something I also did during my first year in college, 1948–1949). After the police disproved this story, Hans and Sophie admitted the truth, but insisted they acted alone; they implicated none of their companions.

[26] For writing this chapter, I am much indebted to Aaron Falbel.

by inner revulsion expressed only to one's most trusted friends. Hans said he could almost immediately "size up" someone he met, and know what he should and should not say to the new acquaintance.[27] Sophie, Hans, and their friends at first lived in a state of mental resistance, then passed on to inner immigration and then, being just over twenty years old, to overt opposition. They thereby favored us with the testimony of martyrs "to the existence of a secret Germany."[28] Those who made up a "secret Germany" may have been few. As John Lukacs remarks, " . . . the guilt (or, rather, the want of civic responsibility) of most Germans was that they found it easy to adjust their ideas to circumstances—as indeed many people are inclined to do."[29]

For me, an American, examining over fifty years later what the White Rose people left behind, I find there is much I can never hope to comprehend, beginning with the principal fact, their death. However, many records remain, important ones being the diaries and letters. These reveal the inner doubts and questions, the certainties and hopes, of those who dared to stand up and shout. Further, the flyers (*Flugblätter*), so dangerously and laboriously written, printed, and distributed, tell much about the perceptions and thinking of those who were executed.

St. Thomas Aquinas discusses the virtue of religion which, for him, is a part of the virtue of justice. Briefly, if I practice the virtue of justice, I pay all my debts. Overall, the debts of religion are owed in three directions. First, I am indebted to my parents and family for the gift of existence. Secondly, I am indebted to my native place, to my land, for the gift of its history, the noble and ignoble deeds of the past. Thirdly, I am indebted to what people call God for the ultimate reality of everything, for the gift of Creation. In each of these areas, I cannot fully repay the debt, but the effort to do so can make up much of the challenge and excitement of my life. Rather than selfishly, I can try to live as a grateful person.

From my reflection on the documents, I conclude that the central thrust of the White Rose was the complex struggle to pay these three debts, an action that cost the principal participants their lives. From what we can infer, each of them could have made a positive contribution to history, beginning with a life well lived, a life to inspire the rest of us.

[27] Dombach and Newborn, *Shattering the German Night*, 29.

[28] Franz Joseph Schöningh, quoted by Jens, *At the Heart of the White Rose*, 302, note #153.

[29] Lukacs, *The Hitler of History*, 252.

One might argue, however, that the manner of their deaths teaches us infinitely more than long and admirable lives ending in old age. As I see it, my task is to contribute a bit to showing how they lived the virtue of religion and what that means for us in our time and place.

The schema of St. Thomas is artificial as, in fact, all understanding. Reality is one, and the transcendental, unicity, explored by St. Thomas, *is* the real. But we are not angels, not simple, rather, we are composites. I can know only by dividing up what is one, and I hope to do this without falling into reductionism or reification. Peter Gay, a distinguished historian who received the Geschwister Scholl Prize in 1999, said in his acceptance speech:

> They [Hans and Sophie Scholl] were heroes, in the full sense of that much-abused word, who in their divine-naïve innocence undertook actions whose failure was guaranteed and who, although an early, cruel death was predictable, continued to struggle against the German mass murderers with weapons alas only too harmless.[30]

Although Gay spoke well, skillfully weaving his remarks in and out of the White Rose witness and his book, *My German Question*, he is unable to recognize the reality of their significance, a truth that reaches far beyond "weapons alas only too harmless."

In looking at the White Rose, I shall concentrate on Hans and Sophie Scholl since everyone maintains that Hans was the leader of the group, and Sophie was closely associated with him. Further, from comparisons with records left by the others, perhaps Hans and Sophie more clearly articulate, in their words and actions, the incomparable meaning of the White Rose. This is especially true because of what Sophie gives us in her letters and diary.

Hans and Sophie are exemplary figures in what each of us is called to do: to rise out of the mire of selfishness. They accomplished this by a complete abandonment of self, enriching the human record.[31] They were able to do this, to be raised to such a height, because of their relationship to God. That is the conclusion I have reached after studying their prayers and reflections, as recorded in diaries and letters. By their actions, they also abundantly manifested their search for the divine.

---

[30] Gay, "My German Question," 21–22. The prize is awarded each year in Munich.

[31] I do not mean they lived as plaster saints. For example, they thoroughly enjoyed skiing trips together, the pleasures of friendship, concerts, fencing (!), and so on.

For example, Sophie, when she was doing her conscripted labor for the State (*Arbeitdienst*), would illegally sneak out of the dormitory early on Sunday morning to go to Mass in a neighboring village.[32] When in occupied Russia, Hans entered an Orthodox church for the liturgy, and described his thoughts and feelings. From the words, one can catch a glimpse of his soul.[33] Many such incidents in the lives of each can be noted.

For Hans and Sophie, experience of the other was particularly powerful. I think one can categorize two "others" in their lives: books and people. Both these youngsters were good readers, that is, the written word had an impact on their lives, they did not read superficially, they were changed by their reading. Perhaps without reflexively thinking about it, they lived the ontological relationship between word and Word. As I will detail below, the books they read helped them form a specific sense of themselves, the other person, history, and the Beyond.

Crucially, they were introduced to people of remarkable integrity and insight, and formed close friendships with them. Perhaps chief among these were Karl Muth, editor of the suppressed journal, *Hochland*, and Theodore Haecker, who assisted Germans to know Kierkegaard through his translations and writing. One must also take into account the importance of their parents, Robert and Magdalena Scholl, in Hans and Sophie's lives. But one cannot know, much less measure, this influence. Therefore, I do no more than call attention to the fact.

I suspect that one of the principal places to begin to get at Hans and Sophie's relationship to history and, specifically, to their homeland, Germany, is through careful attention to the flyers. In this source, for which Hans was the most important author, one can ascertain their sense of the good, what they saw as praiseworthy in their past as Westerners, their fierce judgment on Hitler and the Nazis as destroyers of a Christian ethic, and their uncompromising national fidelity, or patriotism, for which, finally, they were murdered by the State.

The Reality and Intensity of Prayer

Although Sophie and Hans are closely intertwined in their actions and deaths, their unique differences shine out most strikingly in their individual comments and reflections on faith and prayer, and each one's

[32] Jens, *At the Heart of the White Rose*, 296, note #125.

[33] Ibid., 224–25.

seeking God through the desires of their respective persons. But the absolute necessity, without which their journey would lack not only its integrity and inner beauty but its very existence, was their passivity before the movements of God.

Their actions ultimately flowed from their faith. But to know something about faith is extremely difficult, whether it's one's own, or that of another. At times, however, a person will inadvertently say something in which an attentive listener can intuit much. For example, Hans, in a letter to Rose Nägele in Advent of December 1941, wrote that he was experiencing the liturgical season "as a wholehearted Christian for the first time in my life." He went on to describe the very new niche in which he now dwelled:

> I've discovered the only possible and lasting value—the place on one's pillow that never becomes cold, as Cocteau puts it. There are things that are outwardly incomprehensible but inwardly comprehended. I want to travel far, as far as possible, along the road of reason, but I realize I'm a creature born of nature *and* grace, though a grace that presupposes nature.

To emphasize the character of what Hans wrote Inge Jens, the editor of a collection of Hans and Sophie's letters and diary entries, adds two sentences from another letter to Rose, dated earlier in the month:

> For the birth of Our Lord represents the supreme religious experience, because he has been reborn for me. Either Europe will have to change course accordingly, or it will perish.

About a month later, in another letter to Rose, this paragraph appeared:

> I'm now a *homo viator* in the best sense, a man in transit, and I hope I always will be. After a lapse of many largely wasted years, I've finally learned to pray again. What strength it has given me! At last I know the inexhaustible spring that can quench my terrible thirst.

What one says about his or her prayers can reveal something of that person's faith, and vice versa.

Both Hans and Sophie were strongly moved by a photograph of the Shroud of Turin. As Inge Jens points out, both believed the Shroud to be genuine, "the only palpable evidence of Christ's Passion." Hans wrote an essay on the Shroud for the journal, *Windlicht*. Sophie, writing Hans on January 20, 1942, to thank him for the image, said:

> I'm surprised the picture doesn't cause more of a stir, considering that Christians can't but regard it as the face of God, perceptible to their very own eyes. It's marvelous. And to think it had to be technology, of all things, that brought this picture to light.

Karl Muth, Hans's mentor, wrote to Otl Aicher, a friend of the Scholl family, on January 2, 1942, and sent him a photograph of the relic that Aicher had requested. Muth commented on Sophie's reaction to the face:

> I never saw anyone as engrossed as Sophie Scholl was today in the big picture in the main volume I have here. It made an impression on me. She seems to be a very thoughtful and serious girl.[34]

As noted above, the differences between Hans and Sophie are evident in their respective comments about prayer. Sophie is much more detailed, she's much more open to allow us to enter her sacred space. When she was nineteen, she wrote to Fritz Hartnagel just after the Feast of Pentecost, in 1940. She described the glories of nature—the grass, wildflowers, brooks, and a nesting bird. From this date until her apprehension by the Nazis on February 18, 1943, she evidenced a truly remarkable growth in prayer. Fortunately for us, she left a record, she recorded her experiences in a diary and letters.

In a June letter to Fritz, she spoke of a feeling common among those who have begun to pray. "Weariness is my principal possession."[35] About a year later, when she begins her *Reicharbeitsdienst* (RAD) at Krauchenwies on April 6, 1941, she copied out a statement given her by Otl Aicher and attributed to Jacques Maritain: "Il faut avoir un esprit dure et le coeur tendre" (One must have a hard mind and a soft heart).[36]

---

[34] The quoted words are found in Jens, *At the Heart of the White Rose*, 305, note #175, 187; 303, note #157; 308, note #184, respectively.

[35] Ibid., 76.

[36] Ibid., 127. Inge Jens adds that Inge Aicher-Scholl quotes Maritain in his last book, *Le paysan de la Garonne*: "I once told Jean Cocteau: 'One must have a hard head and a soft heart.' Sadly, I added that the world was full of hard hearts and soft 'beans'." See 295, note #115.

From her letters and diary, one sees that the six months at Krauchenwies were difficult for Sophie, demanding a continual practice of a certain kind of asceticism. She was of a different social stratum and both she and the other young women found, on many occasions each day, that they did not feel and act in the same way. Often she was called upon to react as did Thérèse of Lisieux when the nun next to her splashed dirty laundry water in her face.[37] Sophie, whose self-love was not yet so completely obliterated as that of Thérèse, recorded her failures.

Although she was brought up in a Protestant tradition and remained there until her death, she preferred to visit a Catholic, not a Protestant church in the neighboring town. She wanted to be in the church, to assist at Mass, to sing and play the organ with a friend. When the authorities moved her to Blumberg, she continued to visit the Catholic church.[38]

A kindergarten in that town was her next assignment. There, she again recorded the predominant feelings of her soul: "All that I'm left with is melancholy, incapacity, impotence, and a slender hope."[39] From these cries and the disclosures of her letters one can note, at least in the last three years of her life, a marked progress up what St. John of the Cross calls "The Ascent of Mount Carmel." Sophie did not know what she was seeking, did not comprehend that she was asking for the chalice mentioned by Jesus Christ in the Gospel (Matt 20:22). St. John is quite explicit in describing the path Sophie chose: "This chalice means death to one's natural self through denudation and annihilation."[40]

In the early winter of 1941 she recorded her attempts to pray:

> I visited the church on Saturday afternoon, ostensibly to play
> the organ. It was absolutely empty. It's a colorful little chapel.

[37] " . . . I was in the laundry doing the washing in front of a Sister who was throwing dirty water into my face every time she lifted the handkerchiefs to her bench; my first reaction was to draw back and wipe my face to show the Sister who was sprinkling me that she would do me a favor to be more careful. But I immediately thought I would be very foolish to refuse these treasures which were being given to me so generously, and I took care not to show my struggle." St. Thérèse of Lisieux, *Story of a Soul*, 250.

[38] For Krauchenweis, see Jens, *At the Heart of the White Rose*, 130, 147, 296, note #125; for Blumberg, Ibid., 173.

[39] Ibid., 171.

[40] St. John of the Cross, *The Collected Works*, 171. After much reflection on their lives, deaths, and what is revealed in the diaries and letters, I have concluded that citing the writing of St. John of the Cross is neither false nor far-fetched. It is, rather, necessary in order to acknowledge the truth and depth of their commitment.

> I tried to pray. I kneeled down and tried to pray, but even as I
> did so I thought: Better hurry so you can get up before someone
> comes.

A few days later, she returns to the same subject. Each time she writes
about prayer, she reveals more of her soul, and more of her progress
although, to herself, it appears she is forever facing discouragement, forever going backwards.

> Sometimes I feel I can forge a path to God in an instant, purely
> by yearning to do so—by yielding up my soul entirely. If I be-
> seech him, if I love him far above all else, if my heart aches so
> badly because I'm apart from him, he ought to take me unto
> himself. But that entails many steps, many tiny little steps, and
> the road is a very long one. One mustn't lose heart. Once, when
> I'd lost heart because I kept backsliding, I didn't dare pray any-
> more. I decided not to ask anything more of God until I could
> enter his presence again. That in itself was a fundamental yearn-
> ing for God. But I can always ask him. I know that now.[41]

John of the Cross describes what was happening to Sophie. Her
soul " . . . departed on a dark night, attracted by God and enkindled
with love for him alone." But, as with many whom God leads on the
path to the Beyond, Sophie did not know that the " . . . fire of love is not
commonly felt at the outset . . . "[42]

The darkness of the way is a frightful experience for her. She simply
does not understand where she is.

> . . . when I try to pray and reflect on whom I'm praying to, I
> almost go crazy. I feel so infinitely small. I get really scared, so
> the only emotion that can surface is fear. I feel so powerless in
> general, and doubtless I am. I can't pray for anything except the
> ability to pray.
>
> Do you know, whenever I think of God, it's as if I'm struck
> blind. I can't do a thing. I have absolutely no conception of God
> and no affinity with him aside from my awareness of the fact.
> And the only remedy for that is prayer.

She continued to record her experiences of prayer. For example, in
February of the next year (1942), she wrote:

---

[41] For the two quotes, see Jens, *At the Heart of the White Rose,* 173–75.

[42] St. John of the Cross, *The Collected Works,* 119, 383, respectively.

I've decided to pray in church every day, so that God won't forsake me. Although I don't yet know God and feel sure that my conception of him is utterly false, he'll forgive me if I ask him. If I can love him with all my soul, I shall lose my distorted view of him.

. . . Yes, what I understand least about God is his love. But what if I didn't know about it!

O Lord, I need so badly to pray, to ask.[43]

Several times in her writings Sophie related her dreams. On the night before she was killed by the Nazis, she talked to Else Gebel, her cellmate, about her family. The prison authorities kept the light burning all night in the room, and a guard checked every half hour, "to see that everything is still in order." Else wrote that, "The night stretches out endlessly for me, while you [Sophie] sleep soundly as always." In the morning, before they take Sophie away for the trial, she tells Else of her dream that night, and Else includes the account in her letter to the Scholl family.

On a beautiful sunny day you [Sophie] brought a child in a long white dress to be baptized. The way to the church was up a steep mountain, but you carried the child safely and firmly. Unexpectedly there opened up before you a crevice in the glacier. You had just time enough to lay the child safely on the other side before you plunged into the abyss. You interpreted your dream this way: "The child in the white dress is our idea; it will prevail in spite of all obstacles. We were permitted to be pioneers, but we must die early for the sake of that idea."[44]

I think Sophie had another dream that was simultaneously a fervent wish: She wanted to be a university student with her brother, Hans, in Munich. Her frustration because of the various compulsory jobs to which the regime assigned her was manifested over and over. Finally, at the beginning of May 1942 she was able to join Hans at the Ludwig-Maximilian-Universität (University of Munich), and chose to begin her studies with biology and philosophy.[45]

---

[43] The first quote is the draft of an unsent letter: Jens, *At the Heart of the White Rose*, 176–7; the second quote: Ibid., 191.

[44] The quotes are found in Jens, *At the Heart of the White Rose*, 145 and 146, respectively.

[45] Ibid., 201.

The struggle to seek God alone became more intense, as one can see so clearly in her diary entry for June 29, 1942:

> My God, I can only address you falteringly. I can offer you my heart, which is wrested away from you by a thousand desires. Being so weak that I cannot remain facing you of my own free will, I destroy what distracts me from you and force myself to turn to you, for I know that I'm happy with you alone. Oh, how far from you I am, and the best thing about me is the pain I feel on that account. But I'm often so torpid and apathetic. Help me to be single-hearted and remain with me. If I could only once call you father, but I can hardly address you as "YOU." . . . Teach me to pray. Better to suffer intolerable pain than to vegetate insensibly. Better to be parched with thirst, better to pray for pain, pain, and more pain, than to feel empty, and to feel so without truly feeling at all. That I mean to resist.[46]

Another passage from St. John of the Cross helps one "to make sense" of what Sophie writes, for she continually incarnates his teaching in her pilgrimage. St. John claims that

> A genuine spirit seeks rather the distasteful in God than the delectable, leans more toward suffering than toward consolation, more toward going without everything for God than toward possession, and toward dryness and affliction than toward sweet consolation. It knows that this is the significance of following Christ and denying self . . . [47]

In early May Hans and Alex Schmorell wrote, printed and distributed the first flyer. They urged every German to "work against the [Nazi] scourges of mankind, against fascism and any similar system of totalitarianism."[48] It appears that Sophie soon figured out what her brother was doing and insisted on participating. She stepped across a line, actively risking death if caught in what the court later called, "attempted high treason."[49] On August 6, 1942, while helping Hans and his friends publicly confront Hitler and his government, she wrote these paradoxical comments in her diary:

[46] Jens, *At the Heart of the White Rose*, 207–8.
[47] St. John of the Cross, *The Collected Works*, 170.
[48] Scholl, *The White Rose*, 74.
[49] Ibid., 105.

I'm so weak-willed that I can't even fulfill and act on my own perceptions, nor can I ever renounce my personal volition, which I know to be imprudent and self-seeking, and surrender myself to his. Yet I'd like to . . . I pray every night that he may wrest my will away and subject me to him—if only I didn't stand in my own way. I place my powerless love in your [God's] hands, that it may become powerful.[50]

Again, St. John of the Cross illuminates the experience of Sophie. He wrote,

. . . the road leading to God . . . demands only the one thing necessary: true self-denial, exterior and interior, through surrender of self both to suffering for Christ and to annihilation in all things. . . . [and] supported by faith alone . . . [51]

About six years before her death Sophie began writing to Fritz Hartnagel, who was in the army and soon to be commissioned an officer. Her early letters are filled with the adolescent excitement of a teenager writing to a young man four years her senior. But five years later, three months before her execution, the letters reveal an experiential maturity frightening in its insight and truth. For example, on November 18, 1942, she wrote these sentences:

I'm still so remote from God that I don't even sense his presence when I pray. Sometimes when I utter God's name, in fact, I feel like sinking into a void. It isn't a frightening or dizzy-making sensation, it's nothing at all—and that's far more terrible. But prayer is the only remedy for it, and however many devils scurry around inside me, I shall cling to the rope God has thrown me in Jesus Christ, even if my numb hands can no longer feel it.[52]

Sophie was undergoing what St. John of the Cross calls a purgation. He points out that such an infused discipline is "obscure, dark, and dreadful . . . "[53] His words seem so abstract as he methodically details the intricacies, pitfalls and blessings of what is called ascetical and mystical theology. To see his teaching come alive in a specific person is awful and terrifying to behold. Father Zossima, in Dostoievski's *The Brothers*

[50] Jens, *At the Heart of the White Rose*, 209.

[51] St. John of the Cross, *The Collected Works*, 119.

[52] Jens, *At the Heart of the White Rose*, 257.

[53] St. John of the Cross, *The Collected Works*, 119.

Karamazov, claims that " . . . love in action is a harsh and dreadful thing compared with love in dreams. Love in dreams is greedy for immediate action, rapidly performed and in the sight of all."[54] In Sophie's suffering and distress, we are blessed with an intimate view of this heartrending reality.

St. John writes that " . . . in the beginning the soul does not experience . . . savor and delight, but dryness and distaste . . . "[55] One month before the Gestapo arrested her, Sophie expressed this feeling in the diary:

> As soon as I'm alone, melancholy suppresses any desire in me to do anything at all. . . . Extreme pain, even if only physical, would be infinitely preferable to this vacuous inactivity.[56]

From the way Sophie acted when apprehended, during the hours-long questioning in prison, at the staged trial, and as she approached her death one can see that she was not at the beginning of her journey into the light of faith in these last five days. Her calmness and strength, defiance and courage, noted by so many, show she had reached the realm sought by the Psalmist, the peace longed for by every believer.

I've already quoted passages from Hans that indicate the reality of his faith. There is nothing, however, similar to Sophie's Pascal-like outcries and perplexities, almost nothing where one can trace an Ascent of Mount Carmel. But one can easily document the character of his faith as a Christian. For example, while working at a field hospital in Russia he kept a diary and recorded these comments, speaking of Dostoievsky:

> He looked into the darkness and saw because his eyes weren't dazzled by a false sun. He found his way from sin to Christ because one repentant sinner is worth more to God than a hundred thousand of the righteous.

These thoughts could have been made by an intelligent but unbelieving literary critic. Several days later in that August of 1942 Hans described an intensely personal experience that leaves no doubt about where he stood as a believer:

---

[54] Dostoievsky, *The Brothers Karamasov*, 65. Dorothy Day often quoted this truth. See Day, *Selected Writings*, 264.

[55] St. John of the Cross, 378.

[56] Jens, *At the Heart of the White Rose*, 267.

All I hear day and night are the groans of men in pain and, when dreaming, the sighs of the forlorn, and when I think, my thoughts perish in agony.

If Christ hadn't lived and died, there really would be no escape. To weep at all would be utterly futile. I should have to run full tilt at the nearest wall and smash my skull in. But not as things are.[57]

Hans considered Paul Claudel's *The Satin Slipper* " . . . the greatest event in modern European literature." In a letter to Rose Nägele, written on February 16, 1943, two days before his final arrest, he turned to Claudel to express where he was at that moment:

Nowadays I have to be the way I am . . . because the danger is of my own choosing, I must head for my chosen destination freely and without any ties. I've gone astray many times, I know. Chasms dawn and darkest night envelops my questing heart, but I press on regardless. As Claudel so splendidly puts it: "La vie, c'est une grande aventure vers la lumière" (Life is a great adventure toward the light).[58]

Hans, as unequivocally and certainly as Sophie, shows the state of his soul, the condition of his spirit, in the way he conducted himself at the arrest, during the interrogation in prison, at the trial, and in the way he died. Shouting so that the cry echoed throughout the prison compound, his last words before he lowered his head for the executioner: "Es lebe die Freiheit!" (Long live freedom!).[59]

People and Books

Each of us must die. Some are inclined to reflect for only a brief moment, or for occasional hours, or as a regular practice, and think about their death. That is, How should I live today to die well? Hans and Sophie Scholl confront us as exemplary witnesses to living and dying worthily. The last five days in their lives are the most significant ones;

---

[57] The quotes are found in Jens, *At the Heart of the White Rose,* 133 and 235–36, respectively.

[58] Ibid., 195 and 279, respectively.

[59] Hanser, *A Noble Treason,* 284; Dombach and Newborn, *Shattering the German Night,* 211.

in these final moments of their brief time on earth they reached heights rare in the history of death.

I have emphasized the fact and character of their prayer to throw light on the way they lived and died. This means I suggest the Beyond, I make a claim for their experiential contact with eternity, I believe they wondrously united history and faith, thereby bequeathing an inestimable heritage. They achieved timelessness through their painful assimilation of time.[60] What some claim Kierkegaard attempts, Sophie and Hans strikingly did: In their lives and death they united philosophy and mysticism, they combined intuition and discursive reasoning.[61] Believing in eternity, they founded their timeless and infinite happiness on certain time-bound and obscure facts: Stories based on a hypothetical, wandering Semite, Abraham, and a Galilean, Jesus Christ, who lived on the margins of the Roman Empire.

They were greatly assisted in all this by certain people they met and words they read, to both of which they were especially attentive. As I mentioned earlier, their families, in particular, their parents, must have exercised a great influence on them. Formed by the times and their own acute moral perceptions, they chose to be open with young friends their own age who shared their sense of Western history and of the utter perversity represented by National Socialism. An essential aspect of this movement and party is graphically caught in expressions voiced by Hitler soon after grabbing power in 1933:

> "Historically speaking, the Christian religion is nothing but a Jewish sect. . . . After the destruction of Judaism, the extinction of Christian slave morals must follow logically. . . . I am the Lord thy God! Who? That Asiatic tyrant? No! The day will come when I shall hold up against these commandments the tables of a new law."[62]

Hans was fifteen in 1933, so he and his young friends were not so quick as older persons, such as Dietrich Bonhoeffer, Friedrich Reck-Malleczewen, Karl Muth, Theodor Haecker, and others in discerning

---

[60] See the Introduction by Alexander Dru in: Haecker, *Journal in the Night*, xxxviii.

[61] Dru in Haecker, xxvi.

[62] Robinson, *The Ten Commandments,* xi–xiii. The comments of Hitler were written down by Herman Rauschning, and appear as a Preface in this book. As John Lukacs and others have pointed out, Rauschning's memory is somewhat suspect. See Lukacs, *The Hitler of History,* 8, 121.

the exact nature and effects of Hitler's plans. But after his participation in the Nuremburg Rally (September 1936), Hans began to question, to doubt, and rapidly outdistanced his elders in his uncompromising and radical opposition.

Hans especially, but also the other young people with him, manifested an unusual respect and docility toward certain older men who were firmly grounded in Christianity, specifically, in the Catholic tradition. First among these was Karl Muth (1867–1944), the founder and editor of *Hochland* (1903–1941), a journal devoted to discussions between devout Roman Catholics and prominent artists and scholars.[63] Through their friend, Otl Aicher, Hans and Sophie met Muth in the Fall of 1941 and almost immediately submitted themselves to his personal and intellectual guidance; youth and age were no obstacle; they became intimate friends. Through Muth, they met Theodor Haecker (1879–1943), perhaps almost as decisive an influence as Muth on the young people, principally through his secret manuscript, *Journal of the Night*. It was published posthumously after the war, but before he died Haecker read parts of it to the White Rose group.[64] At Muth's home, Hans and Sophie also met others opposed to the Nazis, including Sigismund von Radecki, also a Catholic, who impressed them greatly.[65]

At times through their own initiative, at times through the suggestions of Muth and others, the young Scholls carefully read certain authors. They had a great love for literature and philosophy.[66] From their comments and subsequent actions, one can say they practiced a certain kind of *lectio divina* with many texts.[67] The words entered them, they entered the words, they were changed in their persons by the reading. Perhaps it is accurate to say they were radically transformed. But to say this is to touch upon the impossible, namely to portray and weigh the relative influence of a book, its relationship to a person through whom

[63] Jens, *At the Heart of the White Rose*, 300, note #153. *Hochland*, started by Muth in 1903, was closed up by the Nazis in 1941.

[64] See Jens, *At the Heart of the White Rose*, 320, note ##265, 266. In 1935, the Nazis put Haecker under a speaking and writing ban.

[65] Ibid., 161, 203, 312, note ##210, 216.

[66] Large, *Where Ghosts Walked*, 327. Several authors also note their appreciation for and practice of music. See also the diary entries of Willi Graf. Graf, *Briefe und Aufzeichnungen*, 41, 68, and passim.

[67] Many books and articles describe and analyze different notions of *lectio divina* in the Christian tradition. See, for example, Illich, *In the Vineyard of the Text*.

they learned about it, and to Hans and Sophie's history—person, familial, and Western. In addition, another absolutely incalculable element, divine grace, acted through all the temporal factors. They were able, through their reading of literature, philosophy, and theology, and through their prayer, to move from acute insights into contemporary society to living in the mystery of the Beyond.

Among the many authors important for them, five particularly were pertinent: Pascal, Claudel, Bernanos, Bloy, and Berdyaev. Principally because of the kinds of questions raised by Blaise Pascal in the *Pensées*, and the way in which he expressed them, his ideas were probably the most conclusive in affecting the minds and hearts of the young people. From the opinion of Hans quoted above, one sees that Paul Claudel's poetry was especially strong in touching the feelings of Hans and Sophie. The drama of sanctity, as portrayed by Georges Bernanos in *Diary of A Country Priest* and *Under the Sun of Satan* made the life of faith appear as a truly exciting adventure for generous young people not hardened and embittered by age and experience. The power of León Bloy's literary skill and life is abundantly evidenced in the title of a major work, *The Pilgrim of the Absolute*, and in his influence on the conversion to Catholicism of Jacques and Raïssa Maritain. Bloy is also credited with saying: There is only one unhappiness, not to be a saint.[68] Nikolai Berdyaev presented a Christian view of history that complemented the broader and more inclusive perspective of Haecker.

Perhaps the four Frenchmen and the Russian who settled in Paris had a greater impact on the persons of Hans and Sophie than any German author, for the evidence appears to point toward this conclusion. It is highly significant, too, that all the authors were men for whom Christianity was central in their lives, four of whom being Roman Catholics.[69]

Others, too, acted on Sophie and Hans: Hitler and his sycophants among the Nazis. The young people's opinion of these persons is probably well expressed by someone they did not know and in words they never heard, Friedrich Reck-Malleczewen. He refers to Hitler with the nickname applied to him after Stalingrad, where the Germans lost about

---

[68] Day, *The Dorothy Day Book*, 97.

[69] The six persons, along with others such as Francis Jammes, Charles Péguy, and François Mauriac, produced a kind of renaissance among Catholic French readers that reached far beyond France to such places as America and Germany. See Jens, *At the Heart of the White Rose*, 292, note #64, and the books of these authors.

300,000 men: "*Gröfaz*, an abbreviation of 'Greatest Field Marshall of All Time'."[70] With no sense of irony, Reck-Malleczewen also speaks of Hitler as the Antichrist, a notion much more elaborated by Haecker who directly influenced the White Rose youngsters. Haecker, a deeply convinced Catholic, believed that *the* great fault was to omit something in his considerations of reality. In *Journal of the Night*, he confronts the dichotomies, faith and history, eternity and time, through what he believes to be a direct conception of truth. He thinks it possible to conceptualize the antagonism between metaphysics and history as an ultimate issue facing every person. According to Haecker, the seemingly impossible chasm can be crossed or bridged by individual thinkers through a synthesis of the Greek and Jewish traditions. A careful reading of the *Journal* indicates that he goes far toward achieving such a resolution. To first clear the ground, he speaks of the German *Herrgott-religion*, a belief system promoted by the Nazis that accepts the success of deceit, betrayal, murder or violence as a proof of the blessing of the German *Herrgott*. He holds that " . . . the German *Herrgott-religion* . . . has never been equaled for blasphemous shallowness and simple brutishness."

> Behind the German *Herrgott-religion* there is vacuity, emptiness and nothing else, the same unending nothing which was, moreover, at the back of German idealism, only that its façade made a finer impression.[71]

One can see, in the diary and letters of Hans, the influence of these ideas. Also, the fourth flyer pits God against Satan, speaks about the reality of demonic powers, and claims the Nazis are "servants of the Antichrist."[72] Haecker was a student of John Henry Newman, who preached four Advent sermons on the Antichrist at Oxford.[73]

Various scholars, such as John Lukacs and Friedrich Heer, discuss Hitler in terms of diabolic possession and a personification of the Antichrist. Pope Pius XII, on June 2, 1945, about a month after Hitler's suicide, spoke about "the satanic apparition of National Socialism." Heer, commenting on this interpretation, says that the Pope is " . . .

---

[70] Reck-Malleczewen, *Diary of A Man in Despair*, 173–74.

[71] The references are to Haecker, *Journal In the Night*, 25 and 74–75, respectively.

[72] Scholl, *The White Rose*, 86.

[73] Newman, "The Times of Antichrist." See also McGinn, *Antichrist*. For a competent overview, see: *Dictionnaire de Théologie Catholique*, col. 179–80, and the more extensive entry in the *Dictionnaire*, 1903, vol. 1, col. 1361–65.

being metaphysical, removing something from history and from the responsibility for history, acquitting Catholics of their responsibilities." Lukacs agrees with this judgment, while maintaining that Hitler " . . . in the coming age of the masses . . . was but the first of Antichrist-like popular figures."[74] The White Rose people made the necessary connections between theological opinions, Christian tradition, moral sensibility, politics, and the consequent action of a German citizen in 1942–1943.

Conclusion

On February 22, 1943, the first three members of the White Rose were executed: Sophie and Hans Scholl, and Christoph Probst. Alex Schmorell and Kurt Huber were beheaded on July 13th. Willi Graf's head was cut off on October 17th. Eleven others implicated in activities of the White Rose, including eight from the Hamburg group, were killed, forced to commit suicide, or died in prisons and concentration camps. Many others were arrested and served prison terms.[75] The only person who was not sentenced to prison but let go free was Falk Harnack, a man who had arranged a meeting between Hans, Alex and Dietrich Bonhoeffer, planned to occur on February 25, 1943. Harnack, not knowing of Hans's execution, waited for him in Berlin on that day.

The Gestapo was extremely thorough and rapid in getting almost all the details of the White Rose accurately, as can be seen from the indictments of the People's Court. For example, the document containing the sentence for Hans, Sophie, and Christoph says this:

> That the accused have in this time of war by means of leaflets called for the sabotage of the war effort and armaments and for the overthrow of the National Socialist way of life of our people, have propagated defeatist ideas, and have most vulgarly defamed the Führer, thereby giving aid to the enemy of the Reich and weakening the armed security of the nation.
>
> On this account they are to be punished by Death.

---

[74] Lukacs, *The Hitler of History*, 265–66. Although Lukacs only implies the difference, there is a complex theological distinction between diabolic possession and the Antichrist.

[75] Jens, *At the Heart of the White Rose*, 281. Of the members of the White Rose executed in Munich, the only one who was not a student was Professor Kurt Huber. Various writings in German document his participation with the younger witnesses. Excerpts of his statement before the court are printed in Scholl, *The White Rose*, 63–5.

Their honor and rights as citizens are forfeited for all time.[76]

The witness of the White Rose was supremely important for the German *Volk* in 1943 when the principal participants were killed and imprisoned by the Nazis. In each of the flyers, Hans Scholl and his friends publicly presented searing accusations against Hitler and the National Socialists. Further, they called upon their fellow Germans to arise and throw off the degenerates. In their last flyer, they placed all hope in their fellow students to take the lead:

> The name of Germany is dishonored for all time if German youth does not finally rise, take revenge, and atone, smash its tormentors, and set up a new Europe of the spirit. Students! The German people look to us. . . . The dead of Stalingrad implore us to take action.
>
> "Up, up, my people, let smoke and flame be our sign!"
>
> Our people stand ready to rebel against the National Socialist enslavement of Europe in a fervent new breakthrough of freedom and honor.[77]

But almost nothing happened. The students did not move; some adults retreated into their tormented shells, others simply tried to survive. Only a few rose up, and their efforts, as with the July 20, 1944 attempt to kill Hitler, ended with death or confinement.

Schools and other public places are named Die Geschwister Scholl, and people generally look upon the White Rose as a courageous but futile and doomed call to wartime Germany. Since they were not connected with the Communists or Social Democrats, some consider them to be apolitical. Since they were not Jehovah's Witnesses, Mennonites or members of the Confessing Church—all opposed to National Socialism—others think them asocial. Since they were only slowly developing an overall plan and structure of opposition, they are sometimes dismissed as romantic neophytes. In a conventional sense, they were certainly not religious. This is evident from the sentiment expressed in a letter of Willi Graf, written the day of his execution: "The love of God surrounds us and we trust in his grace . . . "[78] Perhaps it is only in our

---

[76] Ibid., 114.

[77] Scholl, *The White Rose*, 92–93.

[78] Graf, *Briefe und Aufzeichnungen*, 199. One can make a distinction between religion or religiosity and faith. The distinction is evident in several Graham Greene novels. See also Hoinacki, *El Camino. Walking to Santiago de Compostela.*

time that their witness can awaken a slumbering and distracted, fearful and narcotized society, in Germany and beyond.

Hans, Sophie, and their companions perceived the reality of their world. They recognized that an evil presence, reaching into the Infinite, was attempting an apocalyptic destruction. There are persons today who believe that we—meaning everyone—face a similar presence. But there is a great difference. After the night of November 9, 1938, the date of Kristallnacht, Germans living in villages, towns, and cities who possessed a minimal moral sensibility could see the essence and direction of National Socialism.[79] Today, however, the rottenness and perversity, the evil, are wondrously disguised. Many feel a certain disquiet, but few recognize any attack on the very possibility of being human. National Socialism gradually perfected its assault on the tradition of Western humanism. The insight, logical coherence, and unwavering courage of the White Rose people directly confronted the assault. Although the danger is more fundamental today, it is also more hidden. One must search diligently for clarity.

Many voices attempt to delineate the predominant characteristics of our time, and some acknowledge their evil nature. One of the most incisive witnesses who in his life and work stands out as a clear beacon is Jacques Ellul (d. 1994). Many consider him the principal critic of the technological system under which all of us live. In his many books he describes and analyzes the dire character and effects of technology. He believes technology is total, namely, all-encompassing. It "integrates into itself every phenomenon that arises." It is also assimilative in the sense that all movements are ultimately incorporated into it, nothing can escape it. Increasingly technology, under the cover of humanistic promises, actually works to destroy us as human. Since technology embraces everything, Ellul demonstrates the need for transcendence in order to escape its grip; we need "something that belongs to neither our history nor our world . . . " Each of us confronts an absolute either/or: "We are faced either with technology as our fate or the existence of a transcendent."[80]

Hans and Sophie Scholl were discouraged by the fact that their fellow Germans did not appear to see and acknowledge the enormity of the

---

[79] That night Nazi storm troopers mounted an assault on Jews in Germany. Almost two hundred synagogues were burned. Over seven thousand Jewish-owned shops were destroyed. Nearly a hundred Jews were killed. About ten thousand men were shipped to Buchenwald concentration camp.

[80] Ellul, *Perspectives On Our Age,* 100–101.

evil that existed among them, and did not rise up to combat it. Most in the technological society today actually celebrate what Ellul saw as evil. Critics of "the system" meet incomprehension and denial; Hans and Sophie faced accommodation and fear. The contemporary infatuation with consumption, eating deeply into everyone, runs through the various technological systems, supporting them and being assisted by them. Many have commodified themselves, their work—generally experienced only as employment—their leisure, and relationships with others. Do-gooders and hucksters offer a varied and continual stream of distractions that matches every taste, no matter how sophisticated or gross. To see and recognize reality, one also needs silence and a certain withdrawal from the plethora of goods and services seemingly available to all.

For Ellul, as for Sophie, Hans, Christoph and Willi, the transcendent really exists, it is Jesus Christ. But I don't suggest that either the White Rose youth nor Ellul constitute an apologia for Christianity. Rather, Hans, Sophie and their friends ask us to recognize the evil that is asphyxiating the universe today, and to see it as demoniacally evil. Some believe a form of the Antichrist again walks among us.[81]

The lives of Sophie, Hans, and Christoph manifest an incredibly intense growth in the time between the first flyer and their death nine months later. One can get some sense of the height of their passion, the power of their faith, the purity of their thought, from their prayers and reflections. Simone Weil, who wrote out her insights at about the same time the young people advanced toward their apotheosis, helps us look into their souls. She wrote:

> If we find the fullness of joy in the thought that God is, we must find the same fullness in the knowledge that we ourselves are not, for it is the same thought. And this knowledge is extended to our sensibility only through suffering and death.

In her own way, Simone Weil expresses what one finds in the writing of St. John of the Cross and, existentially, in the lives of the White Rose people. She calls this living awareness "decreation." "We participate in the creation of the world by decreating ourselves."

Simone Weil speaks of creation very much in consonance with the Catholic tradition, especially as found in St. Thomas Aquinas. She says that

---

[81] For example, Ivan Illich in a posthumous book: Cayley, *The Rivers North of the Future: The Testament of Ivan Illich*, 59–63 and passim.

> Creation is . . . an act of love and it is perpetual. At each moment
> our existence is God's love for us. But God can only love himself.
> His love for us is love for himself through us. Thus, he who gives
> us our being loves in us the acceptance of not being.

Sophie, Hans, and Christoph, *because* they were young and talented, had something to de-create: their future, their very lives. By calmly facing their death, they marvelously embodied Simone Weil's notion of decreation: "To make something created pass into the uncreated."[82] The executioner, who afterward worked for the Americans, killing some of the prominent Nazis, said he had never seen people like these three who met their end so bravely.[83]

---

[82] Weil, *Gravity and Grace*, 78–84.

[83] Large, *Where Ghosts Walked*, 352. In 2004, a film, *Sophie Scholl—Die letzten Tage*, was produced. In 2005 a book presenting documents, a short history of the White Rose, the film script, commentaries and photos was published: Fred Breinersdorfer, *Sophie Scholl—Die letzten Tage*.

11

To Encircle Death

OCOTEPEC, IN the state of Morelos, in the country of Mexico. But what is this place? A collection of streets, paths, houses, small businesses—some under roof, some in the streets; a prominent parish church; a busy highway slicing through the village from Cuernavaca to Tepotzlán, cutting it into two halves. Ocotepec is further divided into four *barrios*, and during almost twenty years I lived in one of these each summer, the Barrio del Señor de los Ramos. In those years, street lights were installed and, although Calle de los Dolores, my temporary annual address, is still a mix of cobblestones and dirt, the way is brightened at night; especially helpful in the many nights of rain.

Here and there, new houses of obviously affluent people sit alongside much more modest and numerous concrete block and corrugated tin or plastic dwellings. Walking further up Calle de los Dolores for several hundred meters, you reach an elevation from which you can look out over the town. Since the weather is semi-tropical with plentiful rainfall, greenery fills the eye; trees and bougainvillea hide most of the houses and small businesses.

Each barrio has its own name and a small church or *capilla*. My barrio was named to commemorate Jesus' entry into Jerusalem on what is now called Palm (*ramo*) Sunday, and its chapel is half a block from where I lived. Loudspeakers are on the tower of the tiny church. Now and then, regularly on Sundays and feast days, I heard the bell and recorded music or peoples' prayers broadcast over the roofs, but never loudly enough to really catch my attention or distract me. The bell rings regularly and tolls occasionally. But, in all the years I went to Mexico, I never walked the thirty meters to enter the chapel, nor paid any attention to the sounds sailing over my head.

One Sunday in the summer of 1999, however, something drastically changed my life in Ocotepec. I raised my head from some early morning reading in my room and listened carefully; I was barely able to recognize the voice gently moving the air that day. It sounded like Cruz, the caretaker and handyman of the house in which I enjoyed hospitality each year. Later in the day, I asked, "Was that you I heard this morning, Cruz, leading the prayers?" With his usual affable smile, he answered, "Yes."

Cruz can read and write, but I suspect he does not much exercise these skills. I've found him in his house watching TV but never reading a book or newspaper. I was intrigued, curious I guess, about his early Sunday morning activity. "What do you do in the chapel on Sunday mornings?" I asked. "El Rosario (the Rosary)," he responded simply. "Do you say it every Sunday morning?" "Sí, would you like to come?" "May I?" "Certainly. We start at seven."

The following Sunday morning, eager to celebrate the day, I walk the few meters, approaching the newly mysterious chapel. What awaits me there? First I see a plastered wall, about two meters high, surrounding the property. About ten meters behind the wall, the chapel sits in the middle of the yard. Stepping through the opened iron gate, I immediately come under a curved roof that extends out from the chapel entrance into a patio.

Inside the building, I find three very simple pews on each side of a center aisle; no more would fit. A starkly plain altar, covered with a clean white cloth on which two large candles sit, stands just in front of the pews. The wall in front, which still supports an attached old altar, has six tall candles and large vases of gladioli, and a picture of the Guadalupana—a copy of the Virgin's image displayed and honored in the Mexico City shrine, la Villa. Dominating the front of the chapel, about two meters up, seemingly stepping out into the room itself, a large sculptured donkey walks toward me, carrying a Christ clothed in fine garments of real cloth. Below this figure a smaller version of the very same statue also strides toward me. A huge crucifix completes the assemblage of sacred images. In front of the new altar, a thick Paschal candle stands on the floor.

A young woman enters from the sacristy and lights all the candles. Moments later, she returns with a ceramic bowl containing burning charcoal, which is sprinkled with grains of incense. Slowly swinging this simple censer, she solemnly incenses each of the images, then sets the censer on the floor in front of the Paschal candle. In the meantime, a few people take their places in the pews.

Shortly after seven, Cruz comes out, adjusts a microphone and, standing at one side and facing the images, begins the prayers. After each of the five decades of the Rosary, he leads the people in singing a hymn. When the Rosary, hymns and other prayers are completed, he begins the Litany of the Blessed Virgin Mary. He and the congregation sing the entire Litany—in Latin! I marvel at their ability . . . for I believed these people to be barely literate in Spanish. During the liturgy, an older woman replenishes the supply of incense on the charcoal, to that a continual fragrant smoke carries our prayers heavenward.

After the hour-long ceremony, every person present shakes hands with every other person, including the young children. I then notice that people also stand outside the front door under the covered entrance; they had arrived after the service began and could not fit in the small chapel; they turn out to be more numerous than those inside.

Everyone goes out into the patio, the men seating themselves in a circle on plastic chairs; the women sit in their own separate grouping. Soon, we are served a hot breakfast and drink. It is simple fare but is warm and well prepared. Cruz introduces me to the others. The men, who obviously know one another well, discuss the week's events in the barrio while eating; some, perhaps less shy with a stranger, ask me a few polite questions about myself. They seem impressed by the fact that a foreigner has joined them in their Sunday morning prayers. From the *way* in which they speak and the kinds of things they say and ask, it is evident they believe I did not come to watch them; rather, they sense that I came to pray with them.

Although there was no Eucharistic presence in the chapel—the Blessed Sacrament is not reserved there—the words of the hymns referred to the Real Presence several times. I listened carefully, and found all such references theologically sound. The people had picked *good* hymns, celebratory songs that appealed to them and were faithful to traditional doctrine. Further, all the prayers accompanying the Rosary were noble and fitting. They were beautiful prayers, never jejune or sentimental.

Each Sunday morning after that I returned to the chapel for the early Rosario. Then, one day during the week, I heard the bell tolling, as if someone were dying or already dead.

I ask Cruz, "What's happening?" He tells me a young man has committed suicide that morning, that he was at the preceding Sunday Rosario; at the breakfast, he sat next to me in the circle of men! Jostled by Cruz's good memory, I manage to recall him; he sat on a concrete bench that runs along the wall, and I moved my plastic chair to include him more directly in the circle. His position, almost outside the circle, seemed to fit his actions. I don't remember that he joined the conversation, but I shook his hand when I left to return to my room. After eating and visiting, I was always careful to go around and shake hands with every man, to take my leave. "Hasta luego" (see you later).

I asked Cruz and his wife, Lucina, if they knew of any reason for the man's death. No, there were various stories going around the village, but little evidence that one might be more accurate than another. They were inclined to credit none of the stories and to avoid idle speculation or gossip.

That evening, there was a *velorio* in the chapel, with the body present. I could hear prayers and hymns in my room, as they wended their sorrowful way through the trees, but I didn't feel I should walk over to the chapel. I really am an outsider; there, among the people who know him, I can be only a voyeur. One needs to live here a long time, maybe more than one generation; one needs to belong to this neighborhood, to this community, in order to share more intimately in its sorrow.

Later, I learned that there was a funeral Mass in the parish church, a few blocks down the main street or highway, and a procession to the cemetery, another six or seven blocks further. Cruz also told me there would be a Rosario at his mother-in-law's—the young man's house is too small to accommodate the people—each night for seven days. In two days, it will be Cruz's turn to lead the prayers, and he invites me to go. He also asks me to accompany him and Lucina to a neighbor's house a block away that evening for a *cumpleaños*. I know that the word means "birthday," but I nevertheless feel we are not going for that kind of celebration. Attempting not to be too gauche, I ask him what is being commemorated. He says that it is the first-year anniversary of a man's death, and they are going at ten tonight.

When he asked me, I answered with an immediate "yes" in a spontaneous feeling of something akin to joy. Afterwards, though, I was troubled. Is this a good thing to do? Did I unduly influence him to invite me? How can I, a stranger and foreigner, presume to invade the private space of these families in their experience of pain? But I have known Cruz and Lucina for many years now. And I've gone to the Sunday Rosario to join the people in prayer. Can I not hope to enter their homes in the same spirit? I feel quite certain that Cruz invited me to pray with them, not to observe a folk custom; I decide I can go in peace.

That evening, we arrive in about five minutes and enter the yard through a makeshift gate. The people have strung up a row of light bulbs. A crowd is moving around, talking quietly. Lucina, Cruz and I enter the house and are shown to some battered folding chairs. We sit among the fifteen or twenty people who fit in the small and extremely plain room. The roof appears to be made of corrugated asbestos or felt, and can be seen from the inside, since there is no ceiling.

About two meters in front of us there is a catafalque, a platform about one meter high, with the "body" on top; the covered "head" at the far end, the feet pointing directly toward us. So, the "body" is roughly perpendicular to our row of chairs. A black cloth, with a cross sewn on it, is wrapped around the catafalque itself. A large cross, standing on the floor and made of white gladioli fastened to crossed pieces of wood, leans against the catafalque. A strip of nylon or silk cloth, about three inches wide, is draped over the flowered arms of the cross.

Six candles, three on each side, solemnly flank the catafalque, along with many vases of mostly white gladioli. The tall candlesticks, probably made of wood, are wrapped in aluminum foil. There are also ten or fifteen large glass "vigil light" candles, irregularly placed on the floor. Near the cross, on a brightly painted chair, stands a large color photograph of José Agustín, whose anniversary we celebrate. Around the cross, several fat bowls of food are arranged. They contain mostly bread, a large bottle of Coke, what appears to be a bottle of wine or liquor, and several packs of Marlboros. To one side, there is a huge earthenware cauldron that seems to contain *mole* (a rich chocolate-and-pepper-based sauce for meat), with an enormous wooden ladle resting across the top. A ceramic censer on the floor awaits fire.

A body, covered with a white cloth, appears to be lying on top of the catafalque. A row of bright red apples is placed on top of the catafalque, all around the body. Furthering the illusion of a body, a shirt and trousers, nicely pressed, are stretched out over the raised cloth, and a popular style of Mexican straw hat is placed over the position of the head.

Behind the catafalque, on the wall, I see pictures of saints, with more vases of flowers and tall candles. Bouquets of red roses add color; pots of white mums add variety. People continue to arrive, many bringing big bouquets. I notice a glass of water on the floor, with one flower in it, seemingly a carnation. Later, I will see that it becomes a sprinkler for repeated ceremonial blessings.

Shortly after sitting down, we are given a *café de olla* (Mexican spiced coffee), and a large roll. People quietly chat with one another, while the widow, a tiny stooped lady, sits near the door greeting new arrivals and receiving bouquets from them, before they join the crowd in the yard.

A young man, apparently the conductor of the liturgy, gives unobtrusive directions to remove most of the flowers from one side of the catafalque, opening access to it. All present, both inside and outside the room, then go one by one to bless the body by making the sign of the cross on it, touching its shoulders and chest. Everyone goes to the same side to do this. Cruz gently urges me to go, too, and I do so.

After all the people—maybe close to a hundred—have given their blessing, the young director begins the Rosario. Between each mystery of the Rosary, he leads the crowd in several verses of a hymn, different each time. He also sprinkles the catafalque's head with the carnation dipped in water, and recites several prayers and versicles, to which the people give the appropriate responses. It is clear they know all the prayers well. The youthful moderator then begins singing the Litany of the Blessed Virgin Mary, accompanied with prayers specifically worded to invoke God's mercy for José Agustín.

The ritual president then has most of the flowers taken outside, the glassed candles removed or extinguished, and begins to take up the cloths covering the catafalque, first carefully folding up the man's clothes and placing them on a shelf.

He gathers up all the apples in a basket, and sends it out with the other food. Inwardly, I am excited; somewhat apprehensive, too. I watch closely as he starts to remove and fold up the white cloth, for I don't want to miss seeing whatever is under it. He reveals that the body is made of large loaves of bread and bunches of bananas; it's more food! All these items are placed in boxes and sent out, together with the pieces of the dismantled catafalque.

The color photo of José Agustín is put on a kind of altar at the back wall of the room, alongside the pictures of saints. The cross of flowers is leaned against the altar. The censer, now with lighted charcoal in it, is placed on the floor next to the cross. Grains of incense are regularly dropped in it so that a continuously wavering column of fragrant smoke rises with the peoples' prayers and blesses us all with its aroma. The tall candlesticks are arranged on each side of the cross, their flickering flames silent and evanescent witnesses to the possibility of faith.

When the center of the room is clear, a man and woman come, each taking one arm of the cross; they then kneel on the rough concrete floor, facing us. Each person present approaches the cross, kneels in front of it, and kisses it, but a regular line is never formed; there is no crowding, no hurry. A new person continually emerges from the people, comes up to the cross, makes the reverence, merges back, and then another, until everyone has venerated the cross. During this time a moving hymn celebrating the glory and power of the cross is sung by all. Not needing a push from Cruz, I, too, go up when there is a gap in the stream of neighbors.

The young prayer director takes the cross from its two holders, who must be tired from kneeling so long on the hard, roughly finished concrete, and again places it against the altar.

A hymn with many verses is sung. The word, *adios*, is often repeated. It's late; although the words and melody express a courageous devotion and tough sentiments, I grow tired, and begin to wonder if it will ever end! It does, finally, and Cruz suggests that we go home. But as we near the door, the widow stops us and insists that we stay for another cup of coffee. We return to our chairs, and are served a *café de olla*, again together with a large roll. I don't feel I can eat any more that day. Cruz tells me to put the roll inside my shirt and eat it tomorrow.

More quiet, friendly, and unembarrassed talk; the people move easily from the sacred to the secular. They are familiar with the ritual, and the ritual, with its songs, sentiments, and movements, sweetens the fright of death. After finishing much of our coffee—it's now long past my bedtime and the cups seem bottomless—we arise, shake hands with a few people, and bid the widow goodnight. She urges us to attend a Mass to be offered for her husband in the parish church the next day. It is shortly after midnight; we have sung the proper prayers for a solid two hours, remembering the deceased, and repeating the fact that we shall all join him, hopefully in the faith expressed by the ceremonies of this night.

Although it is quite late for me, I do not go to bed immediately; too many impressions and thoughts are running through me, keeping me nervously awake and expectantly alert. I vaguely feel that I'm on the edge of understanding something for the first time. I don't want to miss the insight or intuition that lurks just outside my consciousness, for I believe it is a special grace.

The evening's ceremonies and the Sunday liturgy were a genuine doxology, simple and meaningful words praising God. I never imagined that doxology could be so rich, so full of *human* elements, so expressive of my needs and of a faith community's sorrows and fears. What I had been experiencing, among unpretentious people in a remote corner of Mexico, far from centers celebrated in the media, unknown to the "larger" world, was a living evocation of transcendent spirits, some fleeting contact with eternity. Through vocalized prayer and sacramental motions, the people praise God, absorb a theologically sound catechesis, are formed and confirmed in the physical, emotional, mental, and soulful dispositions most fitting to face and experience death. Their repetitive liturgy is a learning that is experiential and immediate, not mediated and reflexive. On their own initiative, through their own genius, not from an institutional curriculum; by sensual doing, not by being passively instructed, they learn a living preparation for death, an introduction: how to live now in order to die well . . . tomorrow, or on some later day. This is truly the perfection of a rich ritual, encompassing a genuinely incarnate prayer, a rite that includes common but lovely flowers, ordinary food, the cigarettes and Coke of daily relaxation. Further, and importantly, all is done by the people themselves; no official bureaucrat or hierarchical authority oversees or controls what they do; no institutional power is exercised; no pressure, other than that of their neighbors' good opinion and their own faith, impels them to act.

A dense web of traditions that no one could ever completely unravel, reaching back before the Conquest, inspires and supports them. In a society where I have seen arbitrary violence and spectacular beauty, gross ugliness and imaginative fantasies, these people appear to face death with their feet solidly on the ground.

All the words and ceremonies expressed a certain "peasant" nobility, a wealth in the midst of poverty. Everything the people did was in stark contrast to their surroundings. The natural dignity of low-income persons, the beauty of the flowers, and the integrity of the food were interwoven with cheap plastic chairs (rented for the occasion) filling the yard, the small rough box of a house built of the cheapest materials, and naked glaring light bulbs, highlighting the common, inexpensive clothes and mestizo features of the family's friends.

I was especially taken with the unveiling of the body. The evening's director moved slowly in quiet solemnity, as if a real body were present. There was no intimation of make-believe. After all, each person was thoroughly familiar with the rite. His deliberate and careful actions slowly revealed basic foods, fruit and bread, artfully arranged. A "common" member of the community, selected by those who knew him, assumed momentary leadership. His formal and lovely gestures touched sensible objects known to all but, through the faith of the participants, these reached far beyond the death of José Agustín. I assume the food was shared among family and neighbors.

Two days later, Cruz reminds me of his invitation to the Rosario for Roberto, the young man who committed suicide. It is Cruz's turn, again, to lead the prayers. We walk several blocks to arrive for the ceremony at eight in the evening. The meeting place appears to be a simple, but fairly large garage, narrow but long enough for two cars. Many cases of empty and dusty soda bottles are stacked against one wall. Along both walls rough planks rest on large cans or cement blocks. The people sit on them facing one another. By turning their bodies they can look toward the makeshift altar at the end of the building.

I hesitate at the street entrance door, but someone takes me near the front, and I sit on a plank. When the planks are full, men of the house bring out some of the usual white plastic chairs and place them in the center of the space. I can see through the door going into a patio, and notice that the interior of the house appears quite small, too small to accommodate this crowd. The altar is covered with vases of flowers, now no longer quite fresh, because it is several days into the week of Rosaries.

Cruz again stands at the front, a bit left of center and facing the altar, to lead the liturgy. The Rosary, Litany, hymns, and prayers are similar to those we sang and recited on Sunday morning, with two differences. After each decade of the Rosary, Cruz sprinkles the altar with a water-soaked flower kept in an ordinary drinking glass, as was done at the *cumpleaños* two nights earlier. Further, all the prayers are composed in terms of the man who has died, and his name, Roberto, is often spoken. As on Sunday, the censer is kept supplied with incense, so that smoke continually ascends, while its fragrance envelopes all of us, almost transforming the vulgar space of an ordinary garage.

After the hour-long ritual, each person is given a rectangular Styrofoam plate with three delicately prepared tacos, and a decorated clay cup of *café de olla*—good-tasting food and drink. Looking around me, I count about sixty people. So, this family, of extremely limited means, must prepare a supper like this every night for a week. The flowers are not as abundant as I had expected, but then I realize that many more have probably been left on the grave. Perhaps only birds and the cemetery ghosts see and enjoy them until they, too, die and rot.

I accompanied Cruz and Lucina on one other evening to the garage for the Rosario. Every night the widow's family prepared a different dish for the guests to eat after the ceremony. That evening they served *pozole*, a popular soup. It was delicious, but tasted strange to me, and I asked Lucina why. When I ate it other times, I could savor its pork base, but that evening it tasted like chicken. She explained that pork would not be fitting to commemorate the dead. One had to observe a kind of fasting, and this was achieved through preparing the dish with chicken stock. I noticed, too, that all the responses to the Litany were different than in the Sunday celebration. Instead of "Ruega por nosotros" (pray for us), the people repeated, over and over, "Ruega por él," that is, "pray for him" (Roberto). The prayers were both theologically sound and were framed in terms of these people and this person, Roberto. They were expressed in the best possible proportion; they nicely fitted the occasion and all the people gathered for it.

That summer, I prayed with the people of the Barrio de los Ramos in their chapel and in their homes. But I had been coming to the village for almost twenty years, and never before had made any move to join them in their religious practices. Why did I radically change my way of acting that summer? Did I need all those years of prayer, their prayers, not mine, to be so moved? Was this a dramatic example of the power of prayer? Was these peoples' graceful gift to me related to my years of reticence? An unlearned, unsophisticated people gave me a new experience of prayer. I learned what could never be obtained from all the books I read; the world of scholarship is helpless before such knowledge.

It appears that the liturgy in the chapel and peoples' homes forms some kind of central place in their lives. The chapel is more or less in the physical center of the neighborhood. There is a pattern to the ringing of the bell on Sunday mornings, and a different rhythm when it tolls for a death. What do these rhythms of ringing say to the people? Until a few weeks ago, they said nothing to me. Is that true for some of the villagers too? Superficially, I suppose they all know what the different patterns mean when they hear the bell. But I have no way of telling what goes on in their hearts and minds when they hear or listen to the sound.

I know there is a long and complex history of bell-ringing in the West, and that many traditions are associated with specific bells and occasions. But I feel I've already been granted an excess of insight into the community's meanings that their chapel bell evokes. I'm hardly capable of absorbing all they have already revealed to me; to probe further might violate their world, their sensibilities, their collective and individual selves.

Certain things, though, I do know. It might be misleading to call Ocotepec a village. It is more properly an adjunct to the city of Cuernavaca. Speaking of the place as a village leads me to misperceive what is here, contributes to the creation of illusions and sentimental notions about "villagers." Almost every house, no matter how poor or badly constructed, enjoys electricity and sports a TV aerial. Although very few people own a car, the bus and taxi service to and from the nearby city is fast and frequent; no one really needs a car, a conclusion I've confirmed from my own experience.

The people have employment, schools, doctors, and hospitals. Several apparently well-stocked video outlets provide entertainment packages to supplement the usual TV programming. These did not exist a few years ago. When I first arrived here, there was one public phone; now the main street is cluttered with them. As far as I can tell, none of modernity's large or small goodies is lacking here. I see no way in which those who live here could be termed a traditional people. But at least one part of their ancient wisdom seems to have survived in a powerful if slightly syncretic fashion—their approach to dying and the practices surrounding death.

Death is the ultimate unknown, the most fearful experience each person must face, that which above all inspires terror. In a barrio of Ocotepec, I came to know a people anew, a people who have encircled death with regular and meaningful rituals that involve all, from the youngest to the oldest. An outsider might be tempted to say that they have learned how to die, but I think such a statement is grossly inaccurate. They have "learned" to face death the way one "learns" to walk, by doing it. They are aware of death, reminded again each time a neighbor dies, and on each anniversary. They appear to have no need for instruction or the usual institutional support. It may be accurate to say that they know how to keep their "living with death" alive; they have wisely devised a form to face the fear of death; they do not foolishly attempt to banish death. Under the onslaught of an economist, money-intensive society, where economic man is supreme, they may have abandoned or drastically diluted other traditional beliefs and practices, but they have seemingly held fast to those around death with no great struggle or apparent effort. Such may be a most unusual case in the history of modernization's destructions. Have the people of Ocotepec exercised some sapiential judgment I've never before met and certainly don't understand? Does such a wonder occur in other places in Mexico? In other countries, too? Do many such humble lights illumine the prevailing darkness?

It seemed to me that I again had found that the most profound signs of hope are to be found among the conventional, ordinary, and seemingly insignificant acts of the little people of our world.

If it be possible to imagine a good death as a human creation, then it appeared to me that all its elements are present here. Over the years, the people themselves have chosen and maintained certain acts and prayers to accompany and commemorate death. The whole neighborhood is notified by the tolling bell, what has visited someone they know. Each is then free to participate or not, to respond as he or she thinks is proper. Everyone is invited to reflect on their own death.

Books and articles have been written about the questionable or manifestly bad effects of medicalization. But, reflecting on what I saw that summer, I suspect that I came upon the most horrendous aspect of a specifically modern death. If one is taken away to a hospital or nursing home to die—as happens with seven out of ten Americans today—then the customs in which I participated are usually lost. Everyone is impoverished: the dying person, all the family and neighbors, and the medical personnel. Practices such as those to which I was invited seem to be necessary for the act of dying to realize its possible wholeness, that is, it belongs to me as much as my birth. The rituals in Ocotepec prepared all of us, together, for a final act that each must suffer alone.

For some years I have believed that I was preparing to die: I reflected on the fact of death, formed certain ideas about my own death, and prayed for a good death, a death that would remind me, each day, of how to live. But now I tend to think that all these preparations lack an essential component—I have acted alone, but without appreciating the terrible depth of my solitude. Crucially, I have not enjoyed the uncommon privileges of those rough-appearing people, people in whom the world finds no importance.

From Cruz, Lucina, and their neighbors, I saw that my mindfulness of death, my acting in view of my death, is inadequate. I have tried to get along without a living communal liturgy; I have not recognized the need for repeated communal ritual. Each person in Ocotepec can join his or her neighbors to celebrate the death of someone they know, perhaps more than a thousand times during their lifetime. From infancy, each is introduced to the terror of the real world, the world that includes death, in a communal embrace of memory and celebration, of trust and hope. What must such repeated commemorations do to those people, to their sensibilities, their souls? What kind of person lives in that place? My awareness of reality was unimaginably expanded.

Because of my exposure to the social sciences, I ask those questions ... and foolishly, or perversely, am tempted to believe I can find answers. For, I can study those people! I could work out a research design, devise a methodology, and attempt to enter their world, their hearts, their minds, their very being.

But, I hesitate . . . I already know those people, some of them pretty well, and I've come to feel a genuine affection for them. Would looking at them, observing them, be to *use* them? Is this what it means to study them? And would study necessarily be characterized, above all, as an instrumental activity, turning them into a shabby means for my "exalted" end? If I were an academic, how could my career be advanced without such study?

I'm confused. Are there times and places where such seeking after knowledge is not appropriate? Where it is not even permitted? Maybe the very idea of knowledge today must be challenged. Accepted, even respected, academic practices may demand fundamental questioning. Perhaps the learning that takes place through much of social science, including history, is suspect.

Should I attempt to take seriously the articles on curiosity, as a moral failing, in St. Thomas's *Summa theologiae*?[1] Is it imperative today, not only not to be embarrassed by his teaching, but to expand it, given the luxuriant growth of the knowledge industries? In some sense, knowledge has greatly multiplied, but disorder has increased even more—according to some cultural critics. I think one could propose a proportion: There is a regular and positive relationship between the expansion of available

---

[1] Aquinas, *Summa theologiae,* II II, q. 167, aa. 1,2.

knowledge and the disagreement among academics about what constitutes an education. What does it mean to be well educated today?

Another proportion seems to hold true. Historically, the explosion of knowledge in Western universities accompanied the decline of medieval scholasticism. From a height reached in the works of St. Thomas (d. 1274), one can trace a drying up, an over subtle multiplication of distinctions, an abstract and rigid formalism, which people as different as Descartes, Wittgenstein, and Balthasar recognized as sterile.

A third intellectual movement, related to the above two, also occurred. As the natural sciences developed, the importance of philosophy and theology in universities diminished. These three changes are not independent of one another. What I now suspect, from my experience with the people of Ocotepec, is that these social/intellectual shifts contain an important moral dimension, which I have only partially glimpsed . . . up to now!

Years ago I came to believe that photos of peoples' misery—what one sees in newspapers or on television after every accident or natural disaster—are obscene; one should never take or show such pictures; further, they induce an especially odious form of nosiness. Our wounded nature inclines us to rejoice at the misfortune of the other; I am secretly happy it didn't happen to me. But is research into others' situation, into their actions and inner life, essentially different from more crass forms of voyeurism? Am I led to suspect that social science itself is highly questionable, that is, morally questionable? Or is there a kind of seeking after knowledge that is disinterested or even empathic and, therefore, possibly good? Are there exceptions?

My experience with the people of Ocotepec brought me to ask questions about the acquisition of knowledge that directly touches on good and evil. I am now impelled to feel that, in some sense, the seeking of knowledge of the other is morally problematic, in some instances, perhaps even forbidden.

It seems clear to me that the thrust, the inclination, to know about others, is very often not good. The desire to know may be very much like the desire for food and drink. Most of us seem to have great trouble bringing order into our sense appetites. The same may be true, although largely unacknowledged, of our appetites for knowing. Further, some who have excelled in producing social science knowledge may be the ones most intensely living a life committed to vice, to vicious living. Some may have embraced a life partly dedicated to a sinful curiosity. In fact, the desire to know, because of specific knowledge-acquiring developments in Western history, may constitute an eighth capital sin, a sin especially prevalent in what is termed the Age of Information. It might be called the sin of curiosity.

I know that one human act alone is primary and essential, necessary and ultimate: to love. If I do not love, the other or others, I am dead; in a sense, I am hopeless. All the principal fonts of wisdom contain the same teaching; in general terms, it is not specific to Judaism and Christianty.

I came to that place, to Ocotepec, out of friendship. Perhaps this friendship protected me from being curious all those years. However, during that time, I generally greeted the people I met on the street that ran past the house where I stayed, even though I didn't always know them. And I became quite friendly with the owners of two small shops where I often went to get photocopies made, with the man from whom I bought vegetables and fruit, and with a young woman from whom I regularly bought tortillas. The woman who sold me bread and cheese also knew me, but she was usually too busy in her little store for conversation. My everyday needs took me to these people. I suppose my affection for them led me to speak, to discuss the affairs of the barrio or the world with them. If I were to reflect on our conversations, I could tell you something about them and their families. But I never sought this knowledge; I was never curious about them; as far as I can tell, my affection preceded any knowing.

One day, after many years of my annual presence for some weeks or months in Ocotepec, Cruz invited me to the neighborhood liturgy; it occurred "naturally." But something led me to accept, drew me to the chapel. Dare I believe that Cruz's initiative and my response were due to graces we had received? That all this was, quite precisely, a gratuitous gift?

I know, from many signs, that Cruz and Lucina have a genuine affection for me. And I am quite certain of my respect and affection for them. Perhaps this mutual friendship, perfected over many years, worked on both sides: that he invited me, that I accepted.

As I look back, I realize that each time I went to the Sunday Rosario, each time I accompanied Cruz and Lucina to a neighbor's home for a liturgy of the dead, I went to pray. Although I must have had other motives, too, I am quite sure that the desire to pray with these people was uppermost in my mind and heart.

For the last year or so, I have attempted to observe "the Sabbath" as a Christian, to acknowledge the special character of this day each week through my awareness and actions on Sunday. This attitude appeared to match whatever was in Cruz's mind when he first asked me to go to the early morning prayer service. All my thoughts about liturgy on Sunday mornings at the chapel and evenings in neighbors' houses came much later.

After a good deal of reflection, I conclude that the people of Ocotepec taught me certain truths I hope never to forget. Perhaps the principal one is that doxology is important, but in a way I had never before felt or realized. The summer's experience was more than enough evidence to establish the ontological primacy of doxologic words and actions: all language is, exists, insofar as it is doxologic; one judges it according to how it departs from or goes toward doxological speech. Further, doxology goes far beyond the forms in which I had been looking for it: in the Roman Catholic Mass, in the Eastern Orthodox Eucharist, in Western and Eastern monastic liturgies. Doxology, I also learned, in its perfection often contains a further quality: it is communal; one needs something like a familiar neighborhood to raise one's voice to God. The solitude of death also requires that one live with others. To live a doxologic life, it is good to seek a community life.

The people taught me that ritual is necessary. I saw, too, that ritual takes forms I had not imagined, for example, the incense smoke rising continually throughout the liturgy. I had never seen this in any "official" celebration. Rather, the incense is brought out for a moment or two, then disappears.

I also came to a new appreciation and respect for repetition. I used to think that saying the fifty Hail Marys in a Rosary was some kind of mindless activity, *unless* one could really meditate, be absorbed by, the respective mystery of that decade. Now I see that the repetition itself of the same prayer, quite apart from any real or pseudo contemplation, is essential; as humans, we need to return, over and over.

Although I come from a more cosmopolitan, more so-called sophisticated place each year, the death rituals were, nevertheless, both immediately and on reflection, meaningful. But the unique genius of their elaboration, I believe, was found in their frequency: for those living in Ocotepec, the rites are repeated often throughout one's life. I find it difficult to imagine a good preparation for death that would not include this continual return and renewal.

The Sunday and death rituals forcefully reminded me that the engagement of all the senses is important in doxology; therefore, in living, too. For example, the sound of the chapel bell; speaking, singing, and hearing the prayers and hymns; seeing the beauty of the flowers; smelling the sweetness of the incense; the frequent motions of crossing oneself; touching the "body" and kissing the cross at the *cumpleaños*; the taste of the modest lunch; the "small talk" and shaking hands at the end of the ceremonies. All these "liturgical" actions contributed to the reality of doxologic movement. But the truth and reality of doxology, in its turn, comes back from the uncreated to reinforce, to reinvigorate, my sensual life.

The experience of that summer also brought me to ask a question: Why does the Church generally separate liturgy and catechesis? In Ocotepec, I think, the two are joined. There, reflecting on the content of the prayers and participating in the ceremonies, I came to believe that catechesis may take place more meaningfully through liturgy than through classroom-type instruction. Further and, at first glance, amazingly, all this is accomplished by barely literate lay persons. No priest or ecclesiastic functionary was ever present at any liturgy; they were not needed.

The "shape" of the Church, and its action in the world, now appear somewhat different to me. Jesus spoke throughout his active life; he instructed or taught, he preached, he healed. Although commentators and scholars have found traces of it throughout his life on earth, Jesus especially gave us the form and content of a liturgy only toward the end of his life. Over the centuries, various persons in the Church have elaborated many different liturgical expressions. In Ocotepec, I participated in liturgies created and carried out by the most ordinary believers one could ever hope to find. Through prayerful participation, I recognized that these ceremonies are true, moving, and powerful; and that puts me in a quandary. What do I do with this marvelous experience? How do I discharge the great debt I owe those people?

After leaving Ocotepec that summer, a tentative argument, based on what those plain and perhaps badly educated people do, formed in my mind. Up until then I had thought that the natural sciences, especially chemistry, developed through the impulse of men's disordered appetites, are the principal institutional source for the physical condition of a polluted and ugly world. The hard sciences (the adjective is apt) make technology possible, and hubris respectable.

Reflecting on the experience of Ocotepec, I began to think that the social sciences share the "honors," at least equally. The (soft) social sciences made it possible to view people as objects, and made information about the other logically "necessary."

The idea of an objective comprehension of nature—physical, social, and personal—demands an instrumentalization of what I gaze on, turning observation into scientific voyeurism; the researcher then falls into the illusions of power—over the other; and is constantly tempted to attempt manipulation; acting thus, I inevitably end instrumentalizing my self.

Our world could only have come to be if people make a strict distinction and division between themselves as subject and the other, thing or person, as object. Every other person thereby becomes an object, something to be studied, something with the same moral status to my observing and investigative eye as a fly or a microbe, a rock or a volcano. Visualization, through news photos, "realistic" movies, or documentaries, vulgarly popularizes the other as object, legitimating the pleasures, never innocent, of voyeurism.

The social sciences parallel the devastating action of the natural sciences, turning some (the researcher or author) into opportunistic utilitarians for whom the other is principally the material for career advancement. The other is impelled to collaborate willfully, even gratefully, for he or she thereby becomes famous, some kind of celebrity, no matter how undistinguished or tawdry: "I'm written about in the newspaper, or magazine, or book. I may even appear for a fleeting moment on the screen! Far beyond the obscenity witnessed in concentration camp victims, I am eager to collaborate, to turn myself into an abject object."

That summer in Mexico brought me to certain truths I had never before suspected, truths about dying and death. Further, I think I saw possibilities for practices of the Church that would enrich the lives of her members. Thirdly, I reached a provisional understanding of the various sciences that was formerly only inchoate in my thinking.

But beyond these incomparable gifts, the people of Ocotepec also gave me an inestimable good: They revealed to me that I had been held back, restrained, for about a score of years; somehow, although I was living among them for weeks or months each of those years, I never turned them into objects, and myself into a shameless Peeping Tom. Perhaps it is true to say: I controlled my curiosity!

Much of my adult life has been dedicated to cultivating the stance of a perceptive and acute observer, one of the most honored figures in the academic world, the world shaping a large part of my sensibility and thinking. Through the people of Ocotepec, however, I was able to take a few tentative steps towards making myself a stranger to the modern world and, more significantly, to myself. What a blessing! What a joyful alienation!

12

The Pursuit of Health:
Another Chimera?

I AM UNCERTAIN how to analyze accurately the difference between Prozac and an aspirin, Viagra and a Granny Smith apple; but I feel there is a real and important distinction. I have acquired certain habits, for example, never taking a soft drink, nor eating sugar-laden boxed breakfast cereal. But are such actions really different from others I have chosen, like not having a doctor, not going for an annual checkup? I've heard I should esteem the phrase, *mens sana in corpore sano.* Perhaps a key to unraveling the confusion I face is found in the dictionary translation of the Latin: a sound mind in a sound body. I would seek soundness but am wary of going after health.

As an old man, I fear I might envy a young man; I'm worried I might be tempted by an illusory striving for fitness; or, worse, dreading death, attempt to extend the time given me in this world. Others tell me they are anxious about certain diseases, or not having sufficient insurance coverage for their old age. Although not clearly articulating their thoughts, some appear afraid of being left alone and unloved. Many spend handsomely to buy an ersatz youthfulness through the high-tech body-enhancement of cosmetic surgery. Now the government injects further concerns into the country. Especially in airports, but throughout the land, the specter of terrorists, manipulated by politicians and bureaucrats, results in the destruction of civil liberties and a spreading pervasive fear among the citizenry.

I find myself reading ingredient labels; I note the proliferation of health clubs and organic or "natural" food outlets. I am bombarded with images of "health" and continually warned about disease prevention. In an increasingly sick society I am daily reminded to care for my personal well-being. In far-off times, people struggled against gluttony and lust. Today, I am offered Diet-Coke indulgence and the guaranteed offer of an active sex life right up to senility. Formerly, many worked to save their souls; today, an analogous but similar effort is expended on one's figure. However, commenting on the publicly prominent bulges of obesity, many appear mixed up. Some talk of more healthy eating, others rail at the junk food offered kids in schools, and some blame genetics. Almost no one wants to consider the societal and personal disorders that contribute to the moral character of overeating. Fat is only physical or psychological. Drunkenness is viewed solely as a disease.

Looking out over the affluent world, I see a huge and apparently diverse multiplicity of nostrums and programs, consultants and gurus. But there is an underlying unity: Each offers a kind of salvation. Further, this new leaf manifests a specific character: It is medicinal, or therapeutic. Whether I examine a prestigious urban medical center or a fashionable mountain retreat, whether I meet a charismatic healer or an exotic religious personality, I see the same emphasis: I am promised a new life, here and now. If I take the advice, and lay down a hefty payment, I can make myself over, I can be saved.

The spiraling growth of complementary (often called "alternative") medicines, of allopathic investment and procedures, of psychic or religious visions, marvelously matches the fragmentation of contemporary society and modern persons. For the first time in the history of the West, I can choose a salvation that "fits" my needs (*sic*), and the specialness of my person. If I'm sufficiently enthusiastic, I can also simultaneously embrace multiple regimens or programs, stretching from detailed and painful workouts to fragrant and soothing balms, each designed to match a different wound in my disintegrated self.

I am free to pursue any vanity in my personal appearance; I can be insured against every risk of the unknown; I am offered a dazzling cornucopia of mood-altering or organ-fixing drugs; I can access the wisdom of every tradition's sages. Innovative priesthoods have elaborated the rites appropriate for each person's personal passion, no matter how bizarre or fleeting. Some claim these priests serve a new cult, the cult of self.

Cults, focused religious veneration, have been around for a long time, maybe for millennia. It seems highly probable that ancient people, exercising their imaginations, worked out rituals or ways to relate themselves to some higher power. Apparently through oral traditions, they elaborated myths in the form of explanatory stories. Perhaps these accounts entered individual lives, calming peoples' emotional frights and encouraging more strictly rational wonderment.

A bit of research reveals a complex history of cults and rituals in the Western world.[1] Examining these, I suspect that popular contemporary notions of rebirth or cure can be traced to an ur-source, perhaps shrouded in myth, nevertheless true. Vision quests, aroma therapy, and MRI scans are not derived from the ancient Greeks, the Hopi or Trobriand Islanders. Their source lies in an ancient Western transformation of the heart that led to elaborately repeated formal actions. To examine this source through the eyes of medieval thinkers, of men who preceded the concepts and theories of modern anthropologists, permits insights into the attraction and sticking power of contemporary cults and rituals. Many so-called secular rituals today are not only centered around self, but they also promise a product, a new person, apparently within easy reach, if one is rich enough to pay the bill.

The origins of what is called history coincide with the myths of what has been understood as religion in European thought. Although one can argue that Christian religion was influenced by Hellenism, European religious belief and practice come predominantly from the Jews, not the Greeks. Maybe 3,000 years ago, Abram heard a call, and answered, breaking the circle's grip on peoples' imaginations. After him, time was no longer believed to be cyclically repetitive but, like an arrow, shot out in a line toward a future that was anchored on a promise. Abram, becoming Abraham, founded a people in Canaan, a land picked out for him. Putting his faith in a *personal* God, he definitively broke with the ancient world, bequeathing to all future generations a new understanding of religion: Within a strict covenantal relationship, his God promised salvation.[2]

Although often clouded with failures and aberrations from his time until today, Hebrew and, later, Christian belief and practice fitfully realized Abrahamic faith. This faith, bearing witness to God's Covenant, antedated the appearance of Jesus by about a thousand years. At the

---

[1] For survey articles and bibliographies, see the work on myth in Wiener, *Dictionary of the History of Ideas,* vol. 3, 272–318, and associated entries. An exposition of ritual theory is given by Bell, *Ritual. Perspectives and Dimensions.* Selections from recent thinkers are gathered by Grimes, *Readings in Ritual Studies.* The latest study of ritual, carried out by the grab-bag discipline of anthropology, appears heavily weighted in favor or non-Western and "primitive" ethnographic practices. Earlier research, attempting to relate ritual and myth to culture, often began with a study of the ancient Greeks and Hebrews.

[2] A remarkable book discusses the various contributions of the Jews to Western culture and religion: Cahill, *The Gifts of the Jews.*

beginning of the Christian era, the author of the letter to the Hebrews, acknowledging that a Messiah would come from Abraham's flesh and faith, claimed that Jesus is that person, the fulfillment of the ancient Covenant, of the promises made to God's chosen people.[3]

In important respects, many Christians have lived the beliefs and carried out the practices of their Hebrew ancestors. Believers in both traditions see man and woman as made in the image of God. That is, people somehow share God's spirit, and possess the power to make rational choices: to recognize, then choose, good or evil. This view assumes that people act for an end when they act humanly, namely, fully using their human or quasi-divine powers. Further, as Aristotle believed, everyone naturally seeks happiness. In the Middle Ages, thinkers preferred the term, blessedness (*beatitudo*); ultimately, they said, happiness can only be found in God, in being blessed by him; this was the meaning of salvation, the end or goal of Christian believers.

As a matter of fact, however, some place their supreme happiness in certain external goods: traditionally, the list includes money, honor, fame, and power. Others prefer the internal good of sense pleasures derived from sex, food and drink. In the thirteenth century, St. Thomas Aquinas pointed out why blessedness cannot be found in any created good. The ultimate end, or final good, should quiet every desire. And, in this inclusive vision of human reach, the object of one's rational appetite is universal good. Therefore, I cannot find my ultimate happiness in creation. All created goods are partial, found in both good and evil persons, and are often the result of luck; further, created goods are good only through participation in *the* good, God.[4] This view of reality finally rests on a belief, as do all views. Ultimately, everyone is a believer—in something or someone.

---

[3] One can profitably read all thirteen chapters of the epistle. In one of his letters, St. Paul reminds the people of Rome that "He [Abraham] is the father of us all" (Rom 4:16). But if God is God, why did he choose the Jews over other people of the world? Attempting to answer the question, St. Thomas Aquinas ends by saying that St. Augustine's opinion seems the best available for human understanding: "Quare hunc trahat, et illum non trahat, noli dijudicare, si non vis errare" (If you don't want to fall into error, don't try to second-guess God). Aquinas, *Summa theologiae*, I II, q. 98, a. 4, corp. All Aquinas references are to this book, a compendium of medieval thought. Mastering the Hebrew, Greek, Christian, and Islamic authors who preceded him, and presenting a particularly lucid synthesis of Christian medieval thought in his own disciplined order and style, Thomas Aquinas stands out as an exemplary thinker bringing these traditions together.

[4] Aquinas, *Summa theologiae*, I II, q. 2, a. 8, corp.

Abraham and those who followed him sought deliverance, and this was perceived as salvation, a divine healing. Through a millennia-long tradition, women and men have continued to seek happiness through redemption. This is the principal reason why, until recently, almost all within East and West European traditions were more aligned with Abrahamic Jews than with Platonic Greeks. A therapeutic salvation departs from this tradition since it does not demand repentance and conversion. The salvation offered through the modern notion of health does not require a radical turning oneself inside out. But the experience of generation after generation of salvation seekers has left an indelible mark, a desire, in each person's heart.

Those who attempted to be faithful to the example of Abraham developed a religion, a way to worship God. The medieval Scholastics understood the Hebrews' actions as required and ordered by the virtue of justice. If one feels called to respond to the grace first offered to Abram, one must act; belief requires human acts to be real, to be true. Justice is that acquired habit of acting by which one firmly and always gives to the other what is due.[5] In this action, people establish the proper proportion between themselves and the other. Aquinas calls this a proportionate equality (*secundum proportionis aequalitatem*).[6] Whether discussing justice or the operation of grace, the action of the senses or the structure of ritual, Aquinas sees proportion as a key concept.

Because everything humans are, and have received, is God's gift to them, they are indebted to him; justice demands payment. But, as is the case with one's parents, no one can pay this debt as one ought. I do what I can, and these actions are gathered together, organized, then called a virtue, the virtue of religion. Most directly and simply, such is the origin of Western cult, begun by Abram, who was instructed on how to order a people to the deity. His acceptance of and participation in the Covenant was expressed through cult—from the Latin, *cultivare*, to cultivate. Active Jewish response was demanded by justice. Today, however,

[5] Aquinas, *Summa theologiae*, II II, q. 58, a. 1, corp. Justice is distinguished from the other cardinal virtues (prudence, fortitude, and temperance) in that the measure is objective, outside the person. With the other virtues, the measure is found within the (virtuous) person: For example, prudence is found in a prudent person choosing good means to the proper end sought.

[6] Aquinas, *Summa theologiae*, II II, q. 58. a. 11, corp. For Aquinas, justice means much more than dollars and cents, for which an arithmetical measure would be sufficient. He lived before the birth of *homo economicus*, before the substitution of values for the good, that is, before the attempted mathematization of the good.

many cults do not usually mention justice. Often, the only "debt" is to oneself, the manifestation of self-interest. For this, one does not need a long and arduous practice to acquire a habit of virtue.

Having a twofold nature, intellectual and sensible, we offer God a twofold adoration: spiritual, the interior devotion of my mental faculties, and corporeal, the external humbling of my body. But in all acts of worship, the external is hierarchically ordered to the internal as to the more important. Therefore, all external bodily acts are designed to inform our mind and excite our affection toward submission to God.[7] Humanly speaking, I am moved to these actions through meditation on God's goodness and benefits on one hand, my defects and failures on the other.[8]

Why do this? Why submit to such a course? Can one construct an argument in favor of religious belief and practice? That's been done, of course, by medieval thinkers. They placed great confidence in the powers of the mind, and were convinced that one could know reality, that the real is intelligible. This is true because, in certain crucial aspects, the real stays put; it doesn't move, doesn't change. Therefore, one can speak of nature, and a natural order. In this order, the very constitution of "what is," the inferior or weaker submits to the superior or stronger. An immediate example is that of an infant and its parents. Meditating on such phenomena, medieval men—and a few women—concluded that the examples were individual instances of a general law, what they called "natural law," the very way things exist. Law, therefore, is an analogical, not an univocal term; there are different kinds of law.

The Scholastics emphasized the reasonableness of all law. They could do this because they saw an order in all that is and posited the hypothesis that this order was a reflection of the divine. Perhaps one could dare speak of a divine rationality. Such assumes that the universe and God are one. But oneness or unity is quite other than the modern sense of one as the beginning of a numerical sequence.

All law is a certain rule and measure of human acts and, therefore, an external principle of these acts. Since God governs everything and is outside time, one can speak of an eternal law. Creation, according to this belief system, is ruled and measured, and must in some way participate

---

[7] Ibid., q. 82, a. 3, corp; Aquinas, *Summa theologiae*, I II, q. 101, a. 2, corp.

[8] Aquinas, *Summa theologiae*, II II, q. 82, a. 3, corp. He points out that (male) intellectuals are inclined to attribute their talent to themselves alone. Vanity leaves no place for devotion. (Ibid., obj. 3, and ad 3)

in eternal law. Each creature, according to its own mode of existence and action, has a natural inclination to certain acts and ends.[9] For example, a stone falls, seeking its place of rest; a flower reaches upward, a brute animal eats and copulates, a man might choose to forgive a wrong. This inclination came to be called natural law. On reflection, all rational creatures recognize natural law's ultimate prescription for them: Good is to be sought and done, evil avoided.[10] Human laws are the result of people reflecting on historical experience and their own reasonable inclinations and attempting to respond to the particular needs and circumstances of social life. A person or group exercising what is recognized as legitimate authority conceptualizes, spells out, and applies these directives.

Scholastics reflected on certain verses of St. Paul:

> For in my inner being I delight in God's law, but I see another law at work in the members of my body, waging war against the law of my mind and making me a prisoner of the law of sin at work within my members. What a wretched man I am! (Rom 7:22–24)

They then concluded that one could speak of another law, the *lex fomitis*, an inclination of sensuality that is proper to animals but not to humans who wish to live in accord with reason, cultural norms, or divine inspiration.[11]

All persons, contemplating their faults and deficiencies, resort to someone (in this respect, superior) who can help them or make up what is missing. For example, I might decide to consult a physician if I have a fever that will not go away. If I make a sustained effort to reflect on myself, my possibilities and powers, I come to realize that I am not, finally, self-sufficient, I am not my own raison d'être. But I do belong to an order, and this order is hierarchical. Ultimately, there is someone or something believed to be the source, *the* good. Traditionally, people have named this good God, whether that supreme reality is a bronze bull or one's father, money or a demon. By a completely natural inclination, one

---

[9] Aquinas, *Summa theologiae,* I II, q. 91, a. 2, corp.

[10] Aquinas, *Summa theologiae,* I II, q. 94, a. 2, corp.

[11] Ibid., q. 90, on the nature of law; q. 91, on the different laws: eternal, natural, human, divine, and the *lex fomitis*. One can also see Wiener, *Dictionary of the History of Ideas,* vol. 3, 13–27. This source is strongly influenced by the ideas of Kant on law, namely, seeing law as a rule. This is quite different from seeing law as a principle (Aquinas's conception).

is then driven to subject oneself and honor that god in a fitting manner; therefore, one pays a different kind of homage, depending on whether one worships a sacred shrine or a fat portfolio. But whatever be the character of the god, people always employ physical, sensible actions and things as meaningful signs of their internal respect and submission.[12]

In the centuries following the death of Abraham, the Hebrews developed an extensive and detailed collection of laws covering all aspects of behavior, personal and communitary. Medieval thinkers divided these into three kinds: moral precepts, expressing natural law; ceremonial precepts, elaborating the character, times and frequency of the divine cult; judicial precepts, laying down how justice is to be achieved among people. Ceremonial law determined the organization or structure of divine worship, specifying the details of what anthropologists came to call ritual.

Since the modern notion of law is far removed from what obtained, for example, in the time of the Hebrew Judges (about 1000 B.C.), people today experience great difficulty understanding divine law and its accompanying religious rituals. For both the ancients and contemporary Christians the universe and everything in it was ruled or governed by divine providence. Jesus expressed this truth most simply and dramatically:

> "Are not two sparrows sold for a penny? Yet not one of them will fall to the ground apart from the will of your Father. And even the very hairs of your head are all numbered" (Matt 10:29–30).

A cabinetmaker, for example, has an idea of what he will make through his art. Just so, a ruler (for the medievalist, a *gubernans*) will have a clear notion of the order to be realized by those under his reign. This notion is called law. God is like both the cabinetmaker and the ruler. He governs, in the medieval sense, every act and motion of every creature, that is, all action is as dependent on God as all existence, a truth clearly stated by Jesus and, philosophically, by the Scholastics. This plan and mode of governance, existing first of all as an exemplar of divine wisdom moving everything to its proper end, is the very essence of law, in this instance, eternal law.[13]

Persons are subject to divine providence in a more excellent way than any other creature, since they participate in that providence, car-

---

[12] Aquinas, *Summa theologiae,* II II, q. 58, a. 1, corp.

[13] Aquinas, *Summa theologiae,* I II, q. 93, a. 1, corp.

ing for themselves and others (persons and lesser creatures). I see what, in the first place, this care entails, namely, distinguishing between good and evil; and this seeing comes from the light of my natural intellectual ability or power; the light is nothing other than the impress of the divine light on my mind.[14]

Christians have generally been as assiduous as the Hebrews in perfecting and practicing the rituals of their cult. It can be argued, seeing the way medieval thinkers grasped the rituals of Abraham's progeny, that some modern academics (anthropologists) do not adequately understand the nature of cult. The difficulties are two: First, cult is an intellectually elaborated expression of divine law, once people come to the insight into who they are, namely, creatures gifted with rational choice. As such, they then attempt to conform themselves to "what is," to the very nature of reality; hence, they devise appropriate rituals since they suspect or recognize fundamental hierarchy.

As is evident, all creatures below humans have no need for ritual; from the stone to the wolf, all spontaneously embody eternal law. But Aquinas understood and pointed out that law, as it pertains to humans, tends or goes in one direction alone, to establish friendship, friendship among persons, and of persons to God.[15] For many today this constitutes another difficulty. The essential relationship between law and friendship is one of the many truths moderns ignore, neglect or simply do not know.

A Pharisee, testing Jesus, asked him, "'Teacher, which is the greatest commandment in the Law?'" Not afraid of the trick, Jesus answered bluntly,

> "Love the Lord your God with all your heart and with all your soul and with all your mind." This is the first and greatest commandment. And the second is like it: "Love your neighbor as yourself" (Matt 22:37–39).

For over 3,000 years, Jews and Christians have turned their eyes and hearts toward Yahweh/God, attempting to live in accord with eternal law. Throughout this time, those with the most imaginative religious sensibilities devoted themselves to devising rituals fitting the fostering of friendship. The teaching of Jesus is clear: An essential part of law is

---

[14] Ibid., q. 91, a. 2, corp.

[15] Aquinas, *Summa theologiae,* I II, q. 99, a. 1, ad 2.

love; one cannot obey divine law without loving one's neighbor. Today we would often speak of friendship.

Over the centuries religious innovators worked to fulfill the requirements of achieving a cosmic balance through the ceremonies most proper to move men and women to discharge the human debt to divine largesse. As pointed out above, people in the Middle Ages understood all such action as pertaining directly to justice, rendering to the other his due. When the other is the Other, such action is religion. Its practices, internal and external, bring one to the perfection of being healed, to salvation. For at least thousands of years people influenced by European traditions have sought salvation. Although many today do not openly profess a belief in the Jewish/Christian/Islamic God, a powerful vestige of the seeking is still present in them.

Some would claim that the infinitely repetitious rituals were powerfully mythopoeic. Indeed, I hazard the judgment that these millennia-long practices left indelible marks in the souls of Western men and women. Therefore, desires for healing rituals are powerfully present in people today. In the heart of many persons, no matter how "sophisticated" or ironic their self-presentation, no matter how worldly-wise or bored their outward persona, an unrecognized longing exists, a question is ever present: How achieve wholeness, obtain salvation? The contemporary answer often given, in addition to pointing toward a historical source, also manifests a certain corruption of the tradition. Abram answered a call; his descendants developed a law/ritual leading men and women to friendship. Today's anxiety-ridden modern embraces a pursuit, faithfully practices elixir-tinged rituals, but often ends in agonizing loneliness. The other is absent.

The evidence for this interpretation is, I believe, clear and close at hand. So-called secular moderns, affluent and educated, are just as avid in their specific quests as the ancient Hebrew Psalmist or the most self-sacrificing hermit or monk. Growing numbers of anxious transformation-strivers resolutely commit themselves to the wide-ranging prescriptions of the self-help industry, which offers sure-fire diets for both body and soul.

With many others today, I am conscious of good and bad diets, aware that certain practices and places are unhealthy, realize that GMOs are not a sign of progress, and recognize that an exclusively sedentary existence is not to be followed. But I fear that the contemporary seeking after health is a profoundly disordered fetishization, a decidedly perverse sacralization of personal well-being. What comes first is not firmly in place. As Ivan Illich noted, "the art of celebrating the present is paralyzed by what has become the pursuit of health."[16] Attempting to live in the present, and motivated by friendship, I might see that the only way to achieve my wholeness is through caring for the other, the friend, by nursing him back to health. I do not believe such action is the "pursuit of health."

French, Spanish, and Latin employ the same word—*salut, salud,* and *salus*—to signify both temporal and atemporal welfare or health. Dictionaries list this-world meanings first. But I suspect the other-world meanings are deep and powerful in peoples' feelings. If true, this fact contributes greatly to the vehemence with which people pursue health.[17]

Other possibilities also exist. For example, one can fervently chase after health because one wants to live as long as possible, irrationally hoping to put off death. Or I can thoughtlessly engage in various kinds of risky behavior, thinking that medical science will rescue me if I have an accident.[18]

Inside every heart, fear and doubt have always hovered. As a modern, however, I must courageously ask myself certain threatening questions: What is the character of the health I pursue? Is my seeking reasonable, or irrational? Relaxed, or all-consuming? Am I happy only with Viagra, or is a Granny Smith enough? Is my satisfaction found in this world or should I seek the joy found only beyond my self? Finally, do illusions dominate my beliefs?

Today's myriad of quasi-religious promises is, basically, therapeutic, and the most ominous doubts should originate here. It may be that the tenacious sticking power of my pursuit is perfectly and paradoxically matched by the chimeric character of the salvation offered. Perhaps I am not skeptical enough.

---

[16] Illich, "Do Not Let Us Succumb to Diagnosis," unpublished speech.

[17] In the Vulgate, Psalm 107 expresses Revelation's truth about *salus*, perhaps a last word on the subject:
  Da nobis auxilium de tribulatione:
  Quia vana salus hominis.
  [Oh Lord] aid us in our tribulation:
  For the help of men is worthless.

[18] Suggested by a friend, Aaron Falbel.

Bibliography

Aquinas, Saint Thomas. *Summa theologiae.*

Arana Palacios, Jesús. "José Benjamín, un hombre de su siglo." *Revista de Occidente* 69 (1995) 29–52.

Aristophanes. *Clouds.* Translated by Alan H. Sommerstein. Warminster, England: Aris & Phillips Ltd., 1991.

Aristotle. *Metaphysics.*

Aristotle. *The Nichomachean Ethics.*

Balthasar, Hans Urs von. *The Glory of the Lord.* San Francisco: Ignatius Press, 1989.

———. *Seeing the Form. A Theological Aesthetics.* San Francisco: Ignatius Press, 1982.

Barber, Malcolm. *The Cathars.* Edinburgh Gate: Pearson Education Ltd., 2000.

Bell, Catherine M. *Ritual, Perspectives and Dimensions.* New York: Oxford University Press, 1997.

Bellow, Saul. *Mr. Sammler's Planet.* New York: Fawcett Crest, 1971.

Benda, Julien. *The Treason of the Intellectuals.* Translated by Richard Aldington. New York: W.W. Norton, 1969.

Benjamín, José. *La importancia del demonio y otras cosas sin importancia.* Madrid: Editorial Júcar, 1974.

Bismark, Ruth-Alice Von and Ulrich Kabitz, eds. *Love Letters from Cell 92: The Correspondence Between Dietrich Bonhoeffer and Maria Von Wedemeyer, 1943–45.* Nashville: Abingdon Press, 1995.

Bloy, Léon. *Pilgrim of the Absolute.* New York: Pantheon Books, 1947.

Bonhoeffer, Dietrich. *Letters and Papers from Prison.* Edited by Eberhard Bethge and translated by Reginald Fuller. New York: Macmillan, 1967.

Breinersdorfer, Fred. *Sophie Scholl—Die letzten Tage.* Frankfurt am Main: Fischer Taschenbuch Verlag, 2005.

Breviarium Sacri Ordinis Praedicatorum. Edited by Emmanuel Suarez, O.P. Romae. Ad Sanctam Sabinam, 1952.

Brown, Lester, et al. *The Earth Policy Reader.* New York: W. W. Norton, 2002.

Buber, Martin. *The Way of Response.* Edited by Nahum N. Glatzer. New York: Schocken, 1966.

Burl, Aubrey. *God's Heretics: The Albigensian Crusade.* Phoenix Mill, England: Sutton Publications Ltd., 2000.

Cahill, Thomas. *Desire of the Everlasting Hills.* New York: Doubleday, 1999.

———. *The Gifts of the Jews.* New York: Doubleday, 1998.

Camus, Albert. *Resistance, Rebellion, and Death.* Translated by Justin O'Brien. New York: Alfred A. Knopf, 1960.

Catherine of Siena. *The Dialogue.* Translated by Suzanne Noffke, O.P. New York: Paulist Press, 1980.

Cayley, David. *Ivan Illich in Conversation.* Concord, Ontario: Anansi, 1992.

————. *The Rivers North of the Future: The Testament of Ivan Illich.* Toronto: Anansi, 2005.

Chesterton, G.K. *Orthodoxy.* New York: Dodd, Mead and Company, 1954.

Childers, Thomas and Jane Caplan, eds. *Reevaluating the Third Reich.* New York: Holmes & Meier, 1993.

Coady, Mary Frances. *With Bound Hands: A Jesuit in Nazi Germany: The Life and Selected Prison Letters of Alfred Delp.* Chicago: Jesuit Way, 2003.

Day, Dorothy. *The Dorothy Day Book.* Edited by Margaret Quigley and Michael Garvey. Springfield, IL: Templegate, 1982.

————. *Selected Writings.* Edited by Robert Ellsberg. New York: Orbis Books, 1999.

Deák, Istvan. "Why did they love him?" *Times Literary Supplement* 6307 (2000) 4.

Dictionnaire de Théologie Catholique. Paris: Librarie Letouzey et Ané, 1960.

Domback, Annette E. and Jud Newborn. *Shattering the German Night. The Story of the White Rose.* Boston: Little Brown and Company, 1986.

Dostoievsky, Fyodor. *The Brothers Karamasov.* Translated by Constance Garnett. New York: Random House, 1950.

Dru, Alexander. Introduction to *Journal in the Night*, by Theodor Haecker. New York: Pantheon Books, 1950.

Duden, Barbara. *Disembodying Women.* Translated by Lee Hoinacki. Cambridge: Harvard University Press, 1993.

————. "The Quest for Past Somatics." In *The Challenges of Ivan Illich*, edited by Lee Hoinacki and Carl Mitcham, 219–30. Albany: State University of New York Press, 2002.

Ellsberg, Robert. *All Saints.* New York: Crossroad Publishing Company, 1997.

Ellul, Jacques. *Perspectives On Our Age*, edited by William H. Vandenburg. Translated by Joachim Neugroschel. Toronto, Ontario: Canada Broadcasting Corporation, 1981.

————. *The Technological Bluff.* Translated by Geoffrey W. Bromley. Grand Rapids: W. B. Eerdmans, 1990.

Endo, Shusako. *Silence.* Translated by William Johnston. New York: Taplinger Publishing Company, 1980.

Enright, D.J. and David Rawlinson, eds. *The Oxford Book of Friendship.* Oxford: Oxford University Press, 1991.

Farmer, David Hugh, ed. *Butler's Lives of the Saints.* 12 vols. Collegeville, MN: Liturgical Press, 1995–2000.

Foster, Benjamin R., trans. *The Epic of Gilgamesh.* New York: W. W. Norton, 2001.

Foster, George. "Peasant Society and the Image of the Limited Good." *American Anthropologist* 67 (1965) 295–315.

Fukuyama, Francis. *The End of History and the Last Man.* New York: Penguin, 1992.

Ganzini, Linda, M.D., et al. "Nurses' Experience with Hospice Patients Who Refuse Food and Fluids to Hasten Death." *The New England Journal of Medicine* 349 (2003) 359–65.

Gay, Peter. "My German Question." *New York Review* 47 (2000) 21–22.

Graf, Willi. *Briefe und Aufzeichnungen.* Frankfurt am Main: Fischer Taschenbuch Verlag, 1944.

Graml, Hermann, et al. *The German Resistance to Hitler.* Berkeley and Los Angeles: University of California Press, 1970.

Greene, Graham. *The Heart of the Matter*. New York: The Viking Press, 1948.

Griffith, Richard. *The World of Robert Flaherty*. New York: Duell, Sloan and Pearce, 1953.

Grimes, Ronald L., ed. *Readings in Ritual Studies*. New York: Prentice-Hall, 1996.

Haecker, Theodor. *Journal in the Night*. Translated by Alexander Dru. New York: Pantheon Books, 1950.

Hamann, Johann Georg. *Sämtliche Werke*. Edited by Josef Nadler. 6 vols. Vienna: Herder, 1950.

Hamilton, Bernard. "The Cathars and Christian Perfection." In *The Medieval Church; Universities, Heresy, and the Religious Life*. Edited by Peter Biller and Barrie Dobson, 5–13. Bury St Edmunds, Suffolk England: St Edmundsbury Press Ltd., 1999.

Hanser, Richard. *A Noble Treason. The Revolt of the Munich Students Against Hitler*. New York: G. P. Putnam's Sons, 1979.

Haraway, Donna J. *Modest Witness@Second Millennium*. New York: Routledge, 1997.

Harris, Ruth. *Lourdes. Body and Spirit in the Secular Age*. London: The Penguin Press, 1999.

Hildegard of Bingen. *The Letters of Hildegard of Bingen*. Translated by Joseph L. Baird and Rodd K. Ehram. 2 vols. New York: Oxford University Press, 1994.

Hippocrates. *The Theory and Practice of Medicine*. New York: Philosophical Library, 1964.

Hoffmann, Peter. *The History of the German Resistance 1933–1945*. Translated by Richard Barry. Cambridge: MIT Press, 1972.

Hoinacki, Lee. *El Camino. Walking to Santiago de Compostela*. University Park: Pennsylvania State University Press, 1996.

———. *Stumbling Toward Justice: Stories of Place*. University Park: Pennsylvania State University Press, 1999.

———. "Why *Philia*?" Unpublished essay, 2003.

Hoinacki, Lee and Carl Mitcham, eds. *The Challenges of Ivan Illich*. Albany: State University of New York Press, 2002.

Hopkins, Gerard Manley. "God's Grandeur." *Poems of Gerard Manley Hopkins*. New York: Oxford University Press, 1961.

Illich, Ivan. "The Cultivation of Conspiracy." In *The Challenges of Ivan Illich*, edited by Lee Hoinacki and Carl Mitcham, 233–42. Albany: State University of New York Press, 2002.

———. "Death Undefeated." *The British Medical Journal* 311 (1995) 1652–53.

———. "Do not Let Us Succumb to Diagnosis, but Deliver Us from the Evils of Health." Unpublished speech, Bologna, October 28, 1998.

———. *Gender*. New York: Pantheon Books, 1982.

———. *H₂O and the Waters of Forgetfulness*. Dallas, TX: The Dallas Institute of Humanities and Culture, 1985.

———. *In the Mirror of the Past*. New York: Marion Boyars, 1992.

———. *In the Vineyard of the Text*. Chicago: University of Chicago Press, 1993.

———. *Medical Nemesis*. New York: Pantheon Books, 1976.

———. "Pathogenesis, Immunity and the Quality of Public Health." Unpublished speech, Hershey, PA, June 11, 1994.

Jacobs, Sandra. "Death By Voluntary Dehydration—What the Caregivers Say." *New England Journal of Medicine* 349 (2003) 325-6.

Jens, Inge, ed. *At the Heart of the White Rose. Letters and Diaries of Hans and Sophie Scholl.* Translated by J. Maxwell Brownjohn. New York: Harper and Row, 1987.

Judt, Tony. *Times Literary Supplement* 1053 (1994) 3.

Kaelber, Lutz. *Schools of Asceticism.* University Park: The Pennsylvania State University Press, 1998.

Keneally, Thomas. *Schindler's List.* New York: Penguin, 1983.

Kevles, Daniel J. "Grounds for breeding: The amazing persistence of eugenics in Europe and North America." *Times Literary Supplement* 4944 (1998) 3-4.

Kolakowski, Leszek. *God Owes Us Nothing.* Chicago: University of Chicago Press, 1998.

Lambert, Malcolm. *The Cathars.* Oxford: Blackwell, 1998.

Lansing, Carol. *Power and Purity: Cathar Heresy in Medieval Italy.* New York: Oxford University Press, 1998.

Large, David Clay. *Where Ghosts Walked. Munich's Road to the Third Reich.* New York: W. W. Norton, 1997.

Lasch, Christopher. *The Revolt of the Elites.* New York: W. W. Norton, 1995.

The Lévinas Reader. Edited by Seán Hand. Oxford: Blackwell, 1996.

Levine, Edwin Burton. *Hippocrates.* New York: Twayne Publications, Inc., 1971.

Lukacs, John. *The Hitler of History.* New York: Alfred A. Knopf, 1997.

Marlin, George J., et al., eds. *The Quotable Chesterton.* San Francisco: Ignatius Press, 1986.

Marquard, Odo. *In Defense of the Accidental.* Translated by Robert M. Wallace. New York: Oxford University Press, 1991.

Mauss, Marcel. *The Gift. Forms and Functions of Exchange in Archaic Societies.* Translated by Ian Cunnison. New York: W.W. Norton, 1967.

McGinn, Bernard. *Antichrist.* San Francisco: Harper, 1994.

McNeill, William R. *A World History.* New York: Oxford University Press, 1979.

Miles, Siân, ed. *Simone Weil: An Anthology.* London: Virago, 1986.

Mounier, Emmanuel. *Personalism.* Translated by Philip Mairet. London: Routledge & Kegan Paul Ltd., 1952.

Mundy, John Hine. *The Repression of Catharism at Toulouse.* Toronto: Pontifical Institute of Medieval Studies, 1985.

Newman, John Henry. "The Times of Antichrist." In *Tracts for Our Times.* Vol. 5. London: Riverton, 1840.

Nicholls, William. *Systematic and Philosophical Theology.* Middlesex: Penguin, 1971.

O'Flaherty, Liam. *Short Stories.* London: Hodder and Stoughton, 1992.

Oldenbourg, Zoé. *Massacre at Montségur.* New York: Minerva Press, 1968.

Pascal, Blaise. *Pensées.* Translated by A. J. Krailsheimer. London: Penguin, 1966.

Patrick, J. Max. *Francis Bacon.* London: Longmans, Green & Co., 1961.

Pfaff, William. "Eugenics, Anyone?" *New York Review* 44 (1997) 23-4.

Pickstock, Catherine. *After Writing. On the Liturgical Consummation of Philosophy.* Oxford: Blackwell, 1998.

Pieper, Josef. *Leisure the Basis of Culture.* Translated by Alexander Dru. New York: Pantheon Books, 1964.

Plato. *The Dialogues.* Translated by B. Jowett. 2 vols. New York: Random House, 1937.

Polyani, Karl. *The Great Transformation.* New York: Reinhart, 1944.

Pseudo-Dionysius Areopagite. *The Divine Names*. Translated by John D. Jones. Milwaukee: Marquette University Press, 1980.

Rauschning, Herman. Preface to Armin L. Robinson, ed. *The Ten Commandments*. New York: Simon and Schuster, 1944.

Reck-Malleczewen, Friedrich. *Diary of A Man in Despair*. Translated by Paul Rubens. New York: The Macmillan Company, 1970.

Robinson, Armin L., ed. *The Ten Commandments*. New York: Simon and Schuster, 1944.

Runciman, Steven. *The Medieval Manichee*. Cambridge: At the University Press, 1960.

Sachs, Wolfgang, ed. *The Development Dictionary*. London: Zed Books Ltd., 1999.

St. Augustine. *Confessions*.

St. John Damascene. *Holy Images*. Translated by Mary H. Allies. London: Thomas Baker, 1898.

St. John of the Cross. *The Collected Works*. Translated by Kieran Kavanaugh, O.C.D. and Otilio Rodriguez, O.C.D. Washington, DC: ICS Publications, 1991.

St. Thérèse of Lisieux. *Story of A Soul*. Translated by John Clarke, O.C.D. Washington, DC: ICS Publications, 1996.

Sarri, Sergio. Letter to the *New York Review* 47 (2000) 81.

Scholl, Inge. *The White Rose*. Translated by Arthur R. Schultz. Hanover, NH: University Press of New England, 1983.

Smith, Duncan. "Resistance to Hitler." *Times Literary Supplement* 6307 (2000) 19.

Smith, T. Stratton. *The Rebel Nun*. Springfield, IL: Templegate, 1965.

Sophocles. *The Three Theban Plays*. Translated by Robert Fagles. New York: Viking Press, 1982.

Synge, John Millington. *The Aran Islands*. Marlboro, VT: The Marlboro Press, n.d.

Taylor, Melissa A. "Benefits of Dehydration in Terminally Ill Patients." *Geriatric Nursing* 16 (1995) 271-2.

Thoreau, Henry David. *Walden and Other Writings*. New York: Bantam Books, 1989.

Unamuno, Miguel de. *The Agony of Christianity*. Translated by Anthony Kerrigan. Princeton: Princeton University Press, 1974.

Undset, Sigrid. *Kristin Lavransdatter*. Translated by Charles Archer. New York: Alfred A. Knopf, 1963.

Weil, Simone. *Gravity and Grace*. Translated by Arthur Wills. New York: G.P. Putnam's Sons, 1952.

———. *The Need for Roots*. Translated by Arthur Wills. New York: Routledge, 1952.

———. *The Notebooks*. Translated by Arthur Wills. 2 vols. G.P. Putnam's Sons, 1956.

———. *The Simone Weil Reader*. Edited by George A. Panichas. Various translators. New York: David McKay, 1977.

———. *Waiting for God*. Translated by Emma Craufurd. New York: Harper Colophon Books, 1973.

Wiener, Philip P., ed. *Dictionary of the History of Ideas*. 5 vols. New York: Charles Scribner's Sons, 1973.

Wylie-Kellerman, Bill, ed. *A Keeper of the Word: Selected Writings of William Stringfellow*. Grand Rapids: W. B. Eerdmans, 1994.

Zahn, Gordon. *In Solitary Witness: The Life and Death of Franz Jägerstätter*. Collegeville, MN: The Liturgical Press, 1964.

Bibliography

Zibawi, Mahmoud. *The Icon: Its Meaning and History.* Collegeville, MN: The Liturgical Press, 1993.

CPSIA information can be obtained
at www.ICGtesting.com
Printed in the USA
FSHW020958091221
86812FS